IMAGES of America
ANGELS CAMP AND COPPEROPOLIS

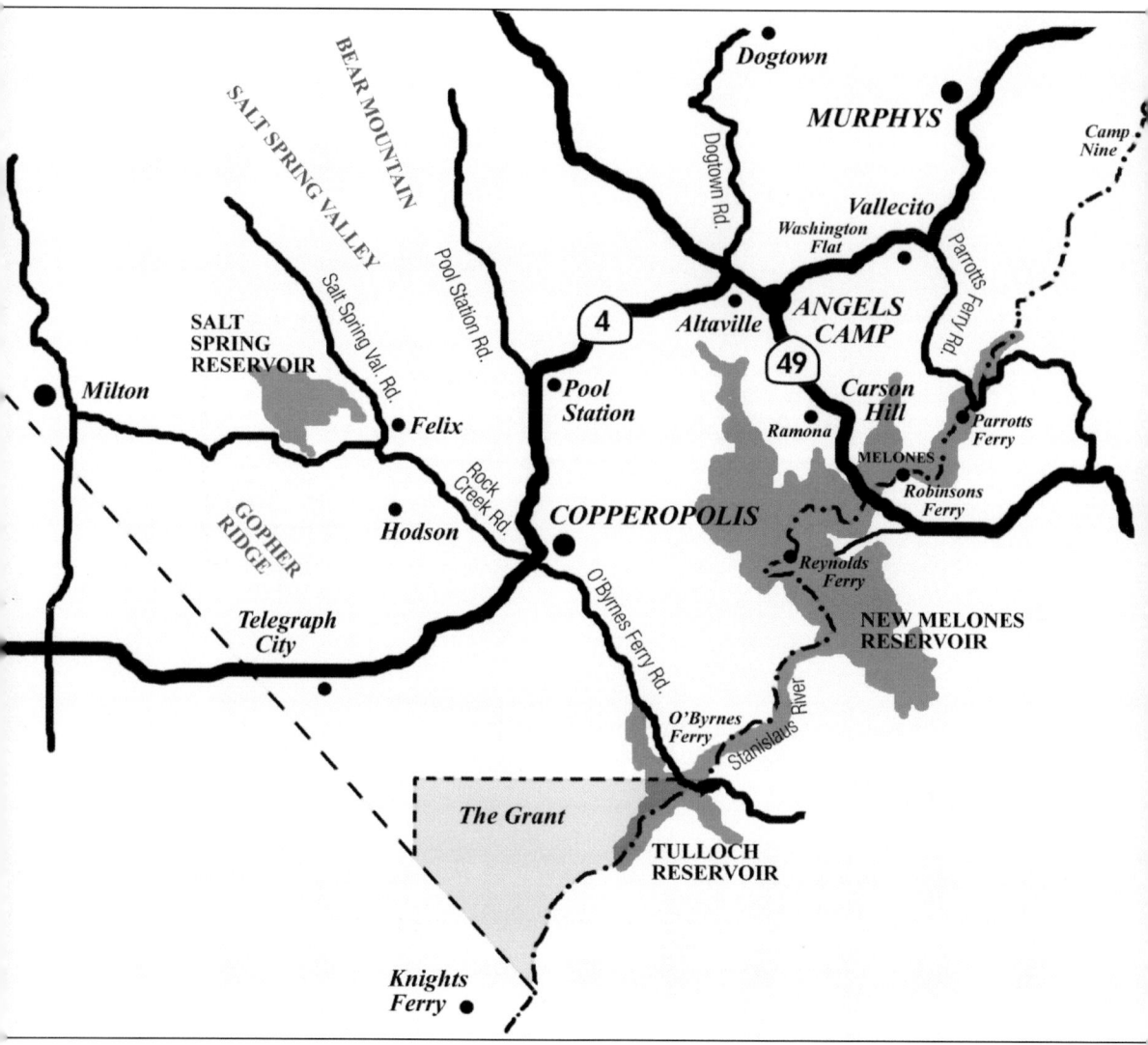

Reaching from the plains of the Great Central Valley to the Foothill Pine Belt, Angels Camp and Copperopolis share State Route 4, while State Route 49 trends north-south along the Mother Lode vein, connecting the gold mines along its route. (Map created by Laura Bowly.)

ON THE COVER: Angels Camp and Copperopolis were all about mining, and these Angels Camp miners appear to recognize this as they pose jauntily in front of the mill at the Utica Mine, to which no one except miners were granted admittance. (Courtesy Calaveras County Historical Society.)

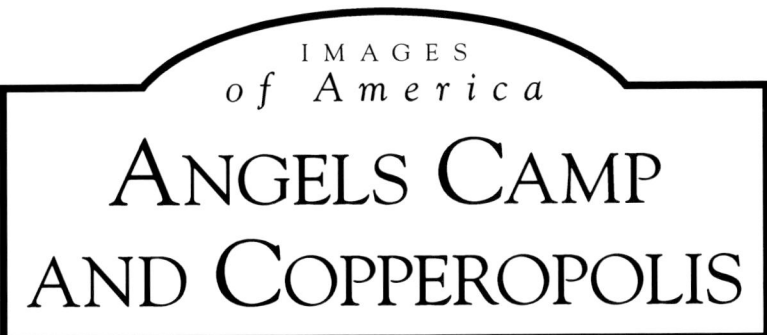

ANGELS CAMP AND COPPEROPOLIS

Images of America

Judith Marvin, Julia Costello, and
Salvatore Manna

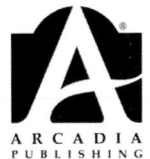

Copyright © 2009 by Judith Marvin, Julia Costello, and Salvatore Manna
ISBN 978-0-7385-5981-0

Published by Arcadia Publishing
Charleston, South Carolina

Printed in the United States of America

Library of Congress Catalog Card Number: 2008931759

For all general information contact Arcadia Publishing at:
Telephone 843-853-2070
Fax 843-853-0044
E-mail sales@arcadiapublishing.com
For customer service and orders:
Toll-Free 1-888-313-2665

Visit us on the Internet at www.arcadiapublishing.com

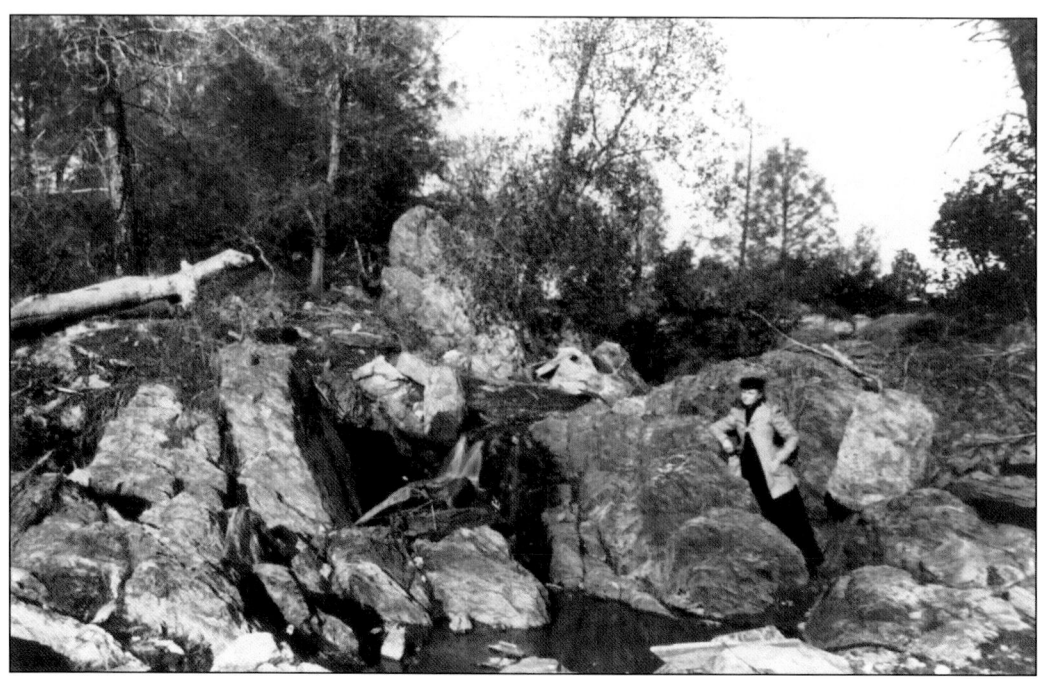

Greenhorn Creek was named for the greenhorn miners who tried their luck in Greenhorn Gulch, only to be laughed at by the more seasoned miners. They had the last laugh, however, as rich pickings were discovered in the creek. The young lady at the falls in Greenhorn Gulch, now part of the Greenhorn Creek Golf Resort, was photographed about 1910. (Courtesy Calaveras County Archives.)

Contents

Acknowledgments		6
Introduction		7
1.	The First People	9
2.	Stanislaus Gold	15
3.	Roads to the Mines	29
4.	Angels Camp and Altaville	37
5.	Copper Country	67
6.	Mines of Madam Felix	81
7.	Ranch Families	97
8.	Black Bart	109
9.	The Iron Roads	115
10.	Frog Jump	121

ACKNOWLEDGMENTS

This volume was made possible by the cooperation of the Calaveras County Historical Society (administrator Kathy Cochran), the Calaveras County Archives (archivist Shannon Van Zant), the Angels Camp Museum (Emily Stemler and Bob Rogers), numerous other institutions, and the descendants of pioneer families. Wally Motloch provided his expertise in reproducing the images, Terry Brejla edited the text, and Laura Bowly drew the overview map.

Of great assistance were previously published articles, including those in *Las Calaveras*, the quarterly publication of the Calaveras County Historical Society; *Calaveras Gold* (Ronald H. Limbaugh and Willard P. Fuller Jr.); *The Tools are on the Bar* (Rhoda and Charles Stone); *Melones: A Story of a Stanislaus River Town* (Julia Costello); and *Madam Felix's Gold* (Willard P. Fuller Jr., Judith Marvin, and Julia Costello). The Far Western Anthropological Research Group, Inc., provided its research on prehistoric peoples. All authors' funds generated from the sale of this book will be distributed to local archives and the Calaveras Heritage Council.

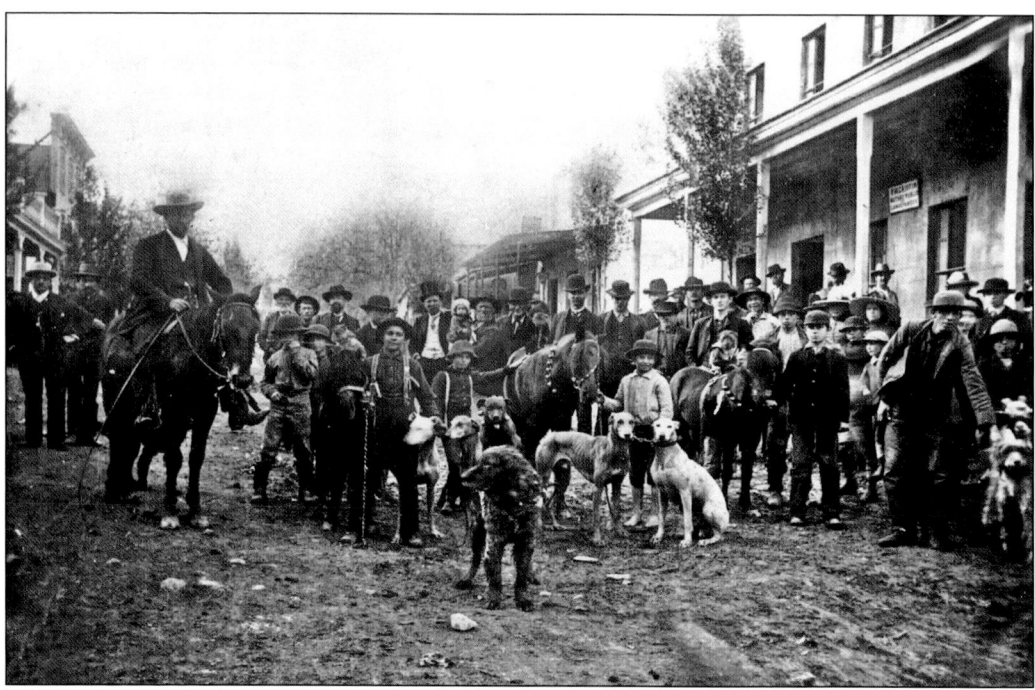

Angels Camp, a town built on hills and underlain with mine tunnels, shares a 4-mile-long main street with Altaville. These townsfolk and their dogs gathered on Main Street in the 1890s when a visiting photographer came to town. (Courtesy Calaveras County Historical Society.)

INTRODUCTION

The histories of Angels Camp and Copperopolis, as well as lesser-known communities in the southwest corner of Calaveras County, are typical of many towns in the California foothills, with their booms and busts, colorful characters, and almost century-long dependence on mining.

Although established on lands occupied for as many as 10,000 years by native peoples, the immigrants of the 19th century ushered in the modern era. The prosperity of the Angels Camp vicinity was first based upon the rich placer gold found along the Stanislaus River and in Coyote Creek, Carson Creek, and Angels Creek and its tributaries of China Gulch, Six Mile Creek, Cherokee Creek, Greenhorn Creek, and their drainages. For the Copperopolis area, its boom was launched with the discovery of copper ore in the 1860s, which helped support the efforts of the Union during the Civil War. Despite a great deal of gold prospecting, it was not until the 1880s that there was any appreciable amount of ore produced in that region.

Called the greatest mass migration in peacetime history, people from the eastern and midwestern United States, every country in Europe, Asia, Central and South America, Mexico, Canada, and Hawaii flocked to the gold fields. Even a little-known writer who went by the moniker Mark Twain took his turn at mining, only to find gold with a story later called "The Celebrated Jumping Frog of Calaveras County."

The Mexicans, the first to arrive, were mostly driven out after the Foreign Miners Tax was enacted in 1852. The Chinese, however, provided the greatest number of immigrants in the 1860s and 1870s. Angels Camp's Chinatown, with stores, gambling halls, opium dens, and gardens, was located along Angels Creek in the southern part of town. Always placer miners, the Chinese established other settlements at Six Mile Bar, Jenny Lind, and all along the Stanislaus River, Angels Creek, the Calaveras River, Littlejohns Creek, and elsewhere.

For thousands of years, Native Americans had traversed this land on routes connecting the Great Central Valley and the Sierra Nevada. Starting in the Gold Rush, those trails were improved into wagon and buggy roads, and the Angels Camp and Copperopolis areas became trading centers for neighboring mines and camps. In all directions from Angels Camp and Altaville would rise the communities of Vallecito, Dogtown, Washington Flat, Albany Flat, Carson Hill, Slab Ranch, and others. Copperopolis also had several satellite communities: Felix, O'Byrnes Ferry, Six Mile Bar, Hodson, Scorpion Gulch, Telegraph City, Napoleon City, and, in the 1870s, Milton, at the terminus of the Stockton and Copperopolis Railroad.

Many decades later, the primary west-east route would evolve into State Route 4, stretching from the San Francisco Bay Area to Markleeville east of the Sierra Nevada crest. North and south, another route—known as the San Andreas and Angels Camp Road, Angels Camp and Sonora Road, and other sobriquets—would become State Route 49, connecting towns along the Mother Lode vein from Mariposa to Auburn in the Southern Mines and extending through the Northern Mines to Downieville.

Close behind the prospectors and miners came the agriculturalists, mainly families who saw opportunities for stock-raising and truck garden operations. While the economy was wedded to the extraction of precious ores, the surrounding rolling hills and open grasslands produced sustenance for the hungry hoards of miners and their stock.

A few of the tent cities that emerged along the major strikes were not abandoned but were instead built up with one- and two-story frame commercial buildings lining their main streets. As these buildings were ravaged by fire many times in the early years, the more determined merchants rebuilt in stone and brick. By the mid-1850s in Angels Camp and Altaville, and the 1860s in Copperopolis, hotels, restaurants, dry-goods and grocery stores, liveries and stables, pharmacies and doctors' offices, barbershops, and the ubiquitous saloons were established. Churches and fraternal lodges were erected, and schools served the growing population of children. Dwellings were constructed around the commercial core, with gardens and picket fences lending permanence to the settlements as they evolved into towns.

Water has always been a necessity for the extraction of ore, and by 1853, water for placer mining was brought into Angels Camp by the Union Water Company. Completed to Murphys in 1853, the system was extended to Washington Flat, Altaville, and Angels Camp that same year by utilizing the bed of Angels Creek. Over the ensuing years, the system was improved numerous times, especially after its acquisition by the Utica Gold Mining Company in the late 1880s.

To the west, Salt Spring Reservoir was completed in 1858 to provide water to the Brushville and Jenny Lind mining districts and was later expanded for use in the Royal, Mountain King, and other mines in the Madam Felix mining district. Reservoirs were constructed along Littlejohns Creek, and water was carried through ditches and riveted pipe to the diggings at Scorpion Gulch and later the Alto Mine. Mining camps and bars along the Stanislaus River turned that water into ditches and built wing dams to work the river beds, while smaller systems were constructed along every creek and drainage where ore was extracted or processed.

Perhaps surprisingly though, the period of greatest mining activity was not during that more colorful Gold Rush but rather the "Second Gold Rush," which began in the 1880s. The consolidation of the mines, facilitated by advances in mining and milling technologies, and the availability of eastern United States and foreign capital combined to warrant large-scale underground mining.

A new wave of migration from southern Europe brought many into the area to work in the mining industry. Angels Camp, the center of industrial mining during the hard-rock boom, became home not only to miners from the eastern United States, England, Ireland, France, Germany, Finland, and Italy, but also the Slavic portions of the Austro-Hungarian Empire—both Croatians and Serbians. A crew of "100 Slavonians" built the road to the Stanislaus Electric Power Company Plant at Camp Nine in 1906–1907, while others labored underground. But mining has never been a consistent industry, and the Second Gold Rush ended with the advent of World War I.

Angels Camp became the county's sole incorporated city in 1912 and gained world renown with its Jumping Frog Jubilee, which continues today. But Copperopolis dwindled, and other settlements became ghost towns. In the late 20th and early 21st century, however, the entire region has experienced a revival fed by a new mass migration—this time of those leaving urban areas for the country. The land they find holds within its borders a rich and fertile history.

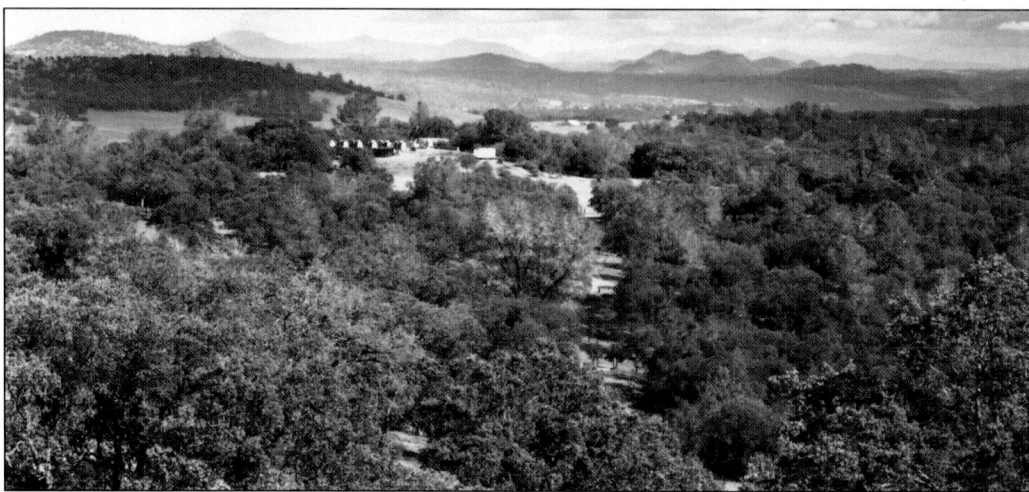

Salt Spring Valley lies between Gopher Ridge on the west and the monadnock (ancient mountain) of Bear Mountain on the east. In the center of the photograph are the ruins of the Royal Mill, which overlooked the pastoral landscape of the 1980s before the recent open-pit mining by Meridian Minerals, Inc. (Photograph by Alice Olmstead, courtesy Foothill Resources, Ltd.)

One

THE FIRST PEOPLE

A Mi-Wuk creation story tells how Coyote-man and Falcon flew over the countryside, planting three feathers at the places where they wanted villages to be established: one feather for Chá-kah, the chief; one for Mi'-yum, the woman chief; and one for Soo-la-too, the poor. The next day, each of the three feathers came to life, and the people lived in the places named by Coyote-man and Falcon.

Archaeologists also try to reconstruct how and when people first came to populate the landscape. One of the oldest sites in California is a 10,000-year-old village discovered in Salt Spring Valley, buried some 9 feet under the surface. Other ancient sites survive at Camp Nine on the Stanislaus River; Texas Charlie Gulch near old Reynolds Ferry; and on Black Creek near Highway 4. About 8,000 years ago, California's climate warmed, reducing stream flows, evaporating small lakes, and driving the Alpine tree line higher. In the San Joaquin Valley, rising sea levels flooded the delta area, creating a vast and rich tidal marsh that supported large, wealthy villages.

Cooler weather returned, and the period from 4,000 to 1,000 years ago is called the "Golden Age" of prehistoric California. Foothill villages expanded, and traders regularly crossed the high Sierra, exchanging obsidian from the eastern slopes for shells and acorns from the west. About 1,000 years ago, the good times came to an abrupt end: many large villages were abandoned, desert rock art traditions ceased, trans-Sierran trade networks collapsed, and conflict and warfare increased. In the foothills, big villages gave way to smaller camps of several families that moved seasonally following available resources. Acorn processing intensified, and multiple—sometimes hundreds—of grinding stones have been found at single locations. The causes of these dramatic changes are likely related to a severe drought, increased population, shrinking resources, and introduction of the bow and arrow.

The greatest disaster was yet to come, however. With the discovery of gold in January 1848, the lives of California's earliest residents changed forever. The tidal wave of miners that swept over the foothills drove away the game, muddied the streams, and introduced lethal diseases. Mi-Wuk survivors retreated to enclaves, and many of their descendants remain in the county today.

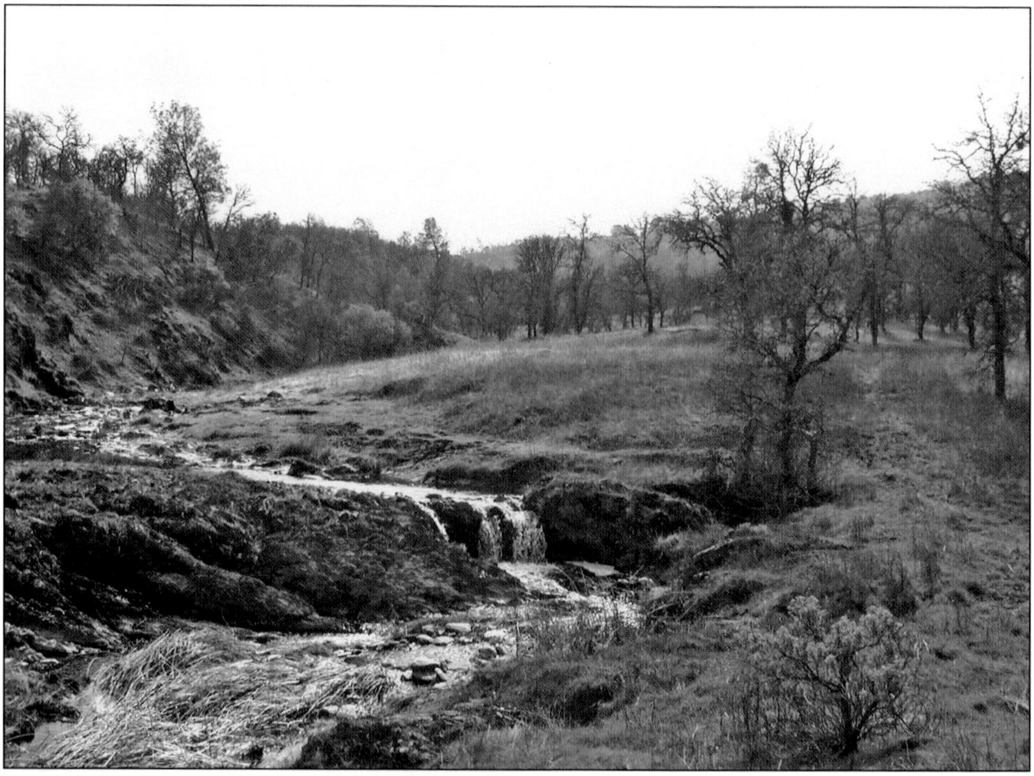

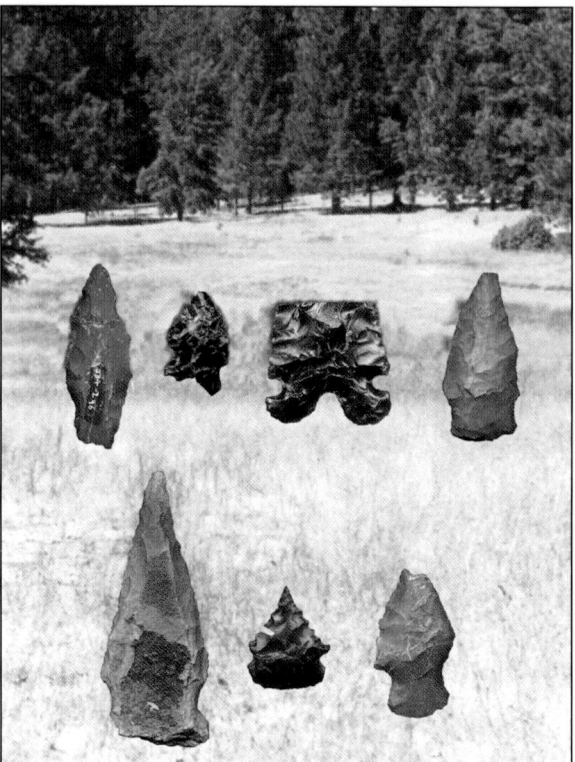

Four of the oldest sites in California are located in Calaveras County's southwest corner. The 10,000-year-old village site in Salt Spring Valley—named "Skyrocket" after an adjacent mining claim—contained hundreds of greenstone tools, milling stones, scraping and pounding implements made from cobbles, and the seeds of oak, grey pine, and wild cucumber. (Courtesy Julia Costello.)

Archaeologists discovered long ago that artifact styles can change over time and have distinct periods of popularity. The arrowhead (center bottom) appeared in California about 1,200 years ago when the bow and arrow—invented on the East Coast—arrived. This new and deadly weapon upset power balances, causing widespread disruptions and conflicts. (Courtesy Far Western Anthropological Research Group.)

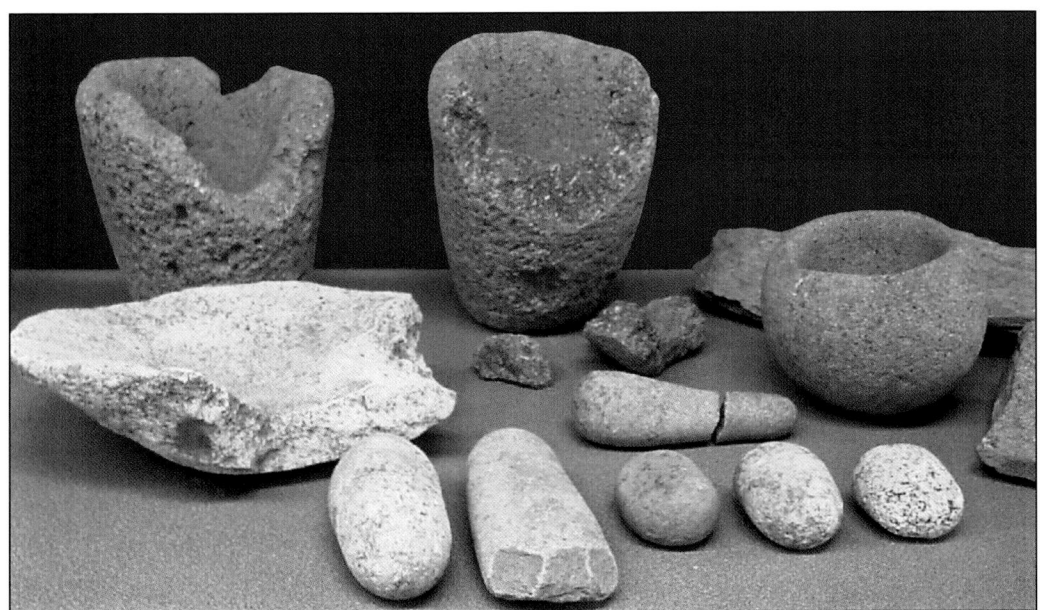

A variety of grinding tools were used by prehistoric peoples. The low, curved grinding slabs were used at the most ancient sites and at smaller camps. Larger bowl mortars were first seen about 3,000 years ago, found at large village sites where families spent more time crafting utensils. Grinding holes carved in bedrock were not common until as recent as 1,000 years ago. (Courtesy Far Western Anthropological Research Group.)

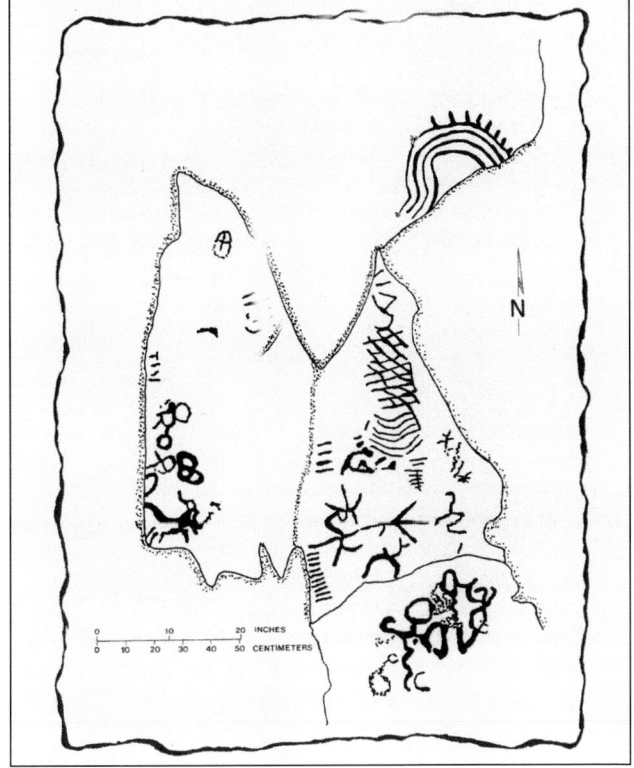

Petroglyphs (designs pecked or carved into rock surfaces) can be found throughout the Sierra Nevada foothills and are associated with the Mi-Wuk, Maidu, and Great Basin traditions. The designs pictured here are from an outcropping next to the river at Melones, carved through the reddish patina to let the lighter-color rock show through. Reproductions of petroglyphs at Horseshoe Bend are displayed at the Calaveras County Museum. (Courtesy U.S. Department of the Interior.)

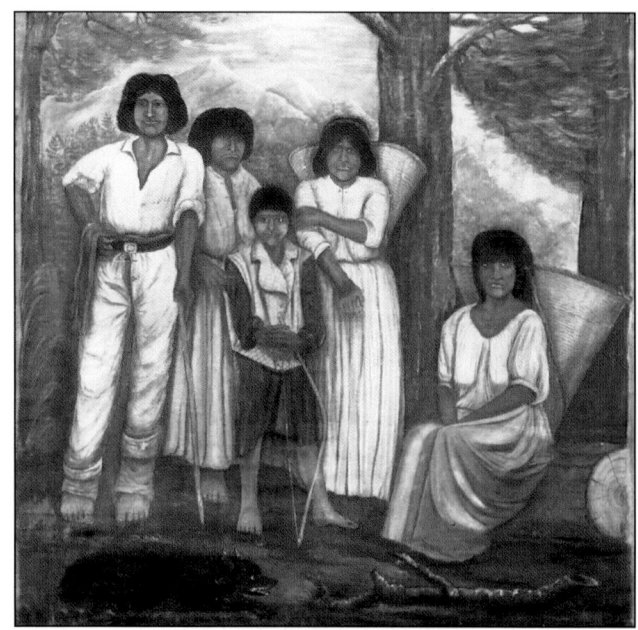

At the time of the Gold Rush, Mi-Wuk territory stretched from the edge of the San Joaquin Valley to the Sierra Nevada crest. This range provided all manner of foods, including seeds, berries, wild grapes, acorns, bulbs, greens and roots, mushrooms, nuts, fish, deer, rabbits, and birds, as well as medicinal plants. This rare depiction of Vallecito Mi-Wuk was made by Isaac W. Baker from sketches created in 1849–1850. (Courtesy Bancroft Library.)

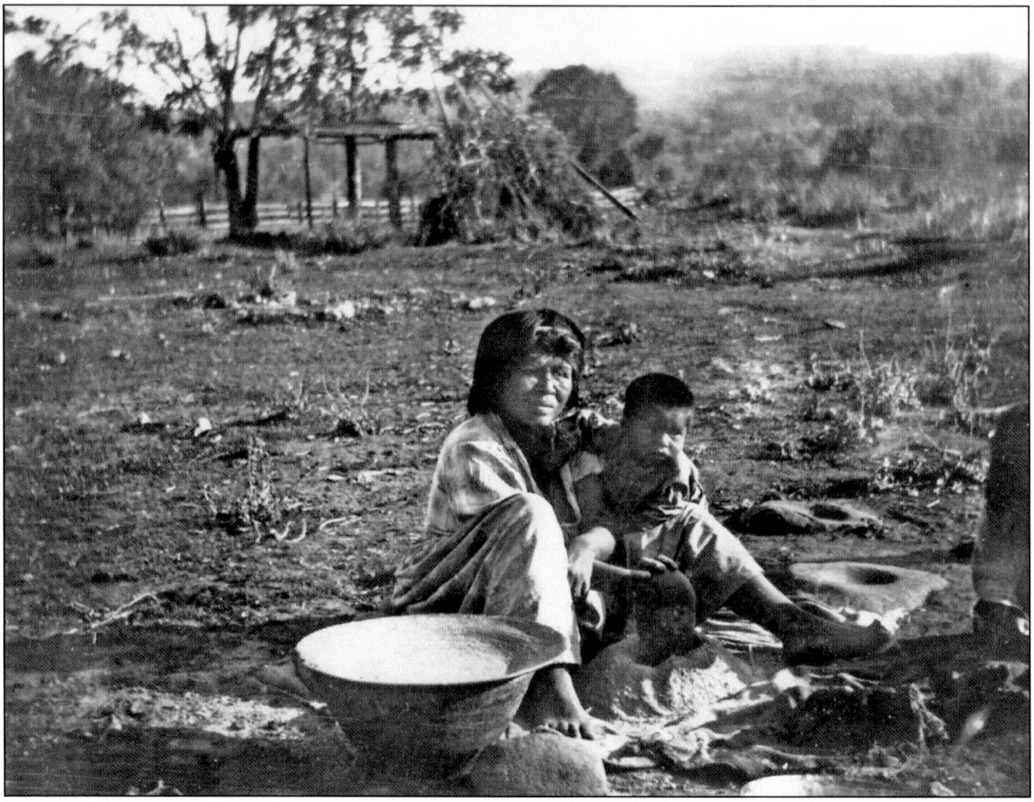

Six Mile Village, near Highway 4 east of Angels Camp, was occupied from about 1830 to 1930. It had both a roundhouse—said to be larger than the one at Murphys—and a dance house. This Six Mile resident and her son were photographed grinding acorns in a mortar (buried under the pile of flour) in 1898. (Photograph by W. H. Holmes, courtesy Smithsonian Institution.)

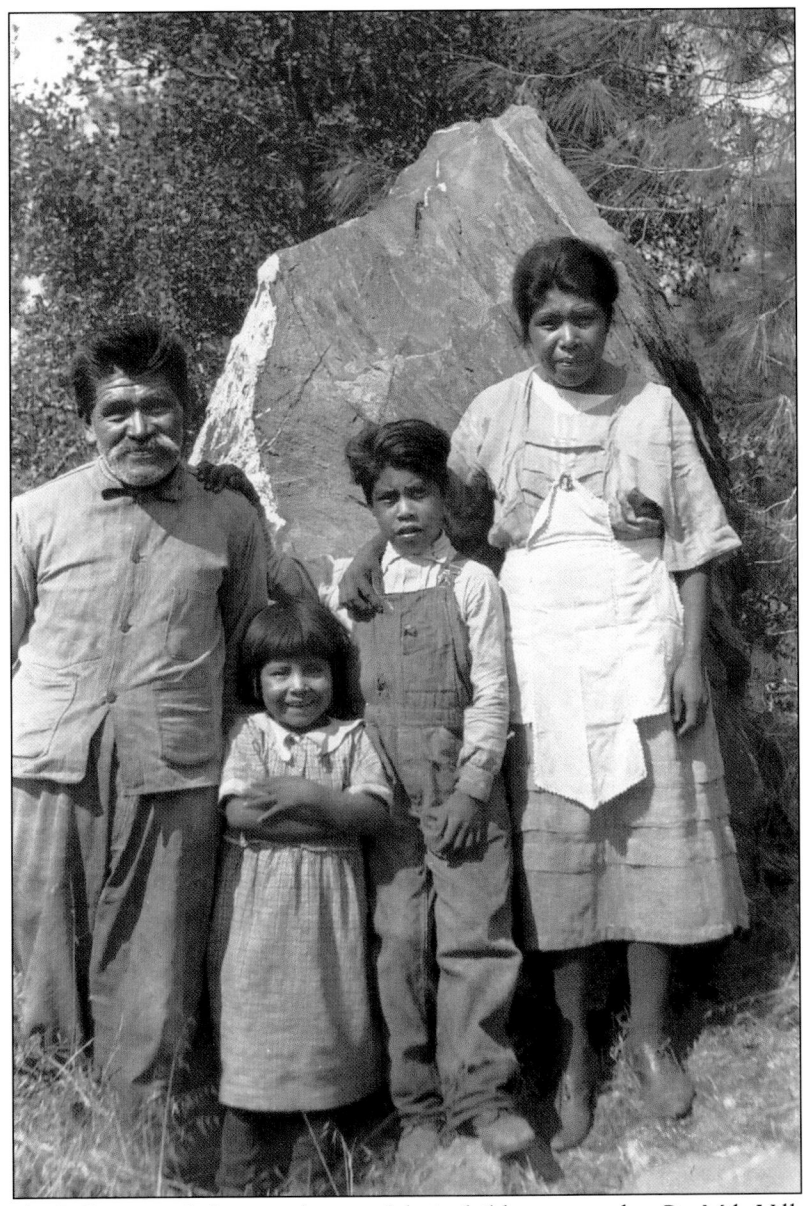

Tillie and John Jeff, pictured above with two of their children, moved to Six Mile Village in 1909, joining her elderly relatives Old Mary and Jack Hardy, who were living there alone. Tillie, born in 1876 at Quartz Hill, near Vallecito, had been previously married to John Carson, by whom she had one son, Jim Ray. John Jeff was born in West Point around 1865. Upon moving to Six Mile Village, the couple built a house where they raised their nine children: Hettie, Laura, Manuel, Carrie, Ray, Hempy ("Hamby"), Lennie, Tessie, and Walter. The family gathered black oak acorns, seeds, and berries, and regularly took deer for meat. They also had two vegetable gardens at Six Mile where they grew beans, tomatoes, corn, and potatoes, and they purchased eggs, bacon, bread, flour, and milk from merchants in Vallecito. Their son Manuel Jeff recalls a trip to Camp Nine where they stayed for two weeks, catching and drying salmon. John died in Sonora in 1937 at age 72; Tillie was killed in an automobile accident in 1945 at age 69. Jeff family descendants still reside in West Point. (Courtesy Calaveras County Historical Society.)

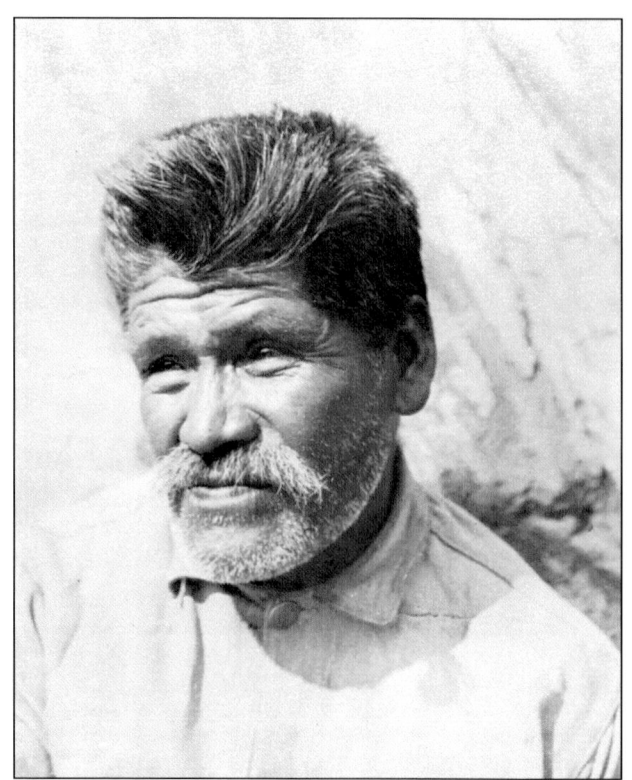

John Jeff's mother was a *mayengo* (chieftainess) from the village Kanusu and his father a *maiyerrgot* (chief) at West Point. John trained as a traditional *sobobbe* (drum major), learning the old songs and native ways from his father, "Indian Jeff," his grandfather, and Pedro O'Connor. He constructed the dance house at Six Mile Village in 1910, which then served as the center of community ceremonies, storytelling, and social events. (Courtesy Loid Haig.)

Ray Jeff, the son of John and Tillie Jeff, was born in 1915 at Six Mile Village. He served in World War II, winning the Silver Star, and died in that conflict in 1945. He is buried under a buckeye tree on the old Saunders Ranch near Vallecito with some 200 members of his tribe. (Courtesy Calaveras County Historical Society.)

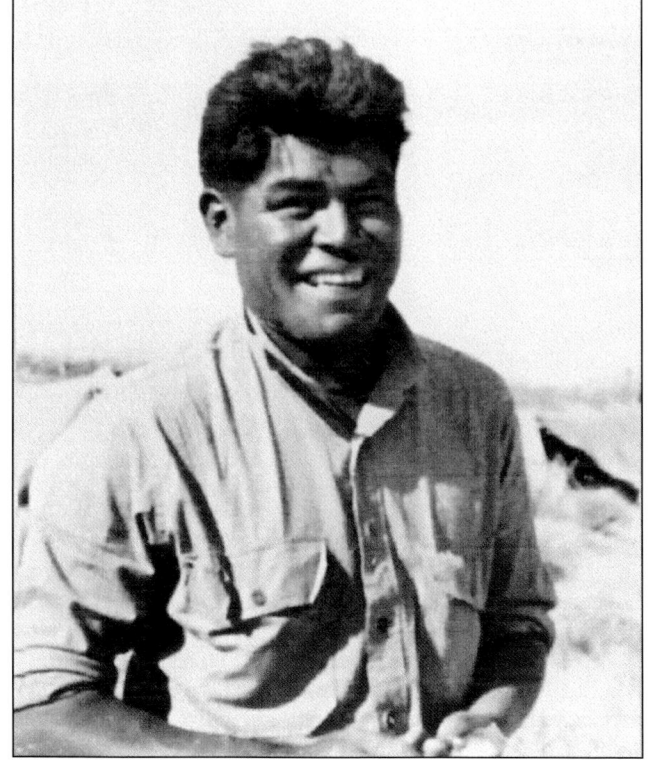

Two

STANISLAUS GOLD

The Stanislaus River has provided sustenance for Native Americans, gold for miners, and water for agriculture, urban development, and recreation. It is named for Estanislao Cucunuchi, who was born at San Jose Mission in 1800. At age 28, he led fellow Laquisemne Yokuts (from near Ripon) in a revolt, refusing to return from a holiday in their homeland. The horse-raiding rebels were pursued by Mariano Vallejo, but after a year, Estanislao turned himself in to his friend Father Narciso Durán and was pardoned. In addition to the Spanish and Mexican Californios, early visitors to Calaveras County included French trappers working for the Hudson's Bay Company—locally headquartered at French Camp near Stockton—and the immigrant Bidwell-Bartleson group in 1841.

The discovery of gold in 1848 unleashed an invasion of miners and settlers that transformed the land. Mexicans from the state of Sonora were likely the first to mine for Stanislaus gold, although the first recorded mining described Native Americans working the river banks for Capt. Charles M. Weber in May or June 1848. During the early years of the Gold Rush, extensive placer mining and prospecting took place in nearly every ravine and gulch. Gold camps quickly sprang up and were just as rapidly abandoned when the ore played out. On the Stanislaus, mining communities at Six Mile Bar, Scorpion Gulch, O'Byrnes Ferry, Two Mile Bar, Bostwicks Bar, and Melones flourished and died. As the economy stabilized, many of the early mining centers developed into permanent towns, such as Knights Ferry, Angels Camp, and Altaville.

The most prosperous and long-lived Stanislaus River mining took place at Carson Hill. The earliest strikes were associated with a Mexican community called Melones, where nuggets were said to resemble melon seeds. The gold was first mined from quartz veins exposed at the top of Carson Hill, where a small settlement developed. By 1900, expansion included construction of a large mill alongside the river at Robinsons Ferry, and the new community was re-christened Melones. Enduring both declines and revivals, the largely abandoned ruins were finally covered by the waters of the New Melones Reservoir in 1980.

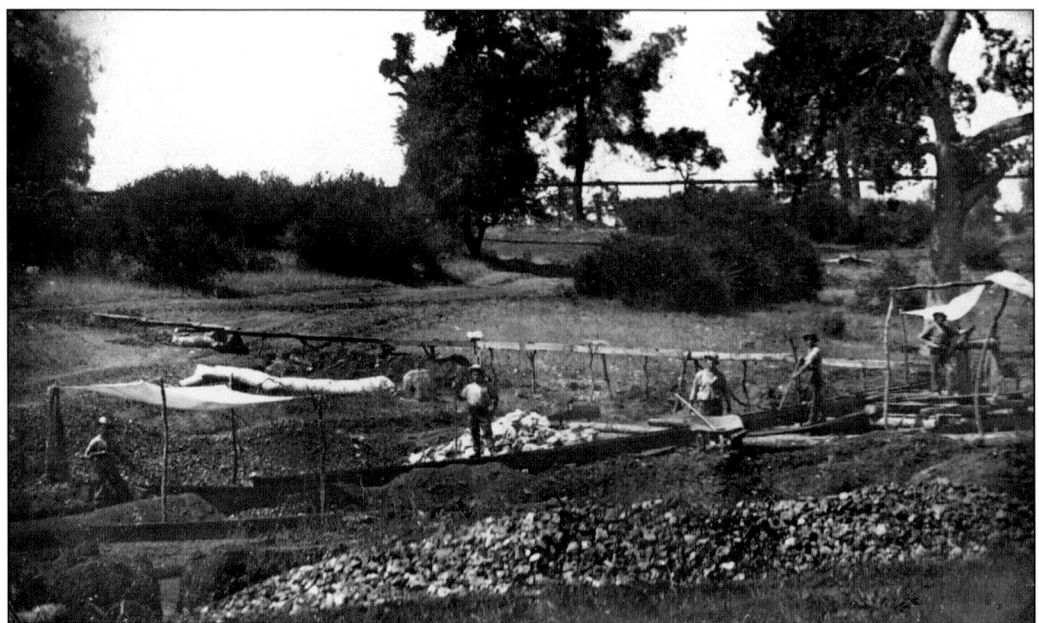

During the early years, placer mining activities were carried out by individuals or small groups of miners using simple gold pans, *bateas* (shallow wooden bowls), sluice boxes, and rockers. Later, when the free gold had been picked up, miners formed companies who built Long Toms, elaborate wing dams, and flutter wheels, and who used inventive means to turn the rivers and expose nuggets in the stream beds. (Courtesy Oakland Museum.)

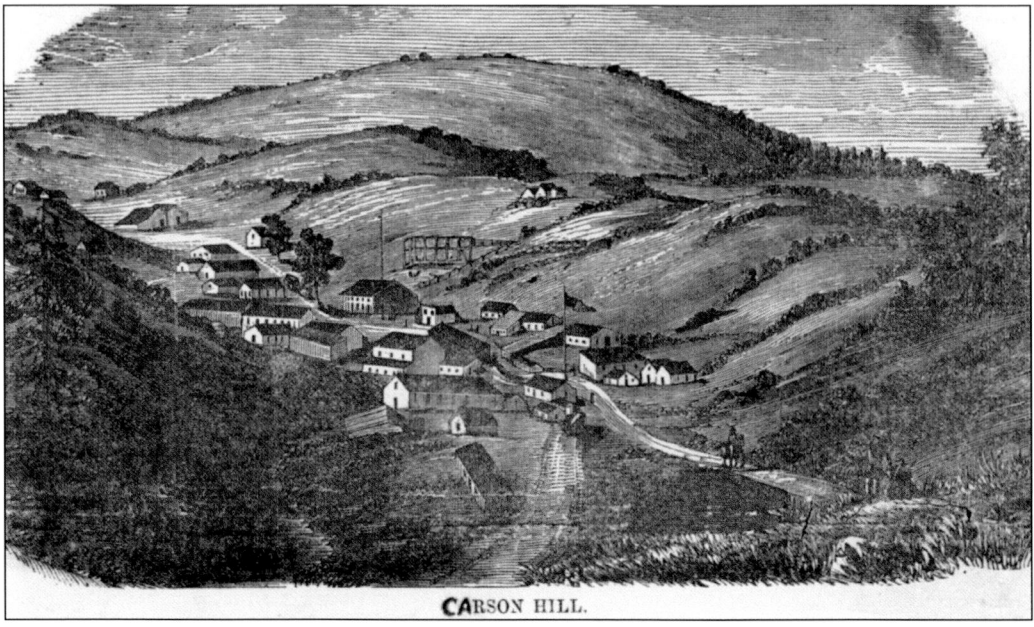

Placer gold was discovered in Carson Creek in 1848 by James H. Carson, whose name was given to the creek, hill, and town. More importantly, in 1850, the quartz lode located on the top of Carson Hill was proven rich, and miners flooded in. In 1854, the Calaveras Nugget—the largest mass of gold found in the United States—was taken from the Comstock claim and weighed in at 195 pounds troy. (Courtesy Bancroft Library.)

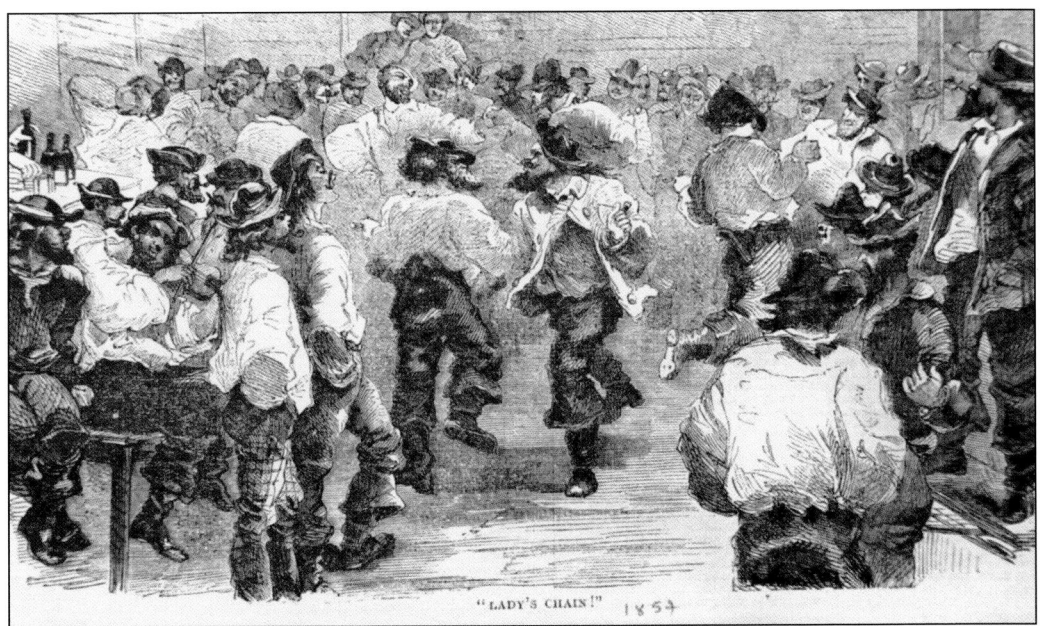

The Mexican miners on Carson Hill lived in their own settlement of Melones, described by Yankee visitors as dangerous and rowdy, featuring murders, fandangos, and gambling halls—accounts undoubtedly sensationalized. Whole families immigrated, and the main street was lined with brush houses and businesses. While the town only existed for about a year, its name survived in mining companies and reservoirs. (Drawing by J. D. Borthwick.)

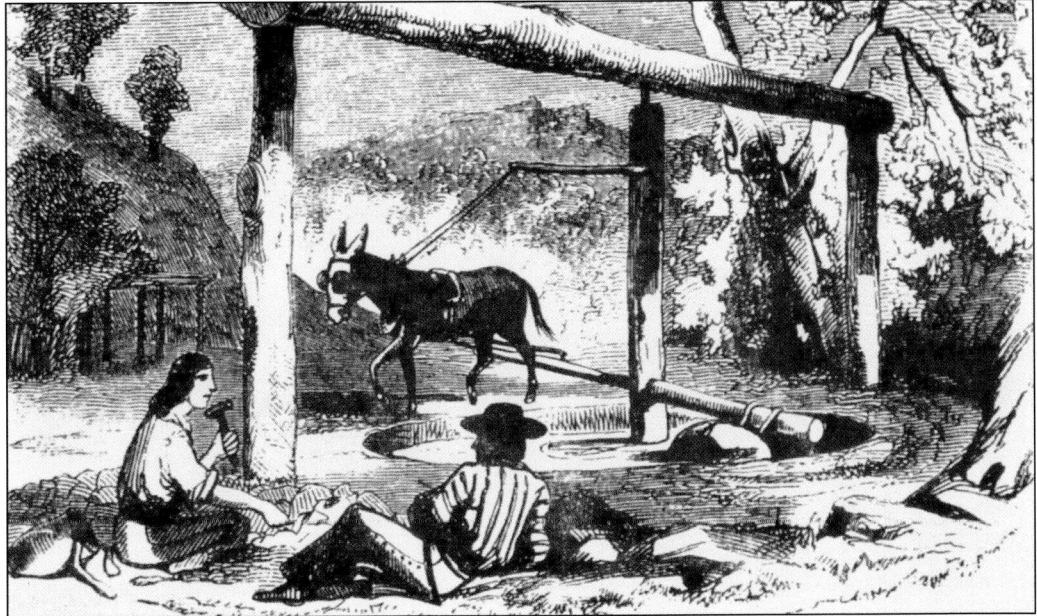

Arrastras, simple ore-grinding mechanisms, were introduced into California by experienced Mexican miners, and several were in use around Carson Hill. They were made out of local materials at little cost and were efficient in crushing quartz. When abandoned, the base stones were pulled up to retrieve gold dust that had filtered through the cracks. (Drawing from *How We Get Gold In California* by William Weeks.)

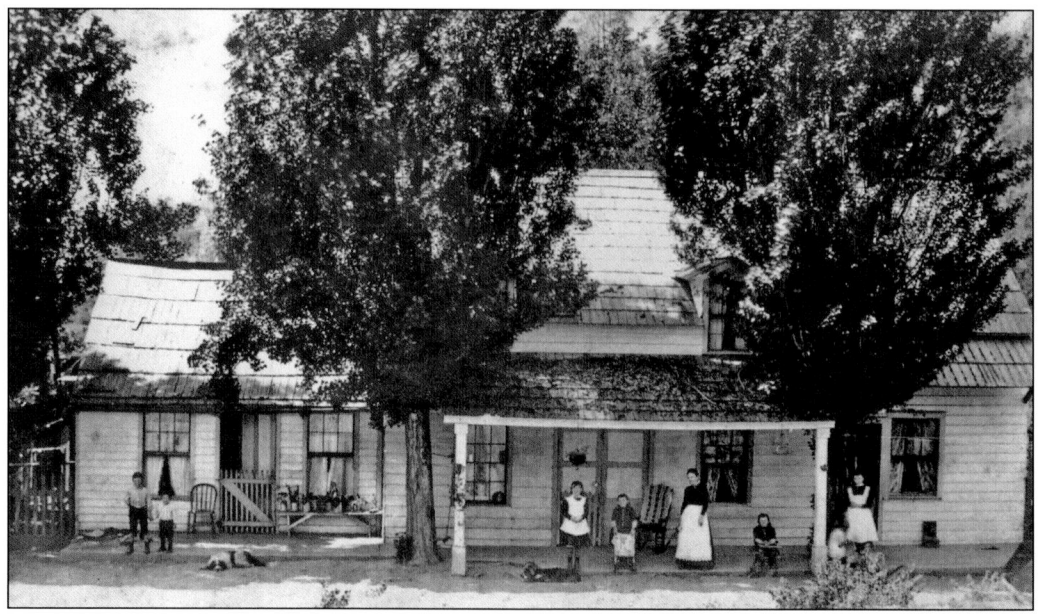

The early homestead of Gabriel Stevenot, called the Melones Ranch, was located on the site of the Mexican town. Pictured here are, from left to right, Fred, Archie, Margret, Nellie, Sarah, Louis, Allie, and Marie Stevenot. (Photograph by Emile Stevenot, courtesy Calaveras County Historical Society.)

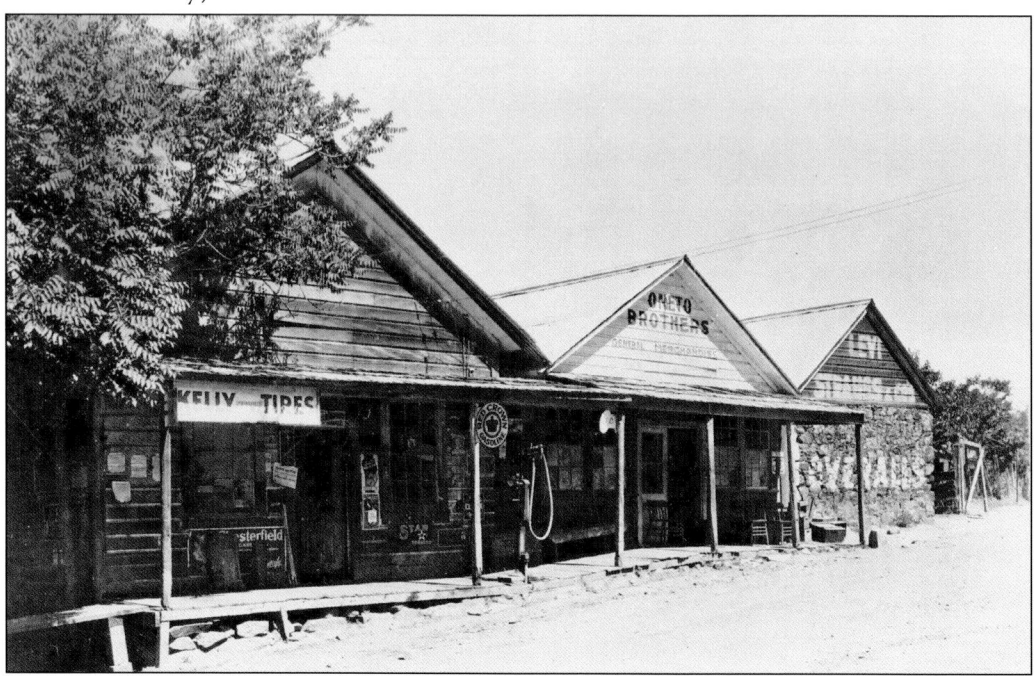

The rich ore of Carson Hill lay largely untapped through the 1870s because of litigation, primitive technologies, and lack of financing. By 1888, a 20-stamp mill had been constructed by the English-financed Calaveras Consolidated Gold Mining Company, although it would be another decade before real development began. The few businesses of Carson Hill (also called Irvine) survived by supplying prospectors and pocket miners. (Courtesy Historic American Buildings Survey.)

At the base of Carson Hill lay Robinsons Ferry, the important crossing founded in 1849 by John W. Robinson and Stephen Mead. It served travelers between Angels Camp and the booming towns of Columbia and Sonora, and thrived with the rich finds on Carson Hill. In this c. 1900 photograph, the two-story ferry house—saloon and lodging—is visible in the center. (Courtesy Calaveras County Historical Society.)

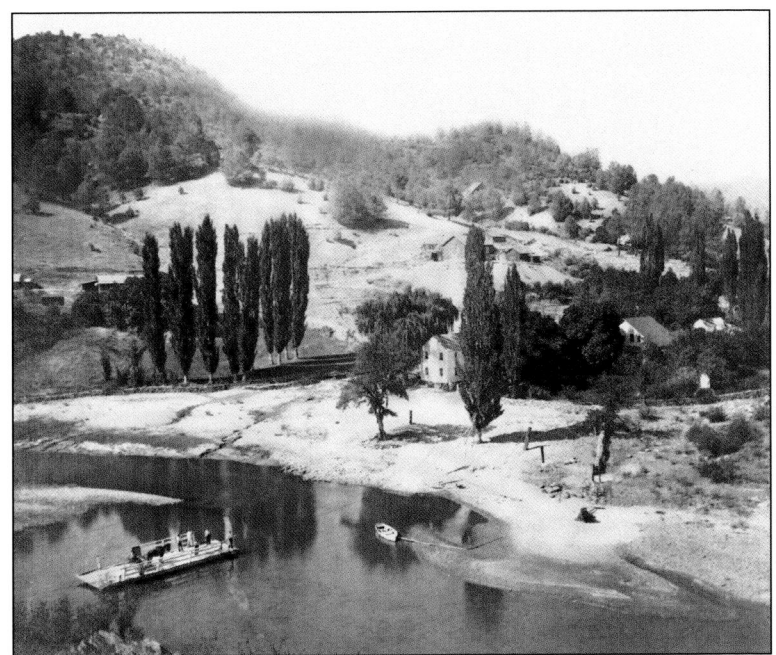

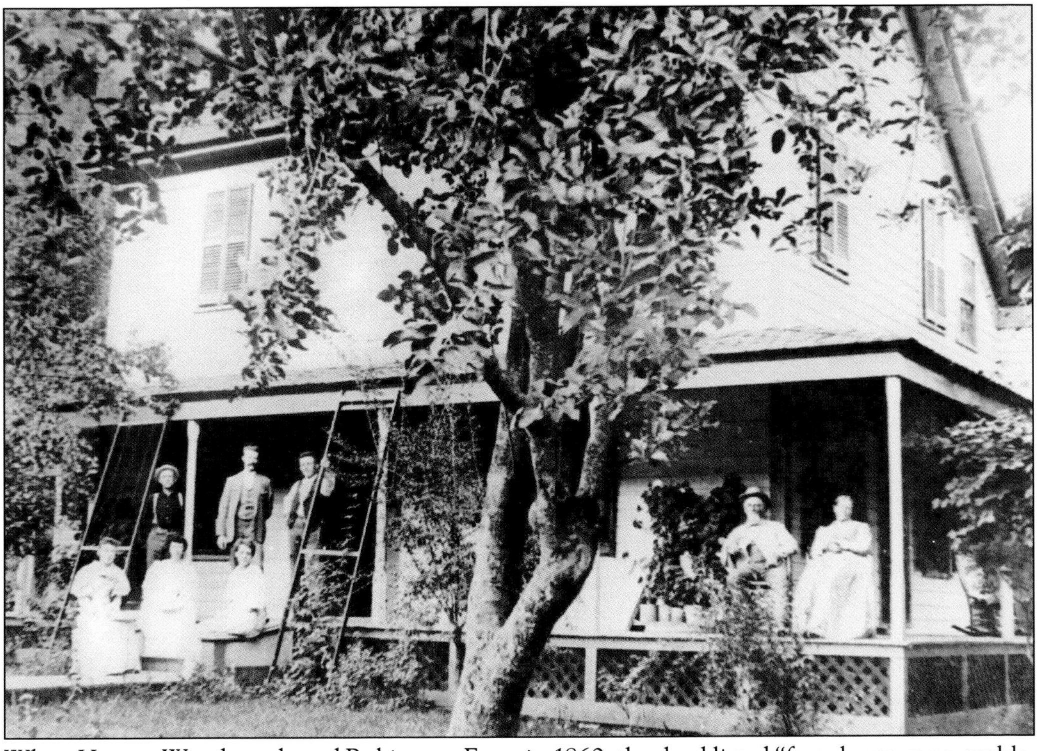

When Harvey Wood purchased Robinsons Ferry in 1860, the deed listed "ferry boats, rope, tackle, ferry house, out houses, bar, bar fixtures, liquors, provisions, and goods of every kind." Pictured around 1890 on the porch of their home are Harvey and Marinda (seated to the right) and (on the left, standing, from left to right) Harvey's brother James and sons Carlton and Percy; daughter Allie is seated to the left of two friends. (Courtesy Calaveras County Historical Society.)

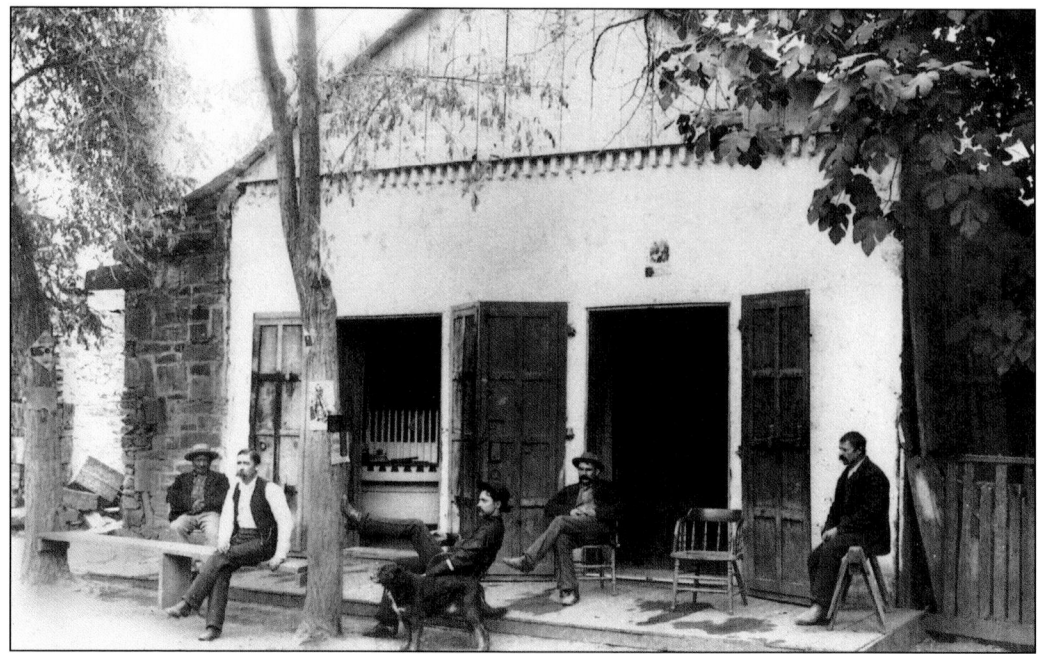

Robinsons Ferry survived the decline of gold mining by serving local ranchers as well as travelers. At that time, Main Street ran along the river and led to Angels Camp by ascending Coyote Creek. Houses and businesses lining this thoroughfare included Manuel Airola's store, captured in this rare 1870 image. (Courtesy Calaveras County Historical Society.)

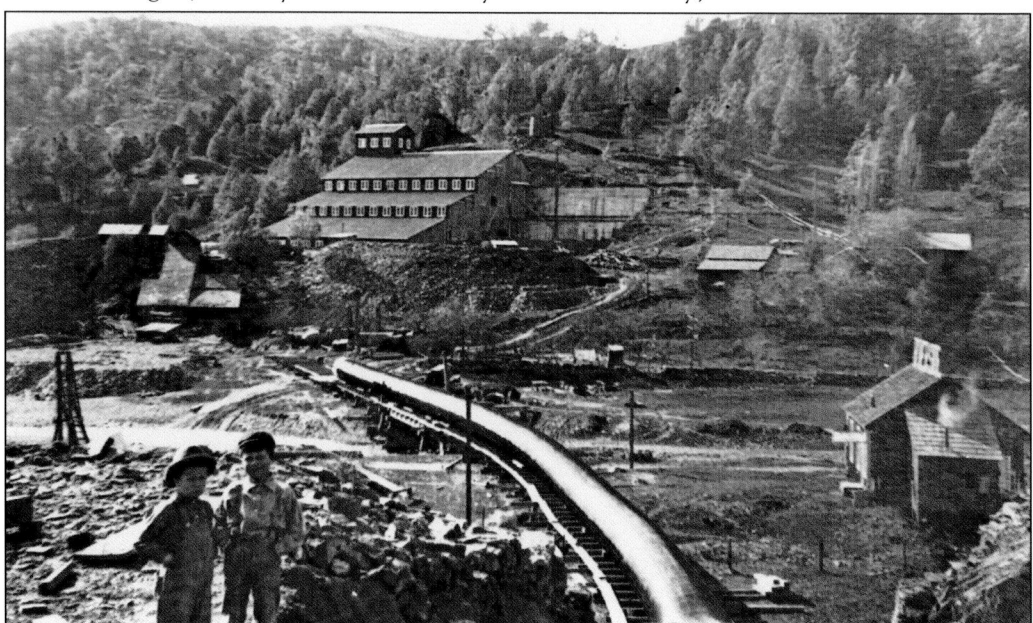

The sleepy settlement of Robinsons Ferry changed drastically when the Melones Company purchased 16 recorded mining claims on Carson Hill and constructed its mill alongside the river at the east end of town. The company also changed the name of the town to Melones. This 1902 photograph shows the first 60 stamps in place with room for 40 more to the right; the large pipe carried water. (Courtesy Calaveras County Historical Society.)

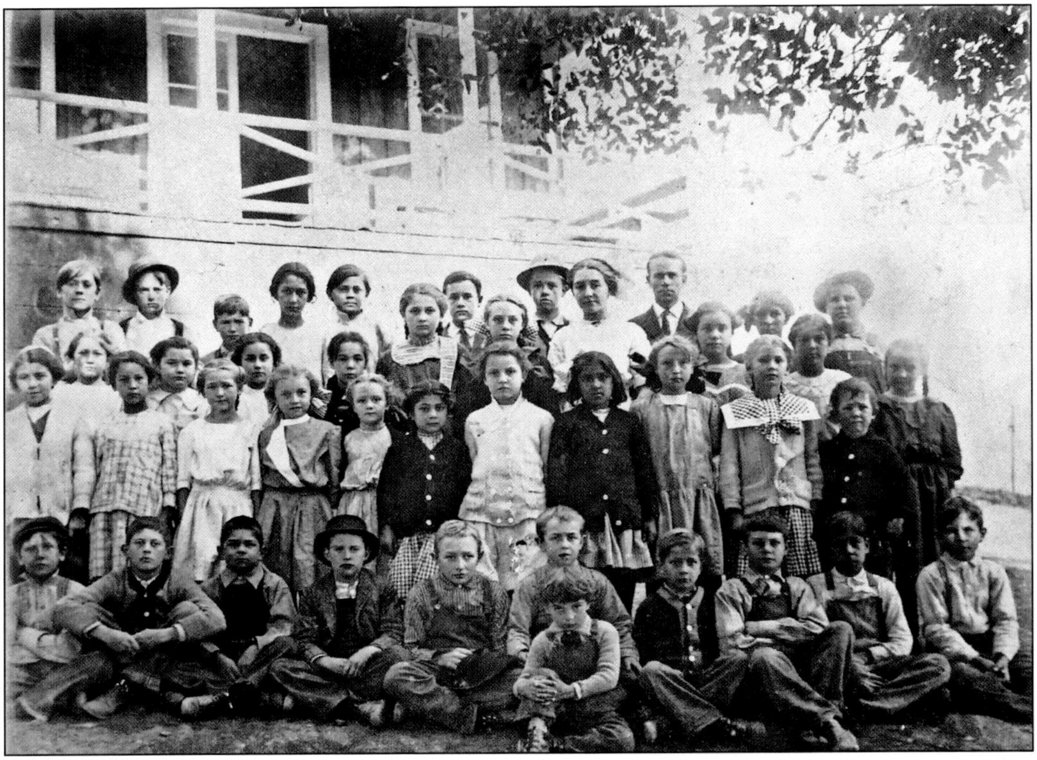

Change in the town's population is evident in the school's population. This photograph, taken in 1911, shows a group of 41 students and their teacher (the man standing in the fifth row, far right) whose names reflect the diverse nature of the community. Old ranch families are represented by Whittakers and Airolas, while new households have arrived from Serbia and Italy. Overall, however, the population of the new mining town of Melones was similar to that of the Gold Rush days: the predominance of single male miners, the large number of foreign-born residents, the high rate of transiency, and the economic dependence on gold. The atmosphere was still more like that of a boomtown than a domestic community. (Both, courtesy West Whittaker.)

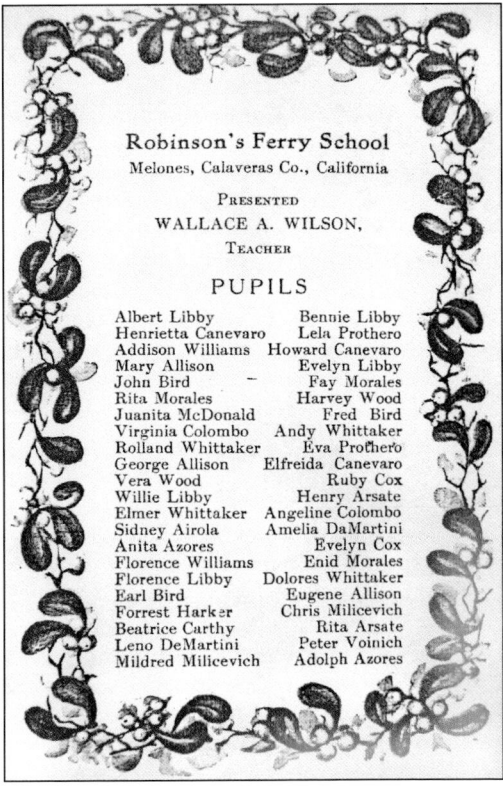

Robinson's Ferry School
Melones, Calaveras Co., California

Presented
WALLACE A. WILSON,
Teacher

PUPILS

Albert Libby	Bennie Libby
Henrietta Canevaro	Lela Prothero
Addison Williams	Howard Canevaro
Mary Allison	Evelyn Libby
John Bird	Fay Morales
Rita Morales	Harvey Wood
Juanita McDonald	Fred Bird
Virginia Colombo	Andy Whittaker
Rolland Whittaker	Eva Prothero
George Allison	Elfreida Canevaro
Vera Wood	Ruby Cox
Willie Libby	Henry Arsate
Elmer Whittaker	Angeline Colombo
Sidney Airola	Amelia DaMartini
Anita Azores	Evelyn Cox
Florence Williams	Enid Morales
Florence Libby	Dolores Whittaker
Earl Bird	Eugene Allison
Forrest Harker	Chris Milicevich
Beatrice Carthy	Rita Arsate
Leno DeMartini	Peter Voinich
Mildred Milicevich	Adolph Azores

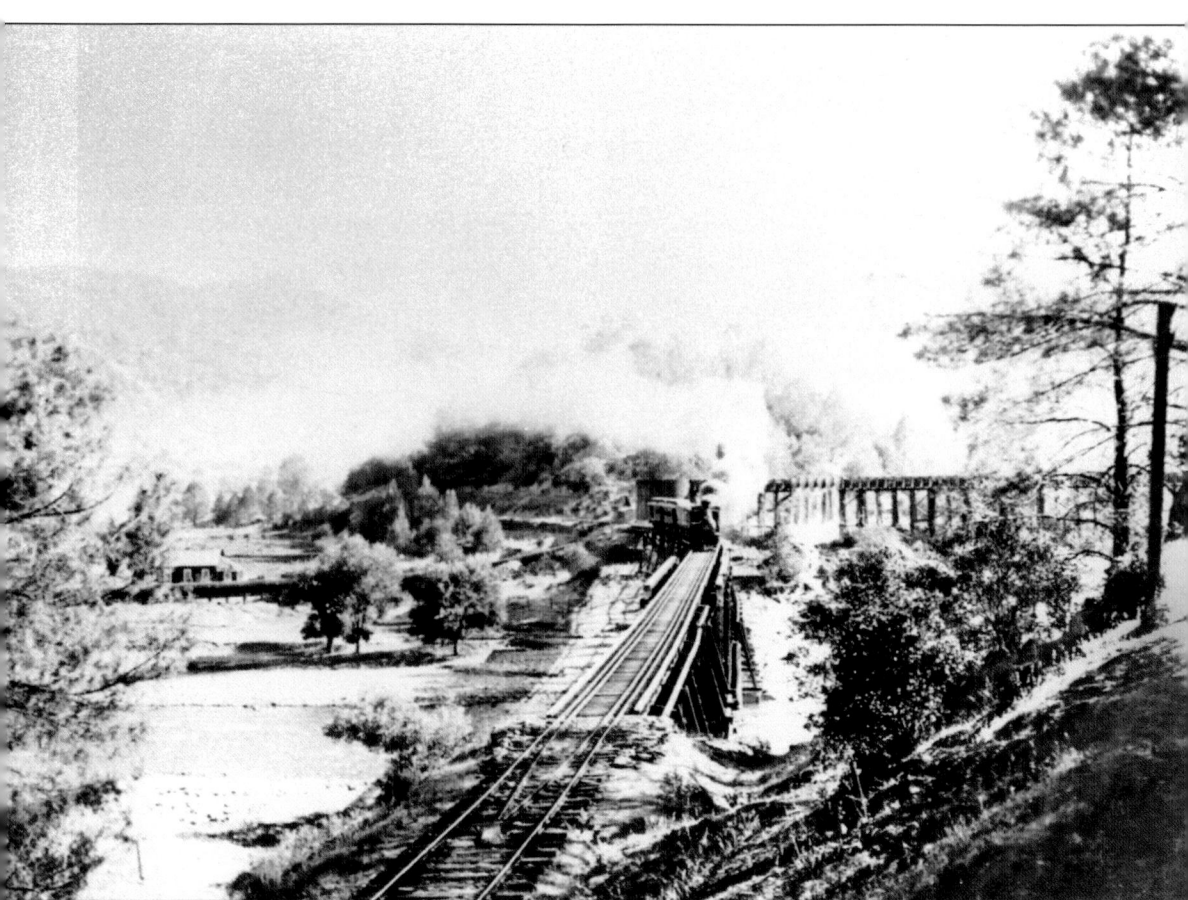

The mining ventures at Melones were greatly assisted by the construction of the Sierra Railway's branch line connecting Jamestown and Angels Camp. Although conceived by investors as a way to reach the vast timber reserves of the Sierra Nevada, the line also hauled supplies and ore for the mines. While the railway reached Jamestown in 1897, the terrain for the Angels Branch was formidable, and it was not until engineer W. H. Newell was hired that plans went forward. Crossing the 700-foot-deep chasm of the Stanislaus River required the use of five switchbacks, grades up to 4.15 percent, and 28-degree curves. The railway crossed the river on a 140-foot-long steel bridge, seen in this c. 1910 photograph (the trestle to the right rear is a water flume). Unexpected benefits of the route included spectacular views of the canyon, which caused awestruck passengers to name one vista "Gee Whiz Point." (Courtesy Calaveras County Historical Society.)

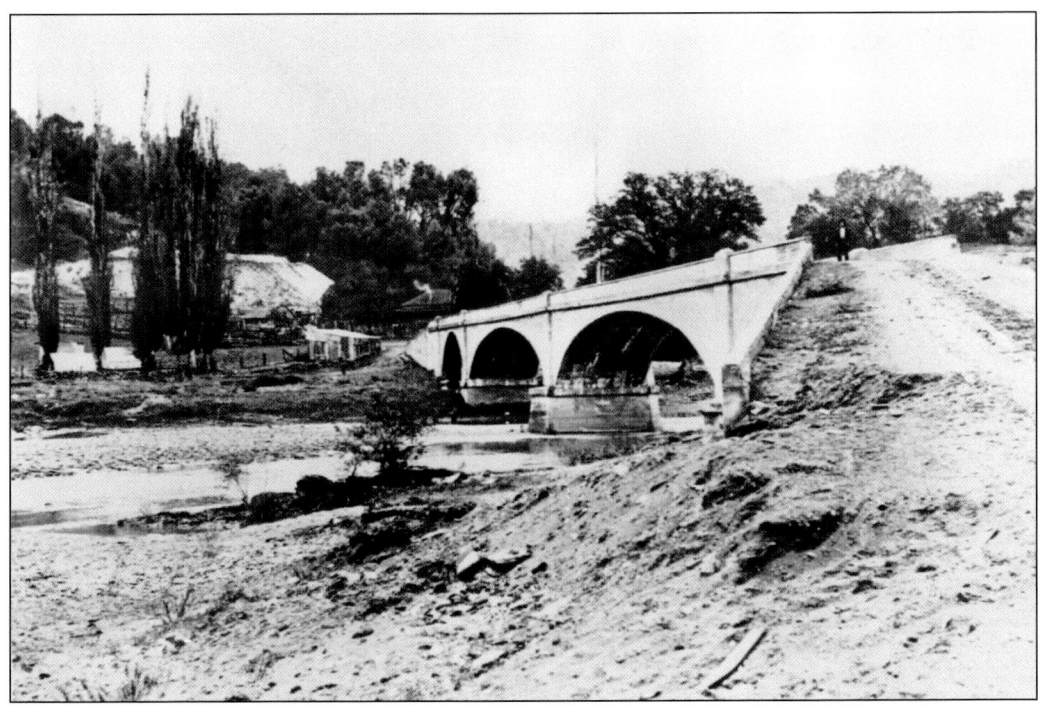

Progress at Melones included the replacement of the old ferry with a toll-free modern bridge, seen here soon after its completion in 1909. The crew constructing the bridge was housed in the adjacent ferry building, and ironically, a workman's cigarette burned the building to the ground. (Courtesy Calaveras County Historical Society.)

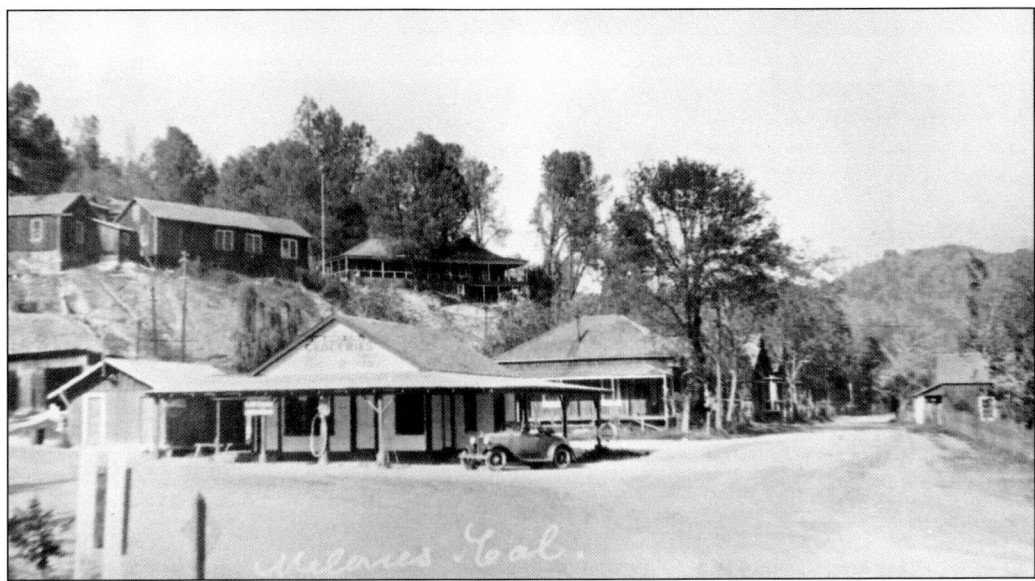

Harvey Wood's son Percy had seen ferry profits decline following the construction of the Sierra Railway, and in 1904, he declined to renew the concession. Modernizing, he opened the only gas station in town, seen here in about 1930. Thus, the Wood family remained in the transportation business. (Courtesy Calaveras County Historical Society.)

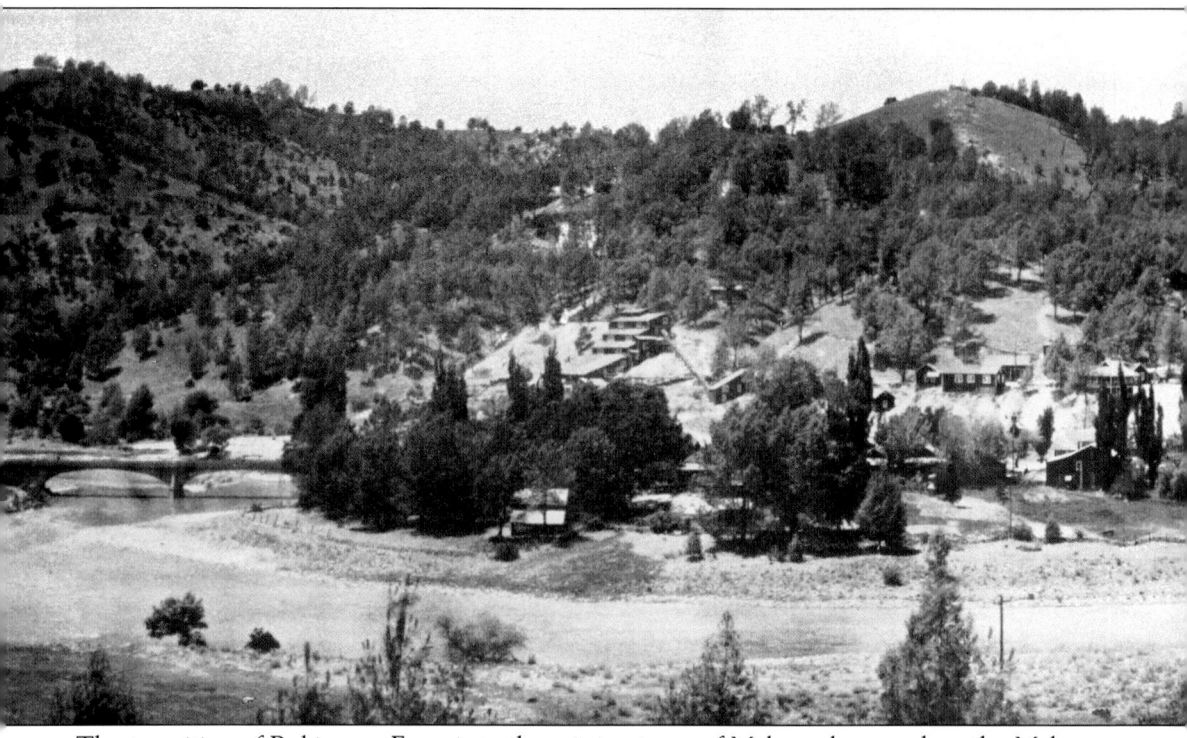

The transition of Robinsons Ferry into the mining town of Melones began when the Melones Mining Company decided to attack the ore body of Carson Hill from below. Driving a 4,500-foot-long adit into the mountain, workers then sank a 3,000-foot shaft into the adit, connecting the old mining workings. Ore was then removed by gravity to the riverside mill, seen on the right in this photograph, and water was readily available. Waste rock piled outside of the main portal is

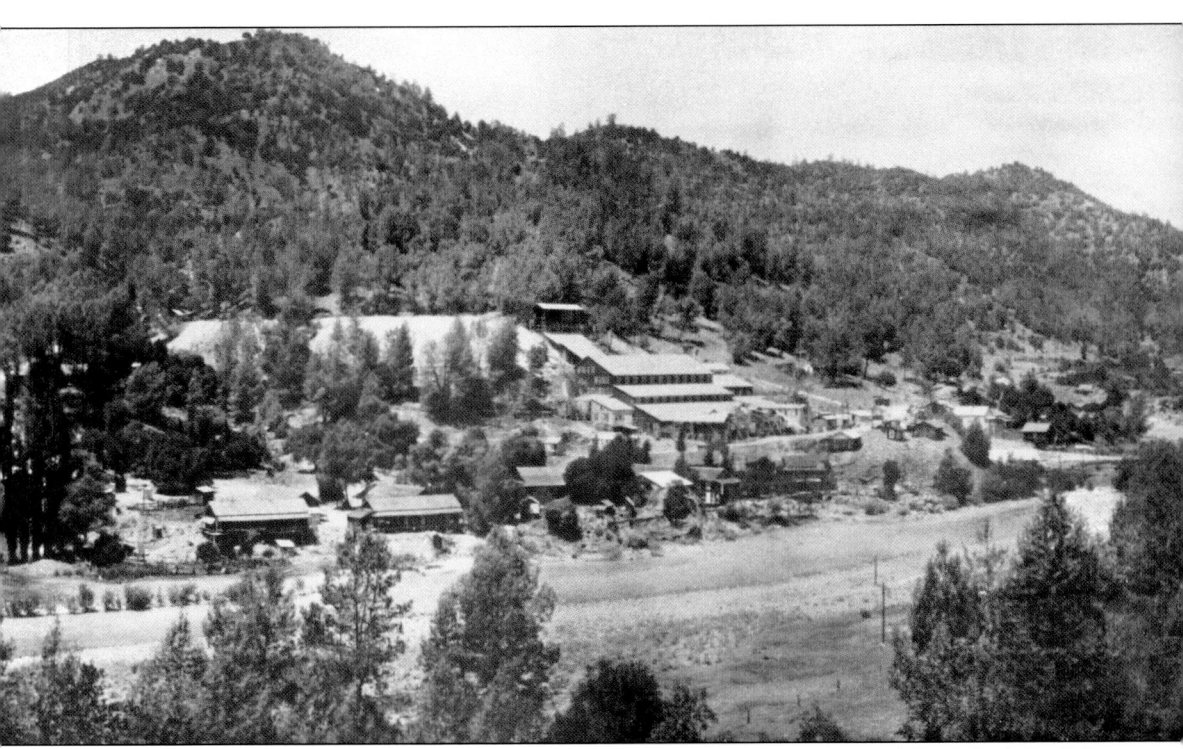

the large white hill adjacent to the mill. Bunk houses for the miners are visible to the left of the mill along the river. This first mill closed in 1919, replaced by the new 30-stamp mill of Carson Hill Gold Mines, Inc., seen here on the west end of town near the bridge. (Courtesy Calaveras County Historical Society.)

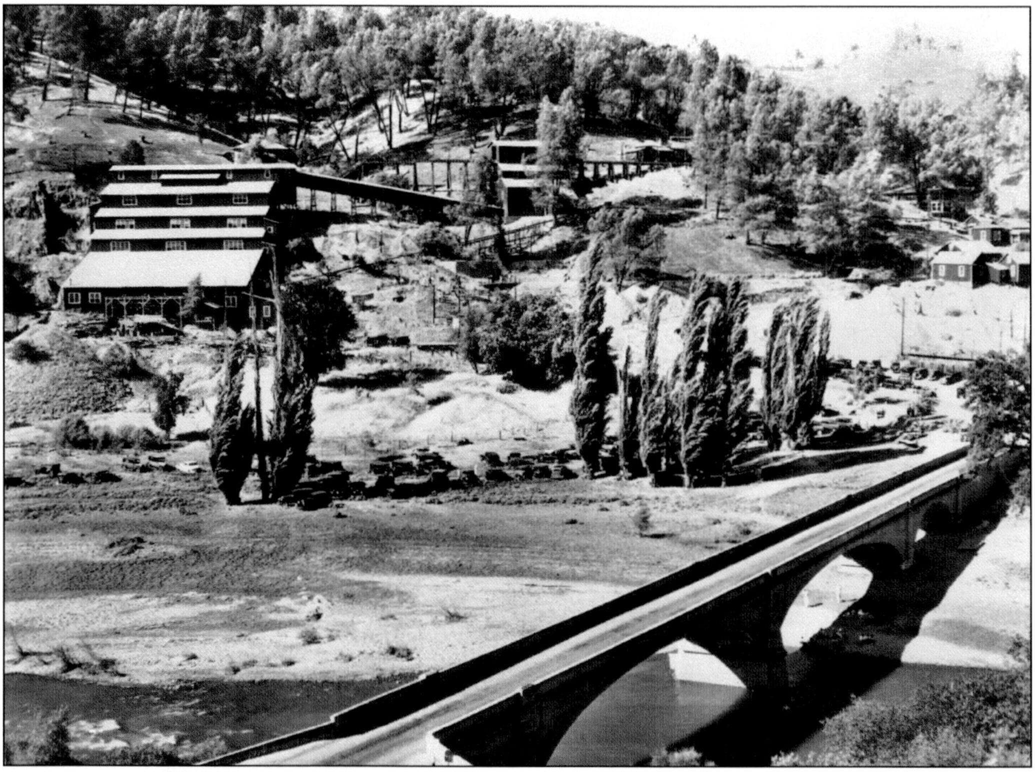

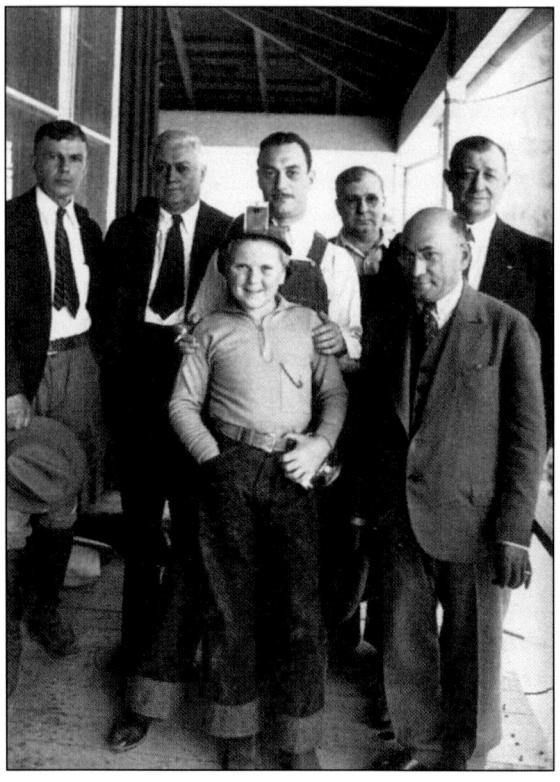

The 30-stamp mill closed in 1926, and Melones seemed nearly deserted after three decades of mining development. However, with an increase in the price of gold, the company reorganized into the Carson Hill Gold Mining Company, and in September 1933, the renovated mine and mill reopened. The photograph above shows attendees' cars parked along the riverbank and a new bridge spanning the Stanislaus. For the festivities, the Angels Camp band played, and child movie star Jackie Cooper, seen in this photograph at left, threw the switch to start the stamps pounding, signaling a return of prosperity to Melones. Also in the photograph at left are, from left to right, managing director John W. Burgess, Lawrence Monte Verda, two unidentified, Sol Grossbard, and Charles Segerstrom. (Above, courtesy Calaveras County Historical Society; left, courtesy Holt-Atherton Library, University of the Pacific.)

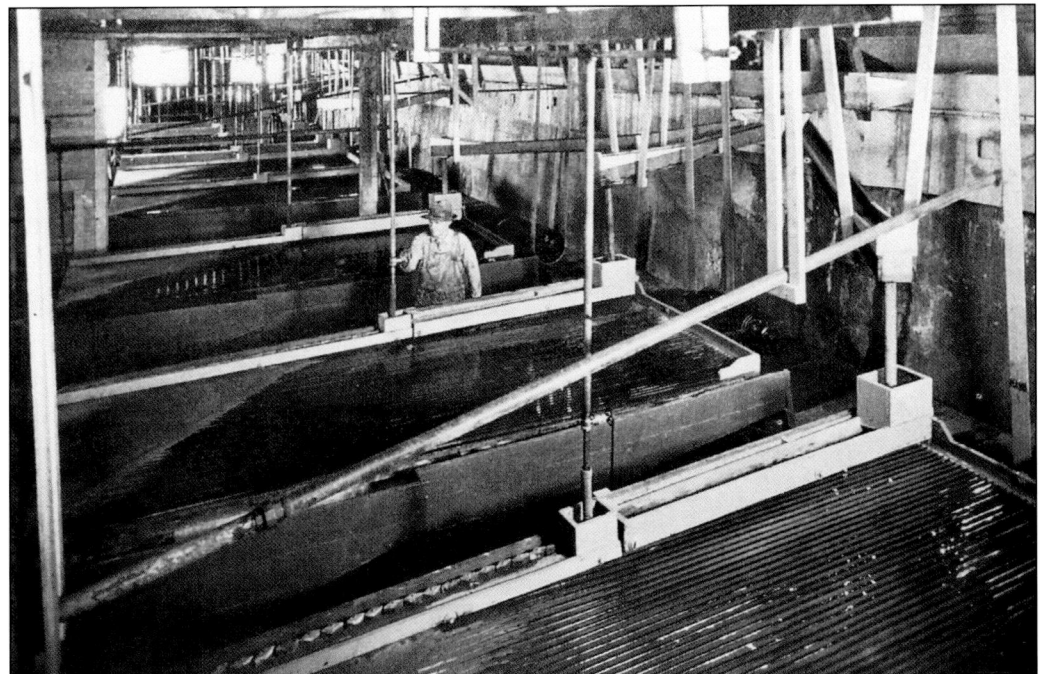
The concentrating tables of the Carson Hill Gold Mining Company mill are seen here processing ore that has been crushed in the stamps. Various chemicals are added to the "pulp" to help recover the gold. (Courtesy Mary Etta Segerstrom.)

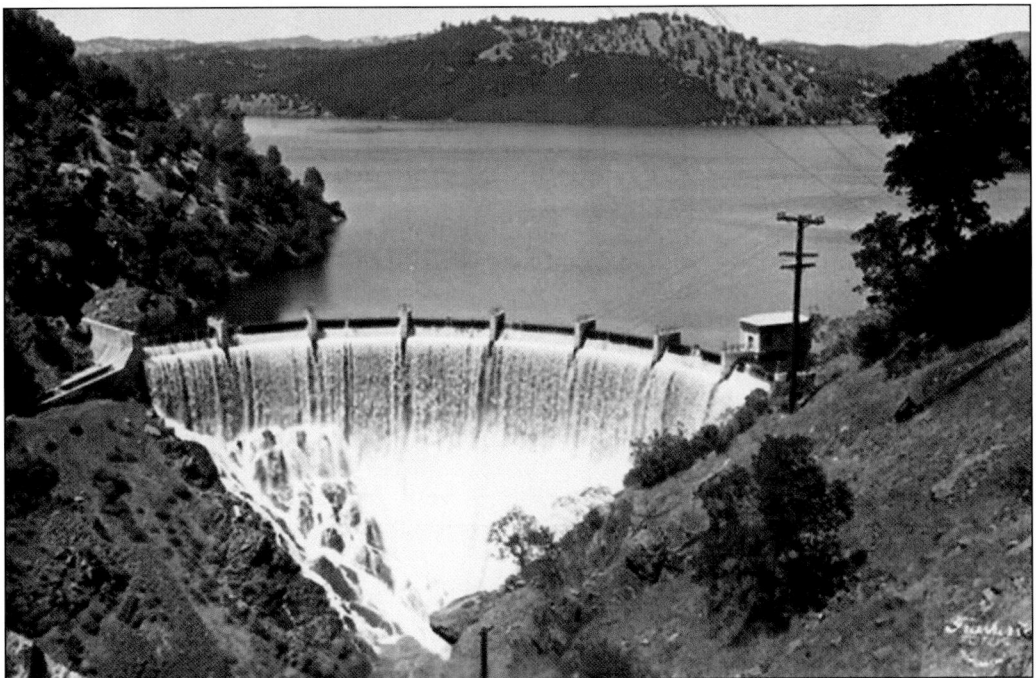
Other changes were taking place along the Stanislaus River. In 1926, the Melones dam was constructed between the old Reynolds and O'Byrnes Ferry crossings, flooding the river canyon upstream as far as the town of the same name. (Courtesy Pomona Public Library.)

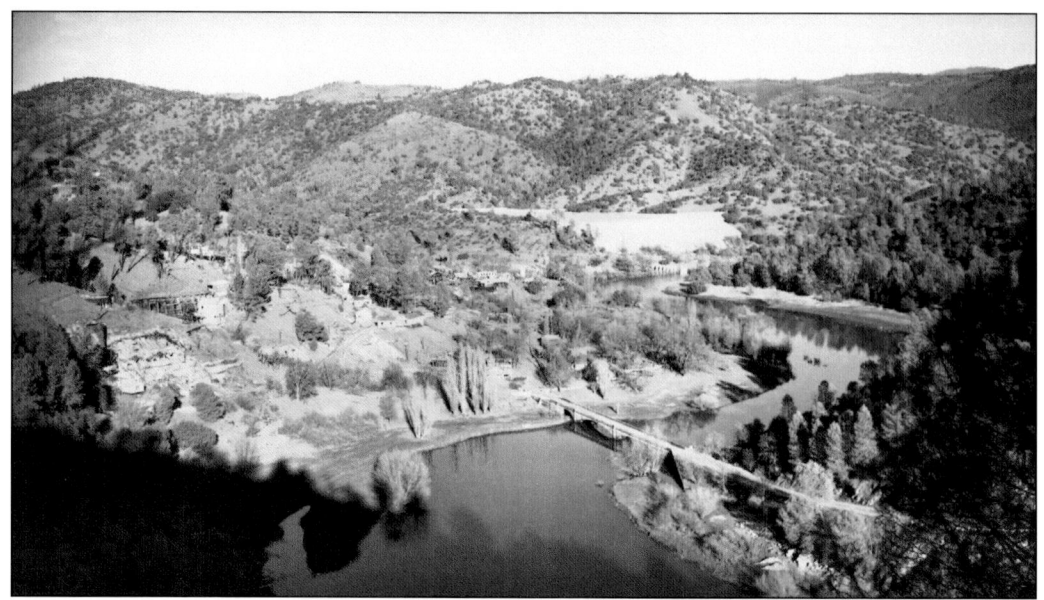

Nine years after it opened, the Carson Hill Mining Company mill burned down in a fire, its remains seen to the left in the photograph above. The flat water of the river is the upper reaches of the Melones reservoir, and the white, flat hill in the background is the tailings pile from cyanide processing used to recover gold. (Courtesy Calaveras County Historical Society.)

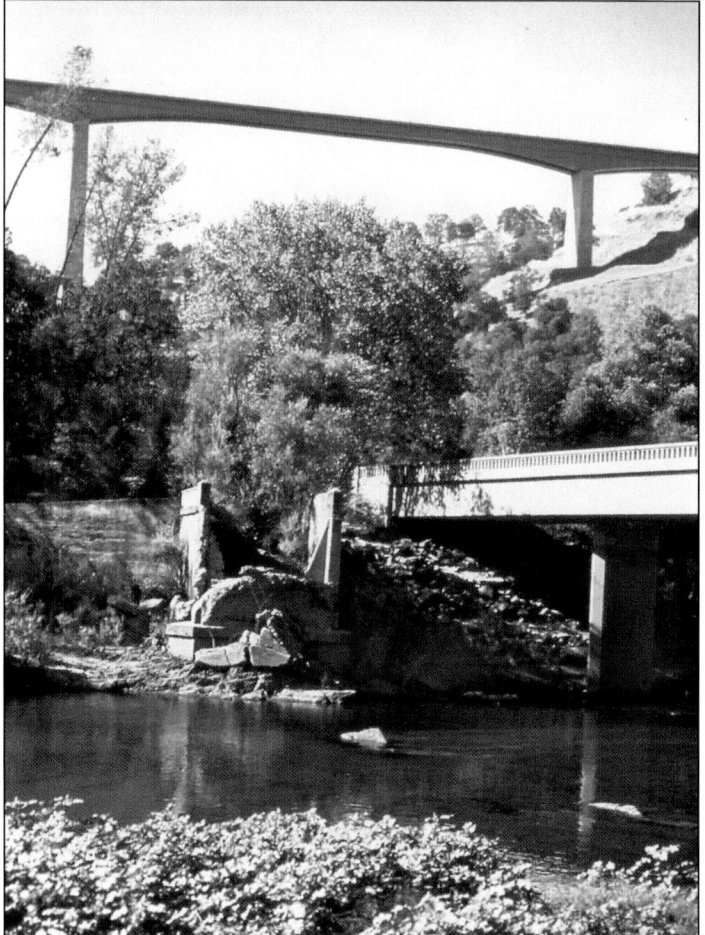

In 1962, Congress approved construction of the New Melones dam, and by 1981, the waters of the Stanislaus River were stilled for some 15 miles. However, under 350 feet of water lie remnants of the mines, ranches, homes, and these abandoned bridges that once served the riverside community of Melones. (Photograph by Julia Costello.)

Three

ROADS TO THE MINES

Following the discovery of gold in 1848, hordes of eager Argonauts swept into the Mother Lode. Although the lands near Copperopolis were not included in the boom-and-bust mining areas of the early Gold Rush, they came to have a front-row seat to the traffic to and from some of the greatest camps of the Southern Mines. At first, travel was by foot or on horseback, and most people used the established Native American route: the Antelope Trail. Also known as the Stanislaus Trail, the Old Stockton Trail, and Marshall's Trail, the route traveled up Rock Creek and through Salt Spring Valley; followed the Bear Trap Trail over Bear Mountain to Nassau Valley; and then went on to Angels Camp, Murphys, and neighboring diggings.

Five of the historic ferry roads that carried travelers from Stockton to Sonora and Columbia passed through or near Copperopolis: two to O'Byrnes Ferry on the Stanislaus River; one to Knights Ferry; and another from Copperopolis to Sonora, the present paved route called O'Byrnes Ferry Road. Reeds Turnpike, constructed 1864–1865, was an improvement over the dusty track from Copperopolis to the Stockton Road. Farther east, roads radiated southerly from Angels Camp, Vallecito, Douglas Flat, and Murphys. Known locally as the "ferry roads," they provided access to the Stanislaus River ferries, the river diggings, and the mines in Tuolumne from Stockton.

Farther east, present State Route 49, which united the early Mother Lode communities, coursed north-south from San Andreas to Angels Camp, then through Albany Flat, Carson Hill, and over the Stanislaus River to Jamestown and Sonora. As the mining population expanded, so did demands for food, mining supplies, and other merchandise. Wheeled vehicles were needed to deliver these materials to the developing towns from where outlying camps and inaccessible mining districts were served by pack trains. Wagon roads, at first few and difficult, were improved, and by the late 1870s, most had been accepted into the county road system.

Located about every five miles, stage stops and ranches along these routes provided layovers and sustenance to the freight teams and passenger stages. Both large important ranches and settlements sprang up along the routes, which are occasionally marked only by the concrete water troughs where horses and livestock once were watered.

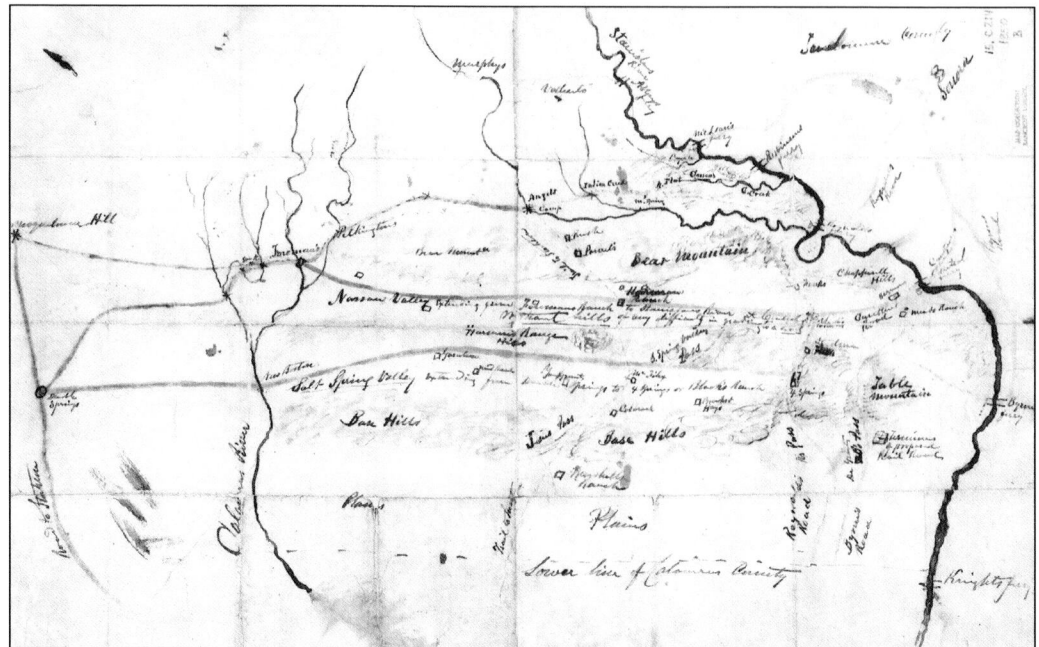

In this earliest known map of Calaveras County, drawn by Thomas Pilkington about 1854, the Stanislaus River and its ferries are prominently depicted on the right side of the image. Although locations are inaccurate, it does depict the major towns, trails, geographical features, and the ranches in the western end of the county, as well as Pilkington's own home at Fourth Crossing and the Calaveras River on the left. (Courtesy Bancroft Library.)

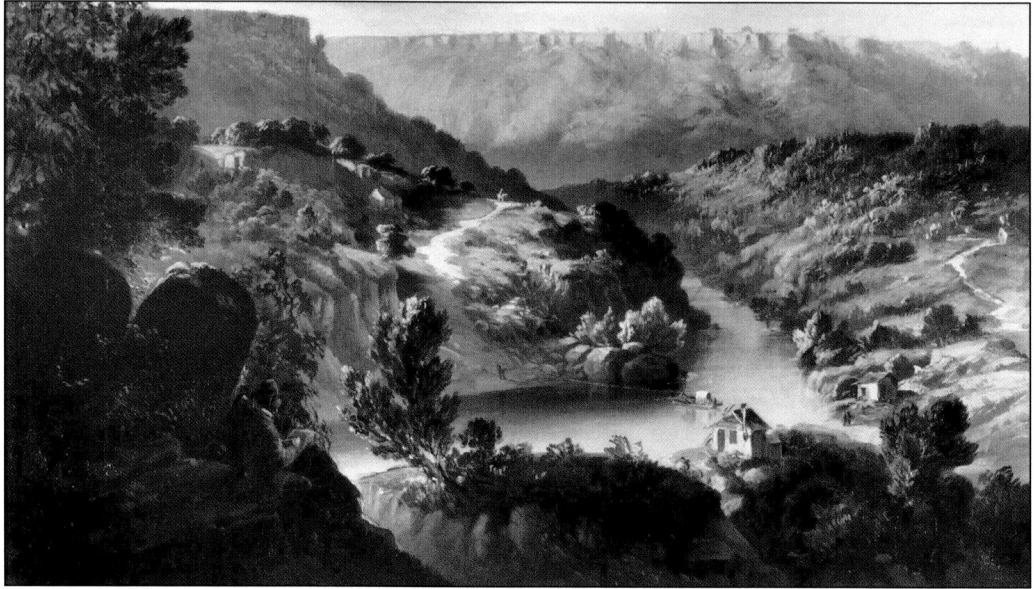

This 1860 painting, by artist Thomas Hill, of O'Byrnes Ferry depicts the site of the earliest crossing of the Stanislaus River. In 1848–1849, a primitive raft crossed the river during high water, but in 1853, P. O'Byrne took over the ferry. He then erected a cable suspension bridge, but that was swept away in the flood of 1862, as was the Gorham family home, also depicted. (Courtesy Bancroft Library.)

By the winter of 1863, a covered bridge was built by the Union Bridge Company and was operated as O'Byrnes Ferry Toll Bridge. It was purchased by Joe Pardies and his nephew Peter Camou, who charged tolls until 1902, when the bridge was purchased by the counties of Calaveras and Tuolumne, and travelers were allowed "free passage." The covered bridge was demolished in 1959 when the current bridge was erected. (Courtesy Calaveras County Archives.)

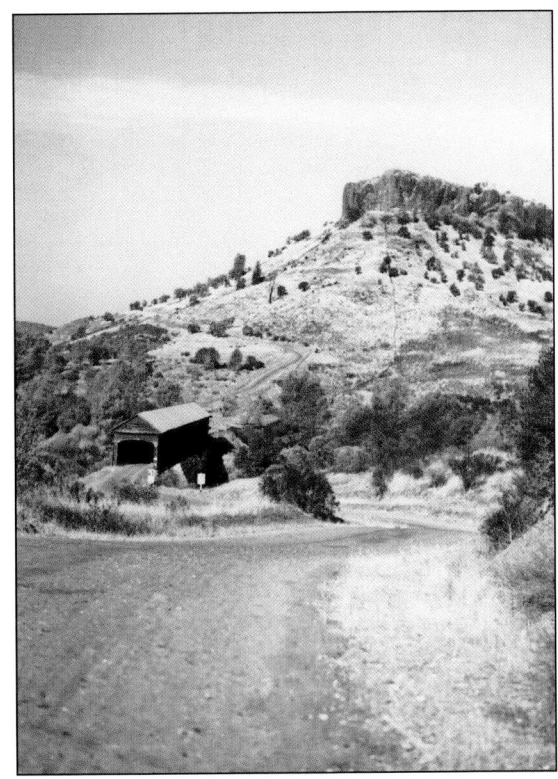

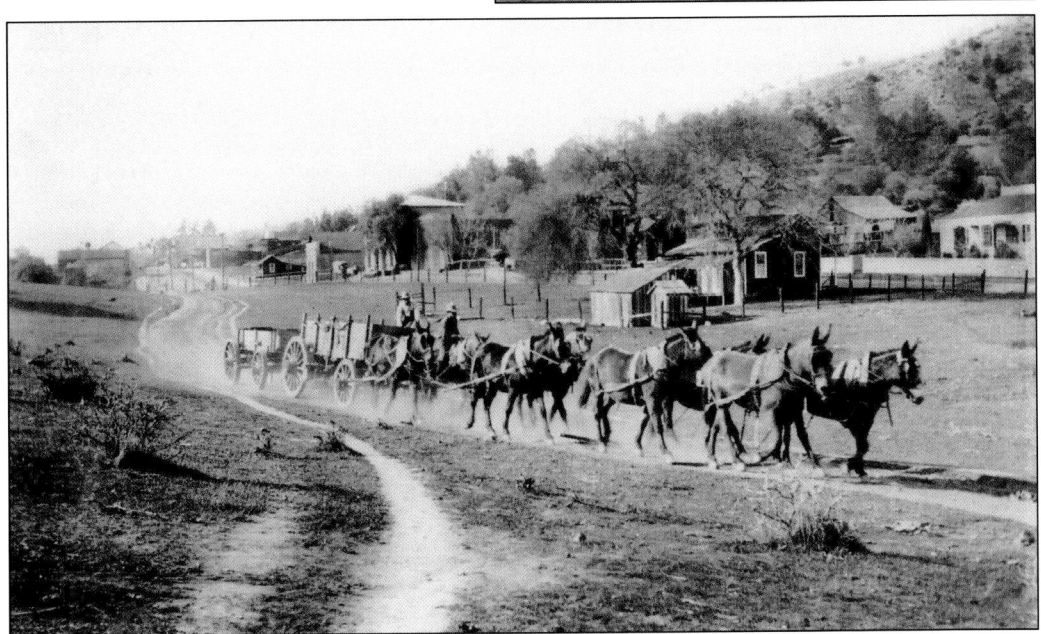

The loaded wagons and mule teams from the Union Mine in Copperopolis start down dusty O'Byrnes Ferry Road toward the mill in this early 1900s photograph. During the early years, many roads were changed seasonally to avoid the boggy areas in winter and rough higher ground in summer. They also altered routes as destinations of mines and camps waxed and waned. (Courtesy Calaveras County Archives.)

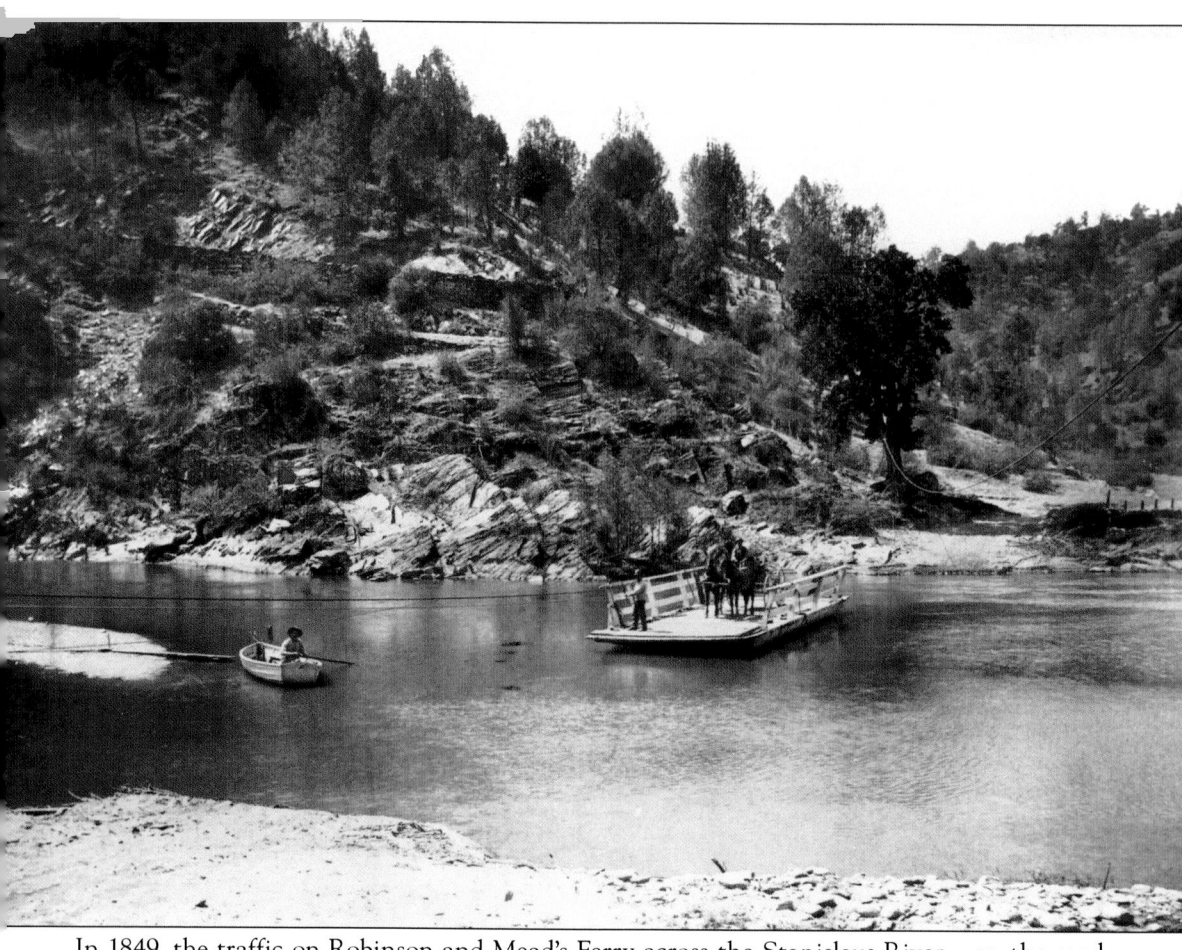

In 1849, the traffic on Robinson and Mead's Ferry across the Stanislaus River—on the road between Angels Camp and Sonora—was so great that $10,000 was collected in a period of six weeks. In this early-1900s photograph, the ferry's cable, attached at both banks, is visible to the left. By angling the boat, the downstream current moves the boat from shore to shore. (Courtesy Calaveras County Historical Society.)

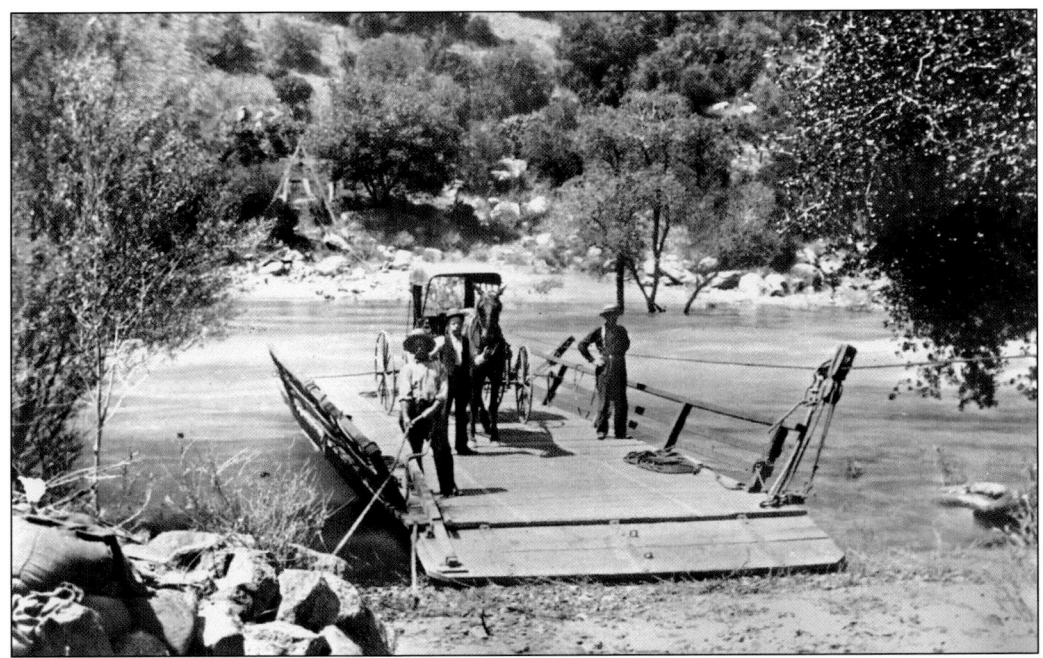

Located on the Stanislaus River between Columbia and Vallecito at Walkers Bar, Parrotts Ferry was originally known as Bradburys Ferry and was sold to J. D. Garland in 1863. By 1867, it was owned by a Mr. Colton and Lorenzo Pendola, who had greatly improved the property. It was sold to Thomas H. Parrott in 1871, with the Parrott family residing on the Calaveras side. (Courtesy Calaveras County Archives.)

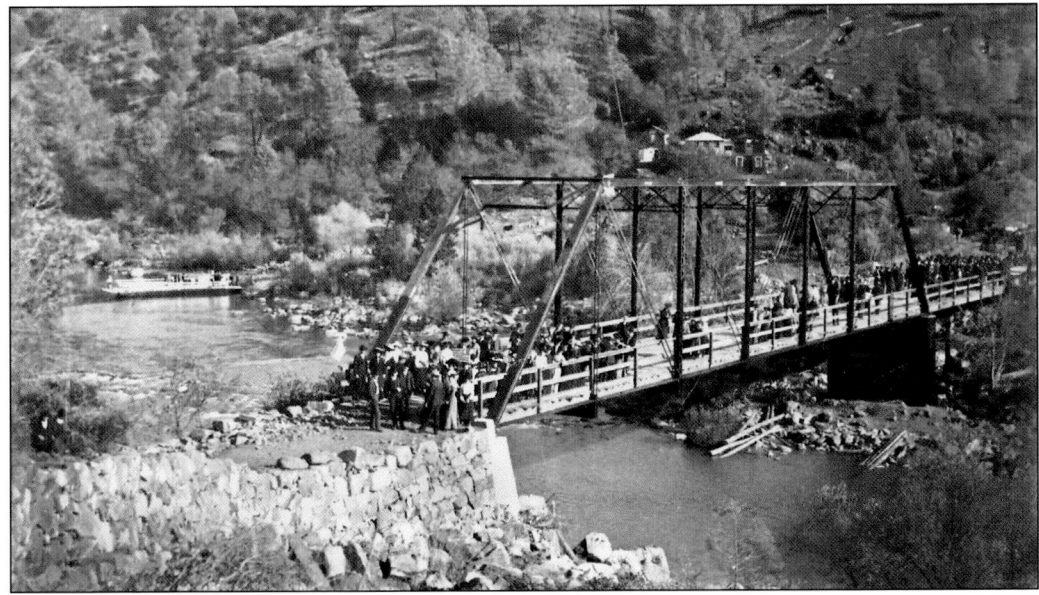

This photograph was taken the day of the opening of the first bridge in 1903, with the now outmoded ferryboat anchored upstream. This steel-truss bridge, erected at Parrotts Ferry by Calaveras and Tuolumne Counties, was washed away in 1937 and was replaced by a new concrete bridge, now under the waters of New Melones Reservoir. A modern concrete bridge now spans the two counties. (Courtesy Julia Costello.)

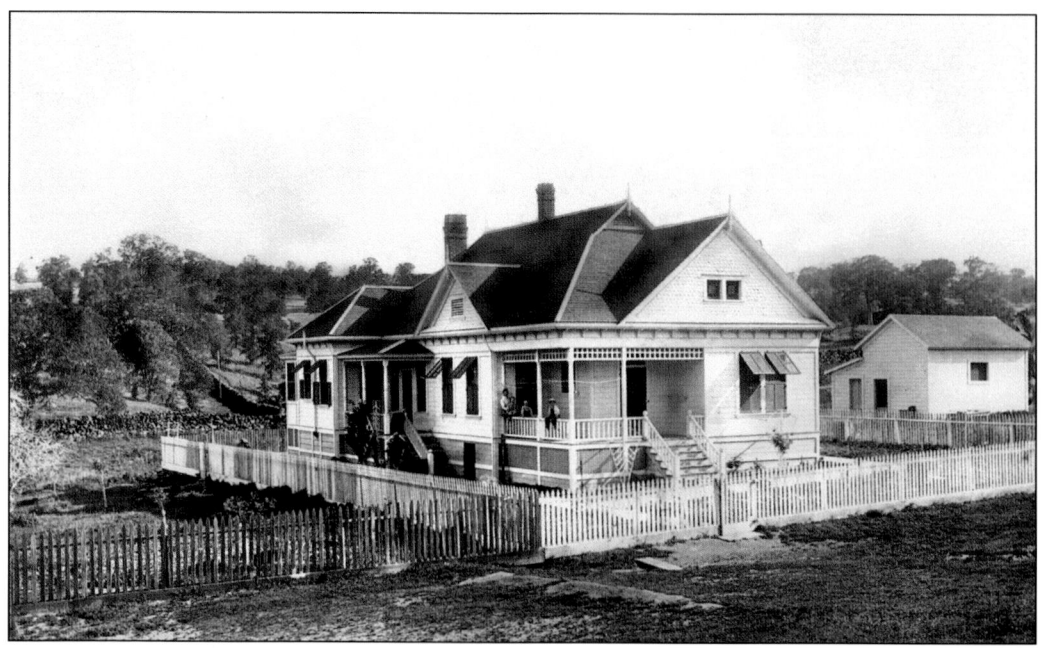

West of Copperopolis, a small community known as Grasshopper City took root around a general store early in 1861. A hotel, blacksmith shop, livery stable, restaurant, saloons, billiard halls, and stage and express station soon followed. After a telegraph line was built along the road in the 1870s, the name was changed to Telegraph City. In 1894, Robert Parks and his wife, Agnes McCarty, built this home on the ranch, selling it to Walter and Chester Murphy in 1919. The Murphy brothers ran 10,000 sheep, as well as cattle, before moving to Milton. Today the rerouted State Route 4 bypasses the site, preserving the historic character of the old road. The carefully constructed stone foundations of Telegraph City and miles of impressive rock fences on the Beardslee, Parks, and Shoemake ranches were built in the 1880s by Welshman Jimmie Sykes with help from the Wirth brothers and itinerant laborers. (Both, courtesy Calaveras County Historical Society.)

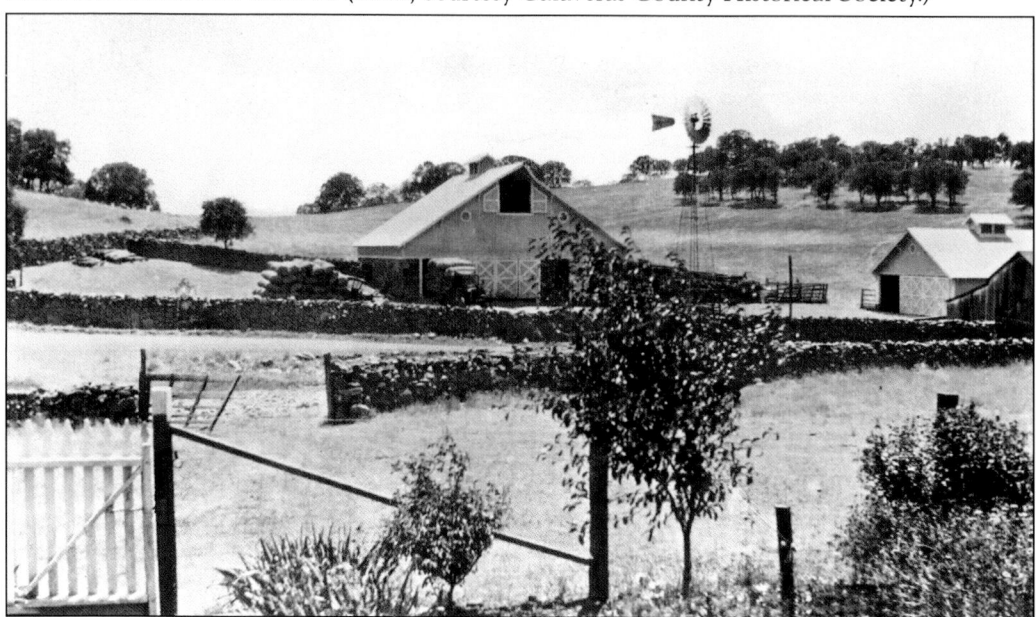

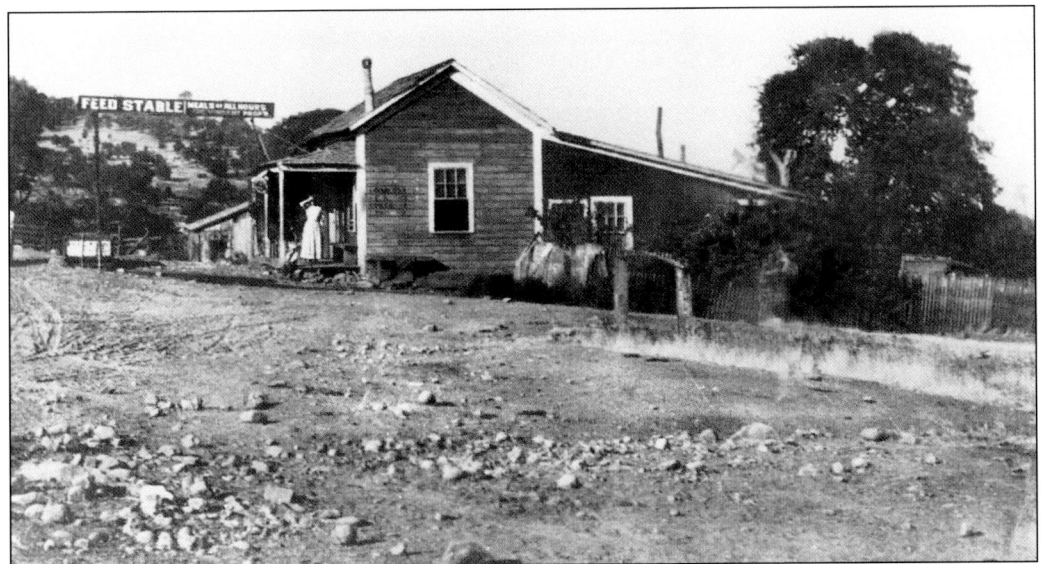

Around the dawn of the 20th century, Leora Tower stands on the porch of the Reservoir House, operated by the Johnson family, on Rock Creek Road near the Salt Spring Dam. The road down Rock Creek to Milton was engineered by a retired military man named Archer and is also known as the Archer Grade. (Courtesy Calaveras County Historical Society.)

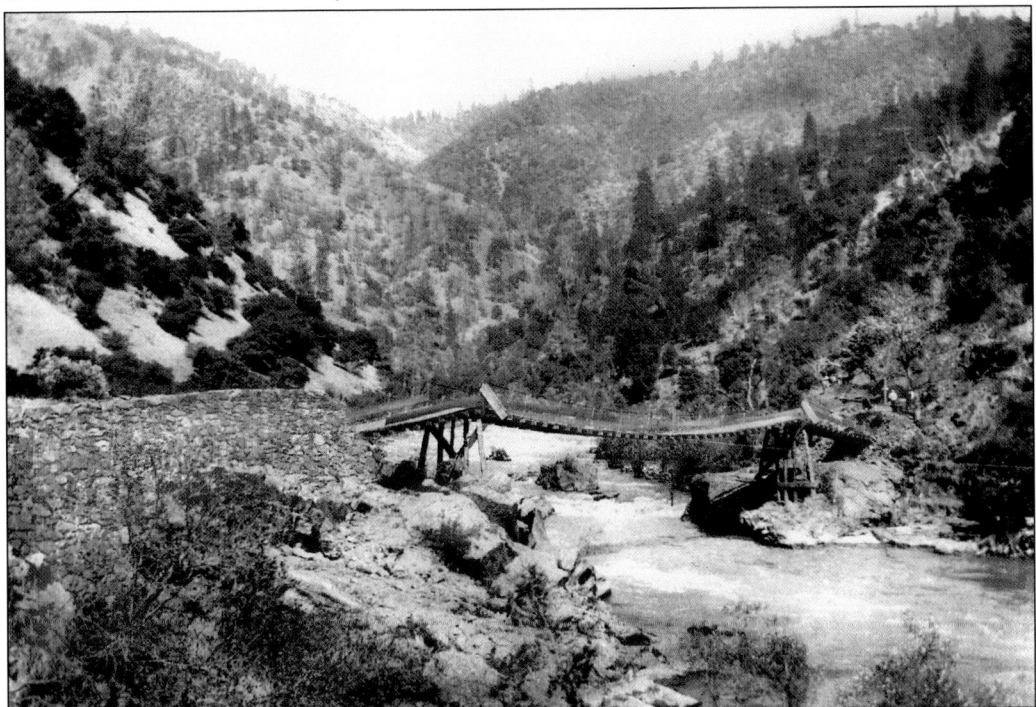

The seven tortuous miles of the road from Vallecito to the Stanislaus Powerhouse at Camp Nine were completed in 1907 by Slovenian immigrants. In this view, their carefully built rock retaining walls are visible, as well as the early suspension bridge across the river. The hydroelectric plant was completed in 1909 and was acquired by the Sierra and San Francisco Power Company that same year. (Courtesy Calaveras County Historical Society.)

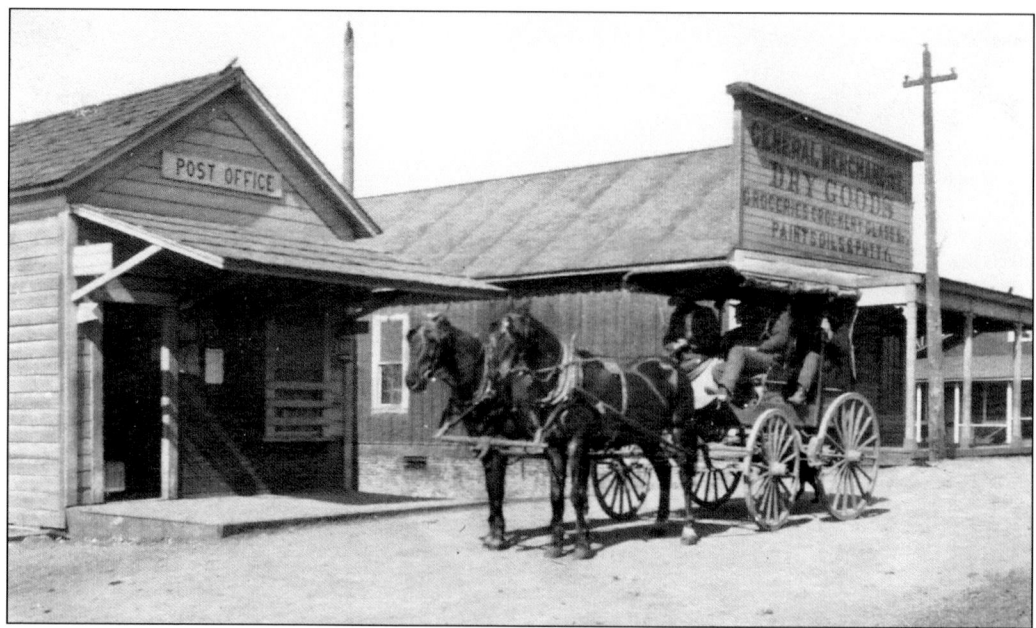

Frank Baker's mail stage is seen here in the early 1900s on Main Street in Copperopolis with the post office and Union Mine Store in the background. Baker covered the Copperopolis-to-Milton run over Reeds Turnpike, built in 1865 as an improvement over the Sonora Road. The turnpike became a county road in 1885 and was superseded by State Route 4 in 1935. (Courtesy Calaveras County Historical Society.)

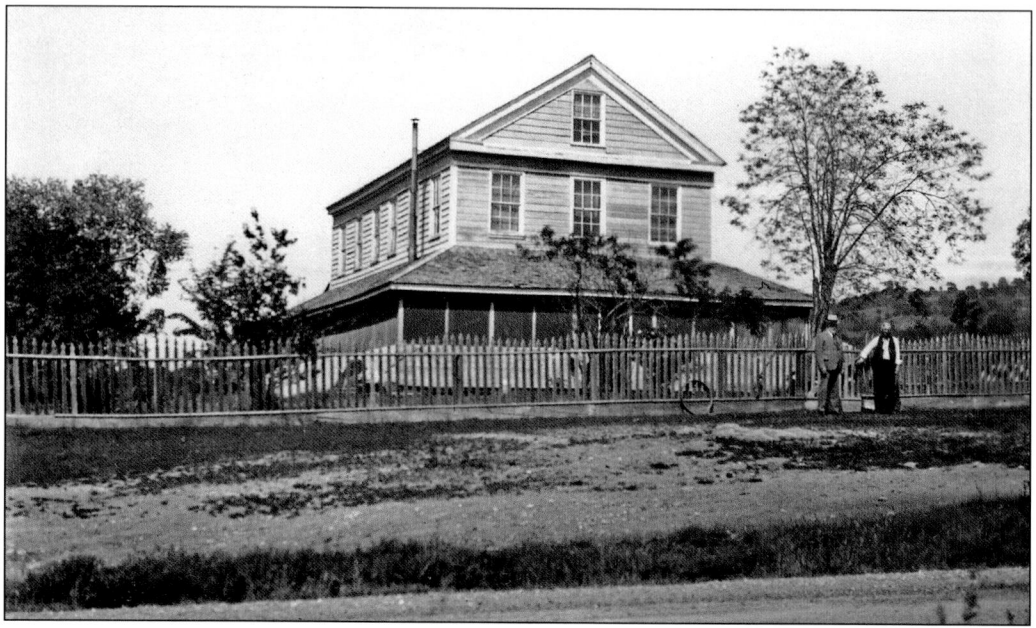

The Hawkeye Ranch and Station, a landmark on the road between Fourth Crossing and Altaville, was named for the nearby gold diggings, where miners from Iowa (the Hawkeye State) prospected in the early days. Built by the Wheat family in the 1850s, the David Maloney family purchased the hotel, store, and dance hall in 1862. The ranch is now owned by their descendants, the Airola family. (Courtesy Calaveras County Historical Society.)

Four

ANGELS CAMP AND ALTAVILLE

With its existence originally based upon placer mining, Angels Camp, named for Henry Angel, who operated an early trading post, had a population of more than 300 by the spring of 1849. It was not until 1854 that the first important quartz locations were made, all on the Davis-Winters Lode where the Winter brothers and Davis and Company were ground-sluicing. This lode roughly paralleled present Highway 49, running southeasterly from Altaville down to Angels Creek. Over the next few years, the vein was developed all the way to the creek, but the low grade of the ore, coupled with the difficulty of processing the sulphurets bound up in it, ended the boom. Altaville, also known as Forks-in-the-Road and Cherokee Diggings, took its present name at a town meeting in 1857. There was intermittent mining activity through the 1860s, and another small boom in the 1870s, but little sustained mining until the late 1880s. At this time, advanced mining and milling technologies, and the availability of East Coast and foreign capital combined to warrant large-scale underground mining. The preeminence of mining in the Mother Lode ensured all other local industries would be auxiliaries. Transportation, lumbering, water, power generation, and ranching have all been directed and influenced by the mining industry. Although not a consistent employer, the industry experienced several significant revivals, particularly in the late 19th century and again in the early 20th century, and provided the lifeblood of the Angels Camp area. Finally, most of the mines in Angels Camp closed during World War I, never to reopen. On the western fringes, the Gold Cliff Mine struggled on for a few more years, as did some of the smaller family-operated mines in the area. Only the Carson Hill Gold Mining Company on the Stanislaus River provided steady employment until it, too, closed during World War II. The City of Angels, the only incorporated town in Calaveras County, was formed by joining Altaville and Angels Camp in 1912, reflecting the hopes of that era for increased prosperity. Although slumbering for several decades, the rolling hills that once grazed cattle now support new families who are making the foothills their home.

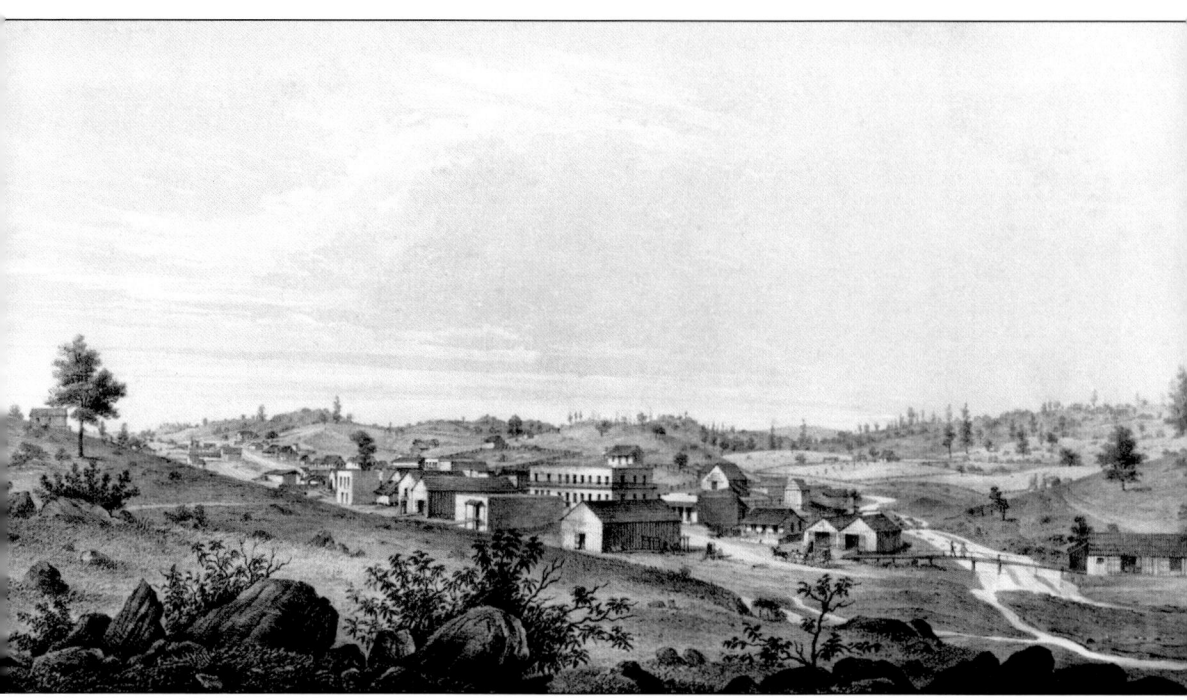

In one of the earliest views of Angels Camp, produced by lithographers Kuchel and Dressel in 1857, the most prominent structure is the two-story Angels Hotel on Main Street, built by pioneer stonemason Allen Taylor. The view is northeasterly, with Angels Creek to the right and Altaville to the left. It was in the latter location where one of the most celebrated hoaxes in the 19th century was perpetrated in the 1860s. Some miners, wishing to play a hoax on state geologist Prof. J. D. Whitney, placed a Native American skull in their shaft on Bald Hill and pretended to dig it out of their claim. Believing it was the skull of an ancient man, Professor Whitney took it to the Smithsonian Institution, where it was eventually discovered to be of recent age. It was so well publicized, however, that Bret Harte composed a poem, *An Ode to the Pliocene Skull*, about the discovery. (Courtesy Calaveras County Historical Society.)

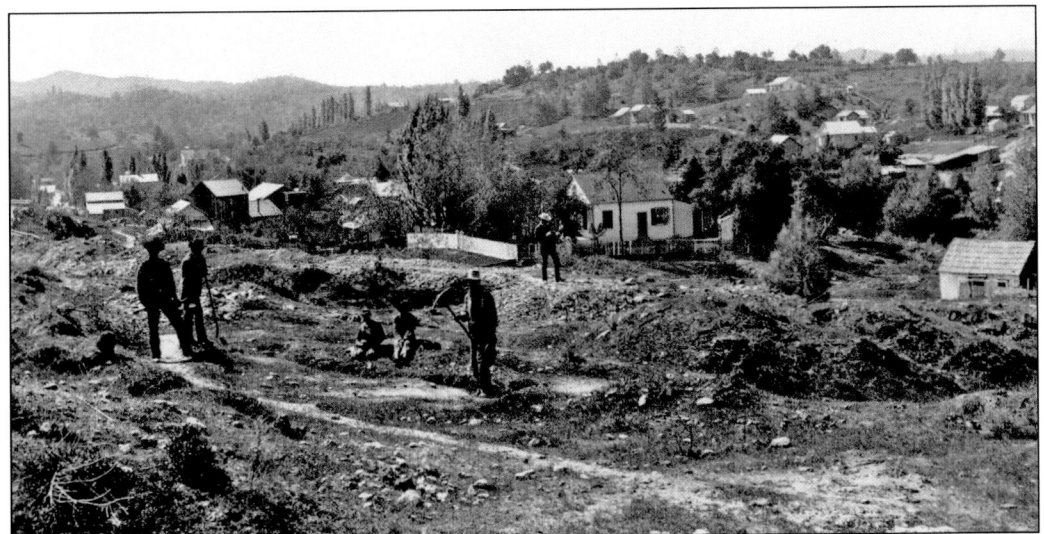

These men are working the placers on the upper end of Main Street in Angels Camp just south of where the Winter brothers first struck the Davis-Winters Lode in 1854. The vein of gold-bearing quartz ore extends southeasterly from Altaville down to Angels Creek, and deep shafts were sunk on both sides of Main Street. (Courtesy Calaveras County Archives.)

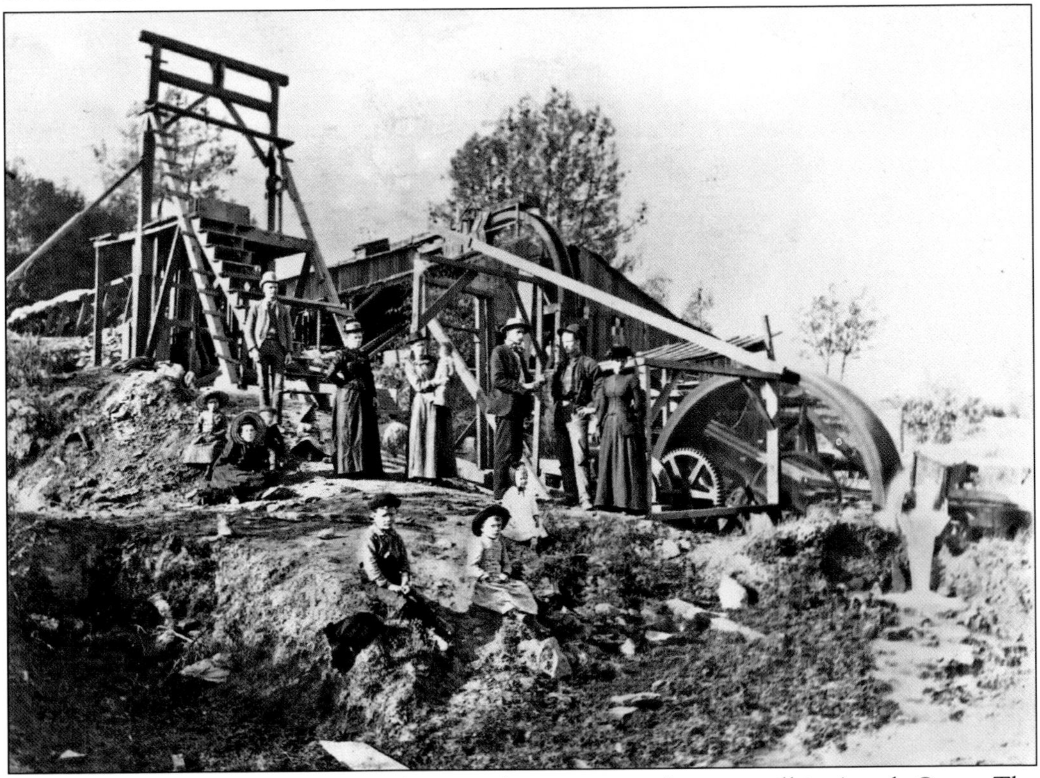

In 1857, William Maltman erected the second water-powered stamp mill in Angels Camp. The overshot wheel was 30 feet in diameter and worked 12 stamps, crushing 15 tons of rock a day. Family and friends are pictured at the mine, with the gallows frame, large flywheel, and hoist in the background. (Courtesy Calaveras County Historical Society.)

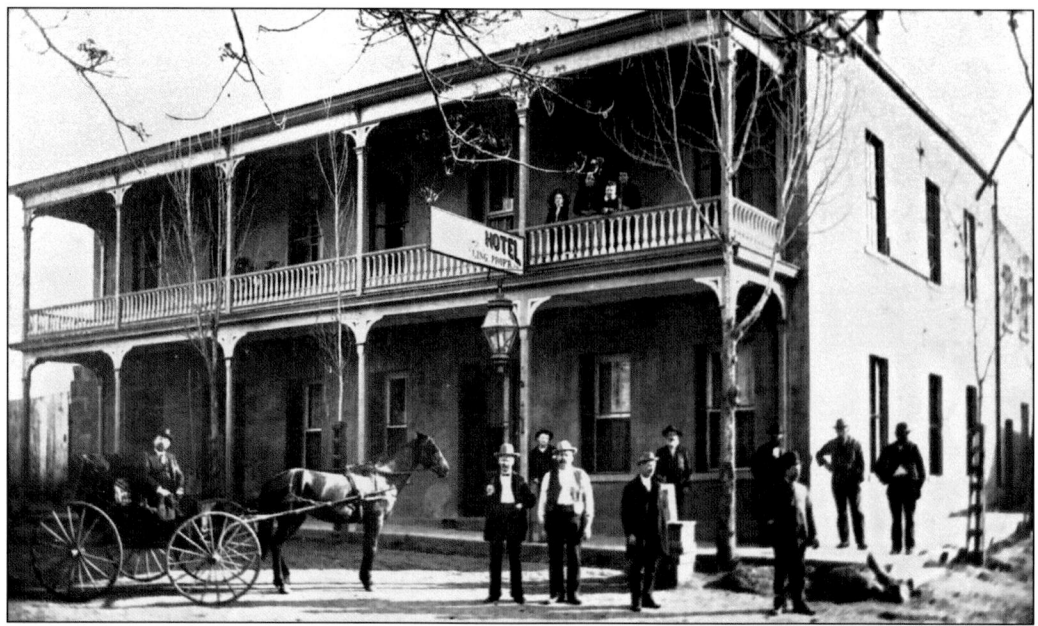

The first story of the Angels Hotel, the first substantial hotel in town, was completed by Allen Taylor for C. C. Lake in 1855 and the second story two years later. In February 1865, Mark Twain heard the "Jumping Frog" story from bartender Ross Coon in the hotel's barroom, where Twain retired that evening. Otto Dolling was the proprietor in this 1890s view. (Courtesy Calaveras County Historical Society.)

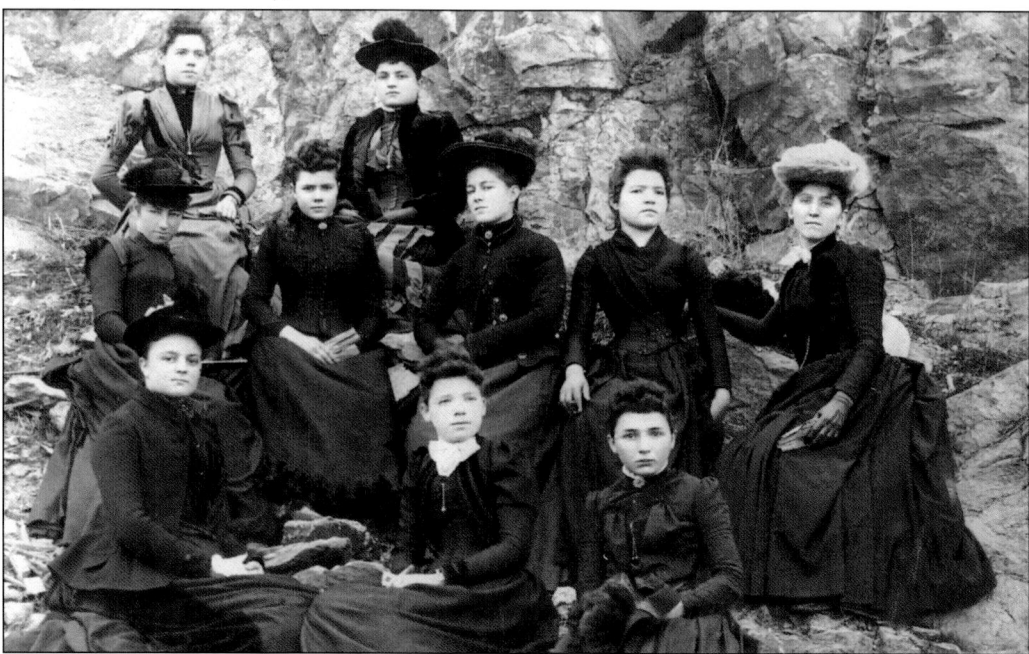

Local young women, including, from left to right, (first row) Josephine Bernasconi, Carrie Huberty, and Lu Rolleri; (second row) Effie Johnston, Lizzie Huberty, Martha Johnston, Mary Huberty, and Kate Zwinge; (third row) Susie Huberty and Minnie Rolleri, pose for the photographer in 1890 dressed in their somber best. (Courtesy Calaveras County Historical Society.)

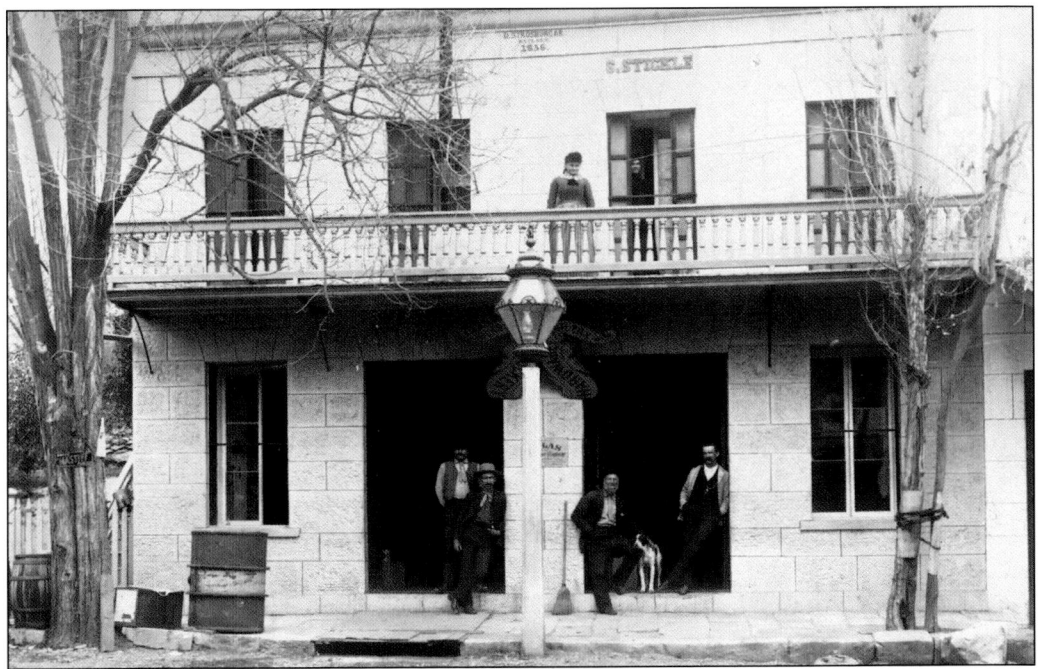

Edward and George Stickles arrived in San Francisco from New York in 1849. In 1852, they opened a mercantile store in Angels Camp and were so successful that they built this stone store in 1856. Erected by David Strousberger, it is one of many stone buildings in the community made of rhyolite tuff quarried from the outcrop north of town. (Courtesy Calaveras County Historical Society.)

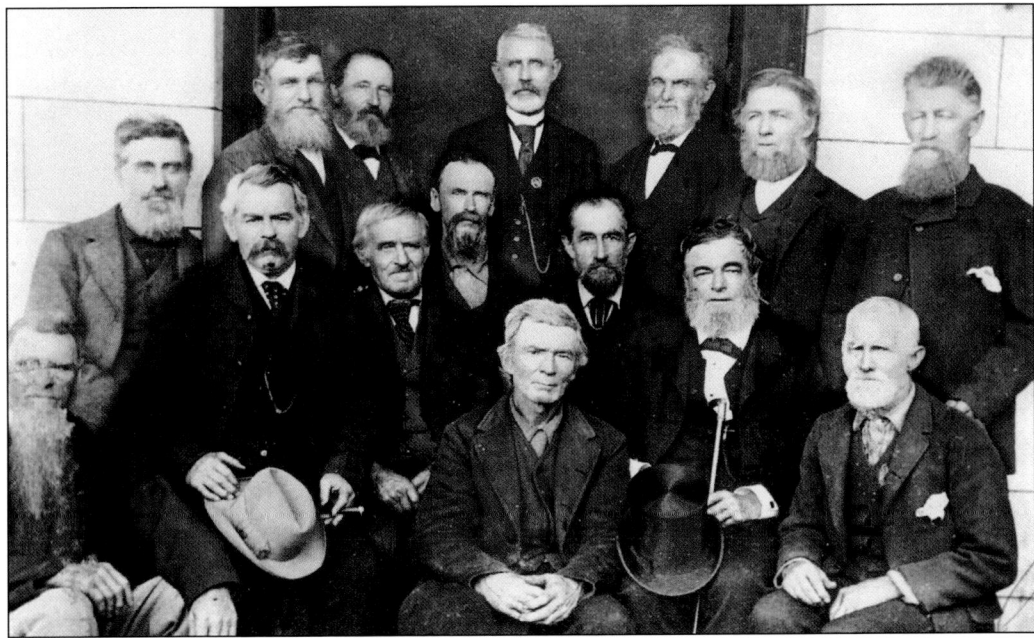

The prominent businessmen of Angels gathered for this photograph in the 1890s. Included in the group are D. C. Demarest, Allen Taylor, George Tryon, John Scribner, G. Raymond, George Stickle, Bud Miller, Joe Ranks, Charlie Gibson, a Mr. Shearer, Tom Hardy, Dr. William Kelley, and a Dr. Sylvester. (Courtesy Calaveras County Historical Society.)

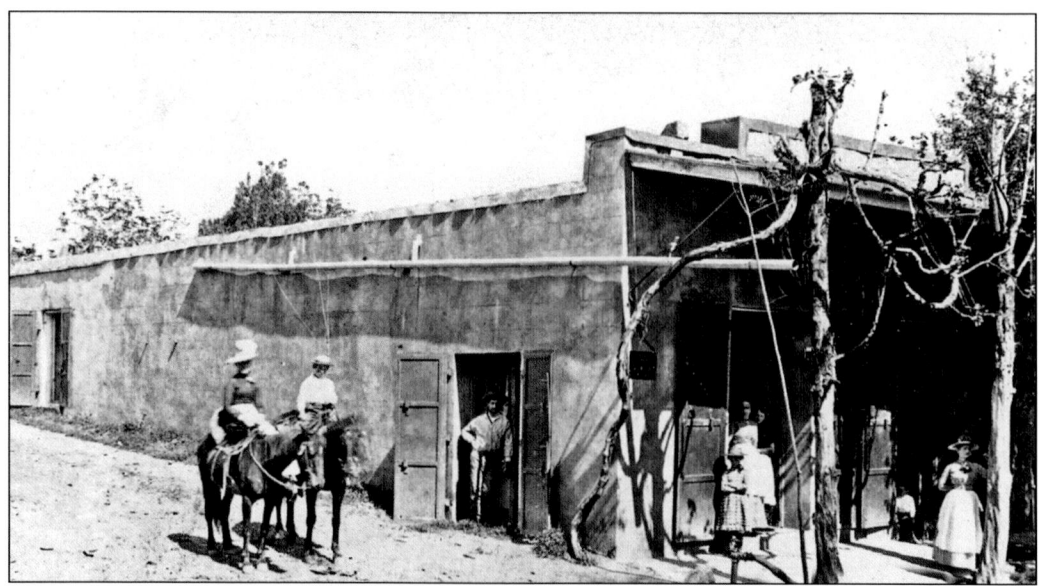

In the early 1850s, John Peirano opened a tent store on the south bank of Angels Creek, later constructing a stone building on Main Street and Chinatown Road (Birds Way). John looked after the grocery and hardware departments while his wife, Julia Podesta, took care of the dry-goods and millinery departments. This view was taken about 1890, when the store was still operated by the family. (Courtesy Calaveras County Historical Society.)

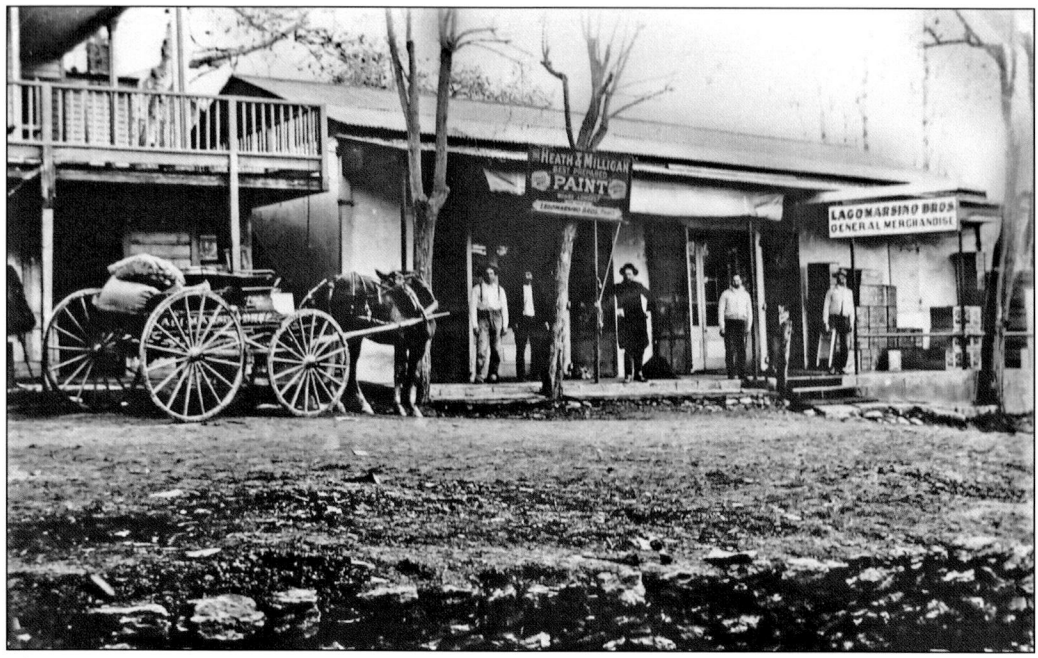

Three Lagomarsino brothers, including John and Jack, along with Frank Bacigalupi, stand on the front porch of the Lagomarsino Brothers Store (later the Lagomarsino and Bacigalupi Store) on upper Main Street in the 1890s. The stone store, built for Joseph Peirano in 1856, was located adjacent to his lovely frame residence. (Courtesy Calaveras County Historical Society.)

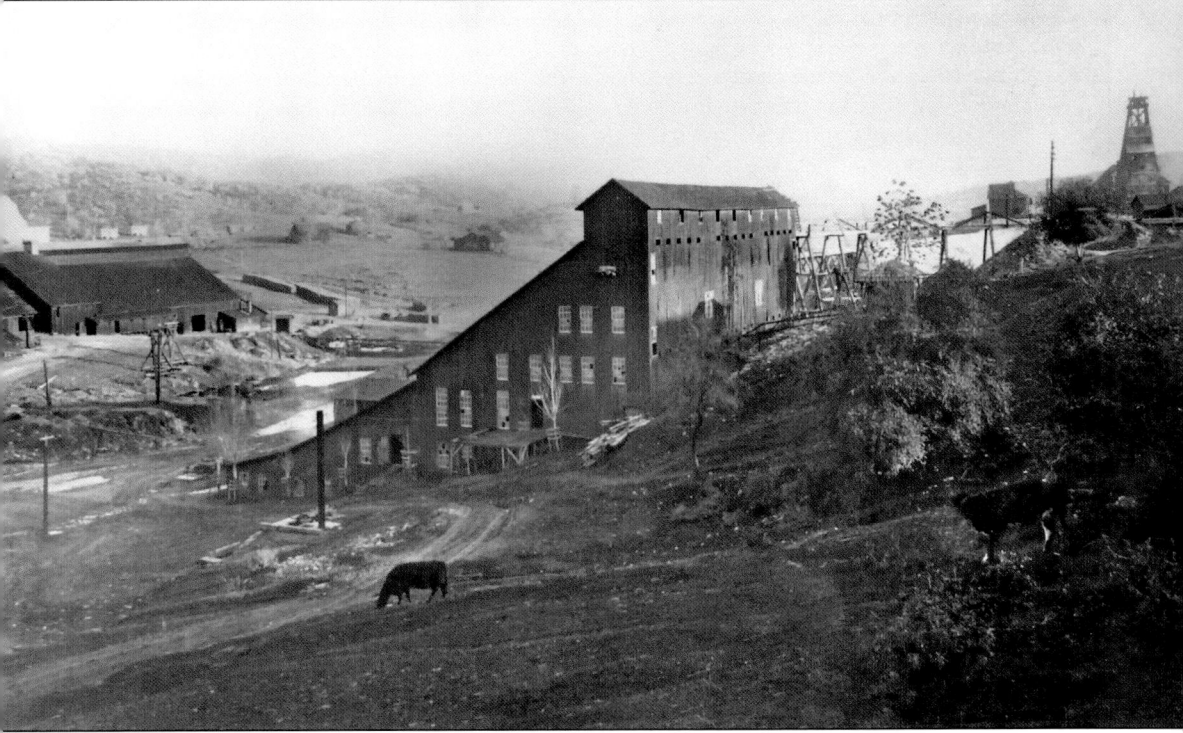

There were a number of stamp mills around Angels Camp, erected in hope and haste, but they crushed out only a small amount of ore and were soon abandoned. The mills that roared on—sustaining the town day after day, year after year, pounding out millions of dollars in gold—were the Utica, Stickles, Gold Cliff, Madison, Lightner, Angels, and Sultana. They were supported by the big chlorination works that extracted the precious ore from the tight grip of the sulphide minerals and the blanket plant that squeezed the remaining values out of the slime tailings. The most important mine in Angels was the Utica, which operated mills totaling 180 stamps and 76 vanners, and encompassed four mines at its peak in the 1890s and early 1900s. In this view, the 120-stamp Stickles Mill, erected in 1903, is in the center, the chlorination plant to the left, and the cross-shaft headframe on the hill to the right. (Courtesy Calaveras County Historical Society.)

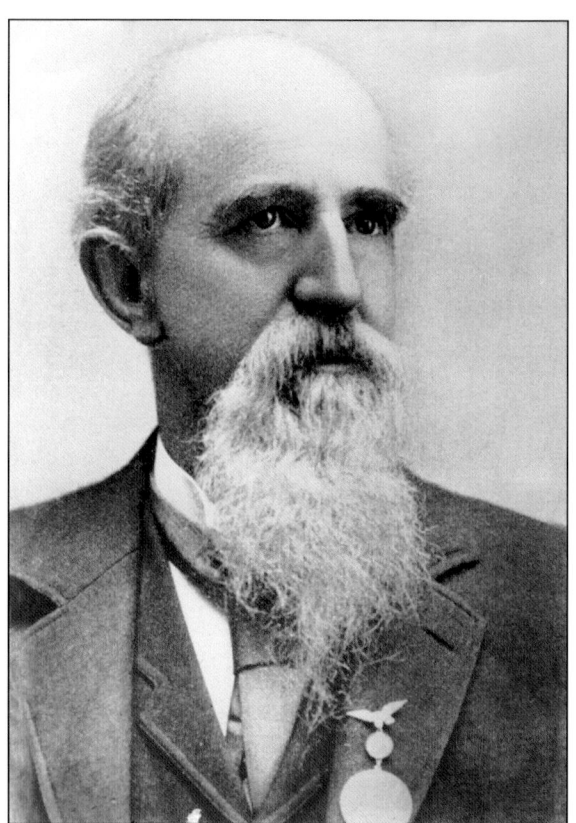

Charles D. Lane, who put the complex Utica Mining Company together, was one of the earliest and most successful mine owners and civic developers of Angels Camp. He acquired the Union Water Company in 1887 (enlarging the canals and flumes that brought water to Angels Camp), constructed new reservoirs and power plants, and brought electricity to the town by 1899. (Courtesy Calaveras County Historical Society.)

Over its long history, several important mining men were involved in the operation of the Utica, including James G. Fair of the Comstock Lode, Robert Leeper, Alvinza Hayward, Walter Hobart, and Charles D. Lane. Under Lane, the most extensive development was made, including sinking the Cross Shaft in 1896, when it was said that "the Utica Mining Company *is* Angels Camp." (Courtesy Calaveras County Historical Society.)

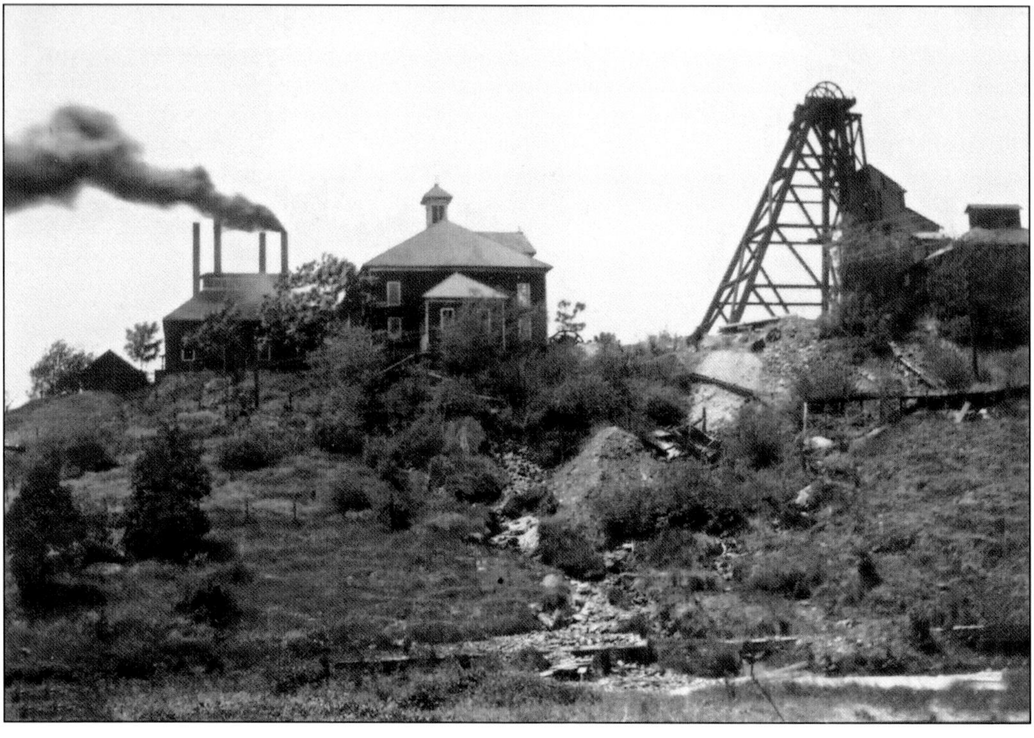

After the Utica and Stickle mines were consolidated, new shafts were sunk at the Stickle and the Utica Cross Shaft, and the old Utica shafts were abandoned. The staff and visitors underground are holding their miner's candlesticks in an area of ground that had recently been drilled and blasted. Men liked working underground because it was cool in summer and warm and dry in the rainy season. (Courtesy Calaveras County Archives.)

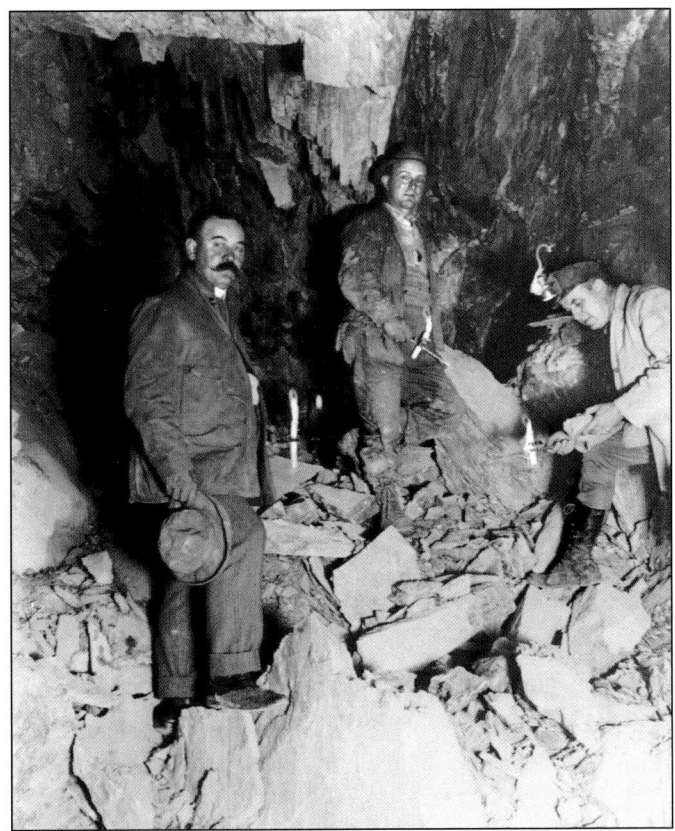

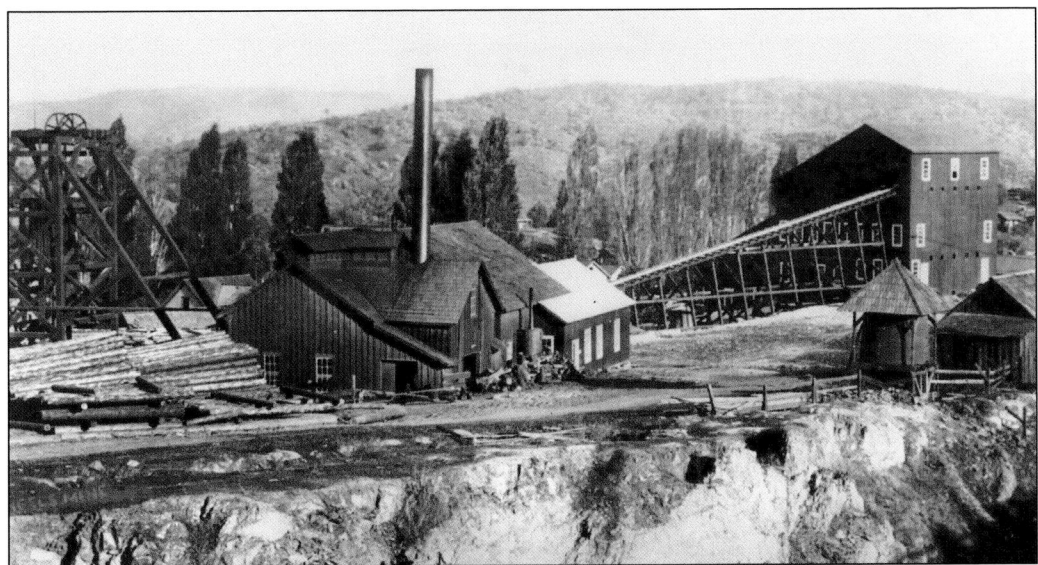

The mill plant of the Angels Mine, consolidated from the Angels, Doctor Hill, Maltman, and Potter claims in 1884, operated between 1890 and 1918. The open vein, shown in the foreground, is located across from today's Angels Camp Museum. Just to the south, the remains of the compressor of the Lightner Mine, which operated its 40 stamps, is now an artifact in Utica Park. (Courtesy Calaveras County Historical Society.)

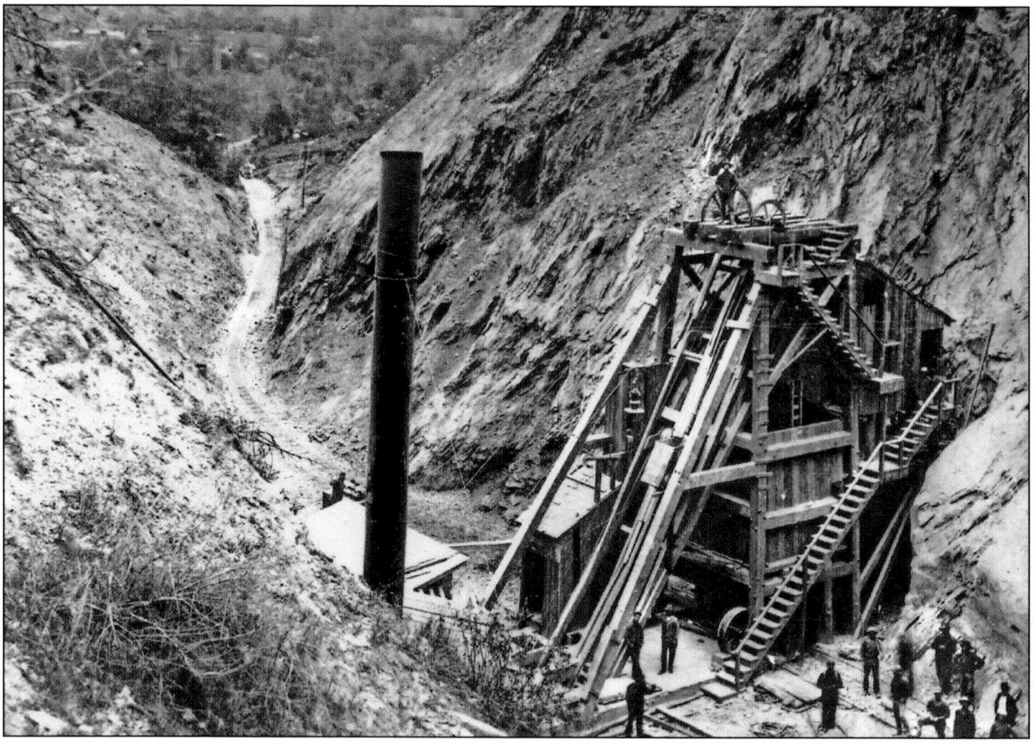

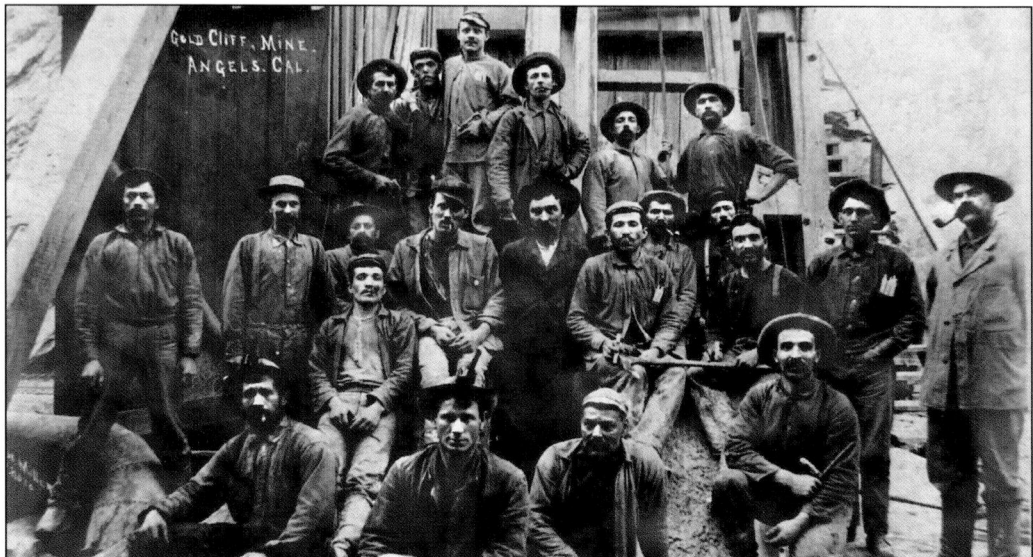

The Gold Cliff Mine, worked from the earliest days, was located on the Boulder Lode west of town. Serious production began in the 1880s with a deep open cut 275 feet long and 160 feet deep. In 1899, the mine was taken over by the Utica Mining Company, which sank a deep shaft that year and worked the ore until 1920. (Courtesy Calaveras County Historical Society.)

A mining crew poses during its shift at the Gold Cliff Mine in 1893. Willie Williams, the man with the pipe at far right, was the shift boss. The miners worked a 10-hour day, seven days a week, and were paid a daily wage, generally once a week. Miners were paid $3.50, muckers $2.50, and skip tenders, timbermen, and engineers received $3 a day. (Courtesy Calaveras County Historical Society.)

After the 1888 death of her husband, Geralomo, with whom she operated a small hotel at Reynolds Ferry, Olivia "Grandma" Rolleri purchased a boardinghouse in Angels Camp. An astute businesswoman, she ran the Calaveras Hotel, cooked her famous ravioli dinners, and purchased the Marks and then the Slab Ranch, where she raised beef, hogs, poultry, and vegetables that provided food both for the Calaveras Hotel and for her butcher shop. (Courtesy Cornelia Barden Stevenot.)

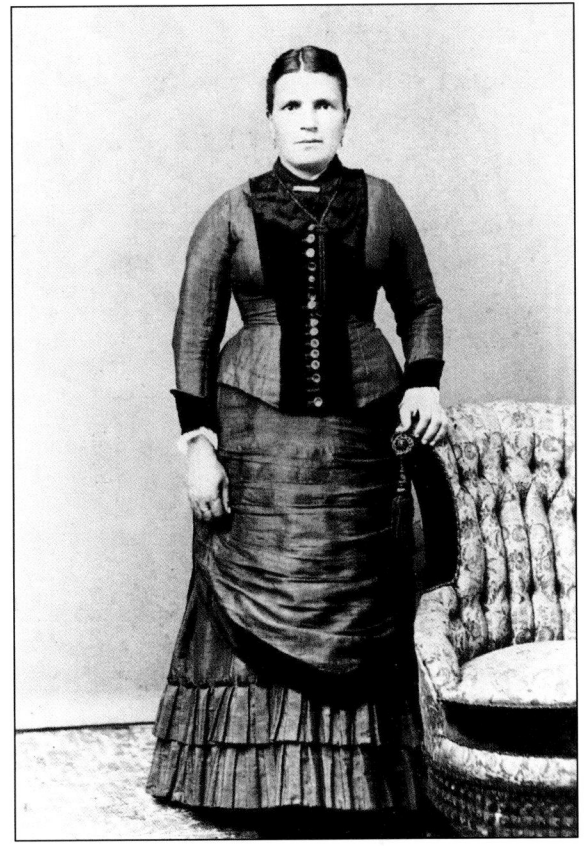

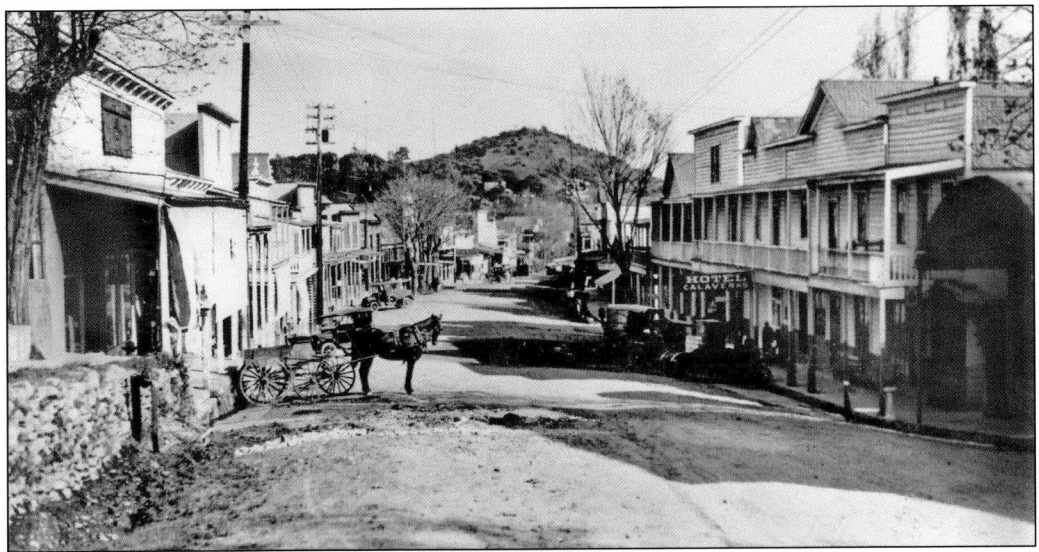

The Calaveras Hotel, depicted in 1900, was the center of Angels Camp's social life for the almost 50 years it was operated by Grandma Rolleri and her daughters. Eventually expanding to occupy the entire block between Hardscrabble and Bush Streets, the hotel had 50 rooms, some for transients and some for family and permanent guests, a lobby, a parlor, two dining rooms, an elegant saloon, and indoor bathrooms. (Courtesy Calaveras County Historical Society.)

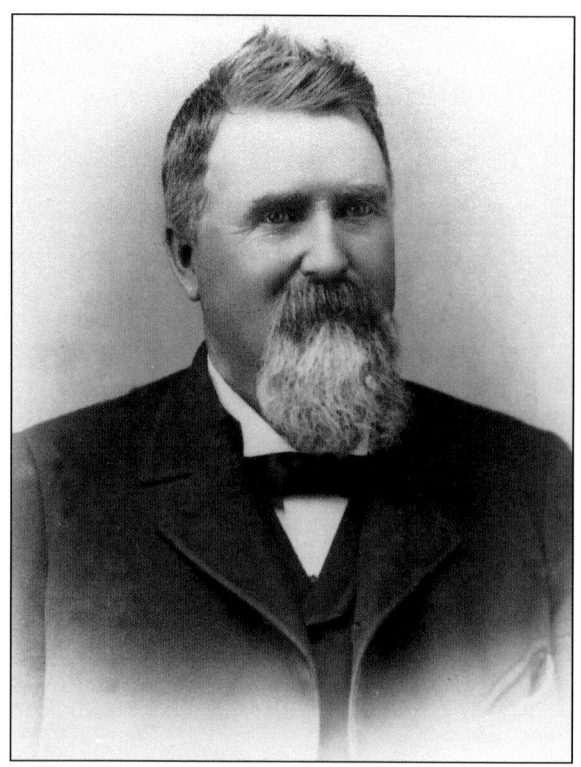

Harvey Blood, a prominent citizen of Calaveras and Alpine Counties, served as an assemblyman to the state legislature in the 1890s. A resident of Angels Camp, Blood and his family operated and maintained the Big Tree–Carson Valley Turnpike over Ebbetts Pass from 1864 to 1910. Bloods Station, located at Grizzly Bear Valley, was a major stopover on the road to the Washoe mines. (Courtesy Calaveras County Historical Society.)

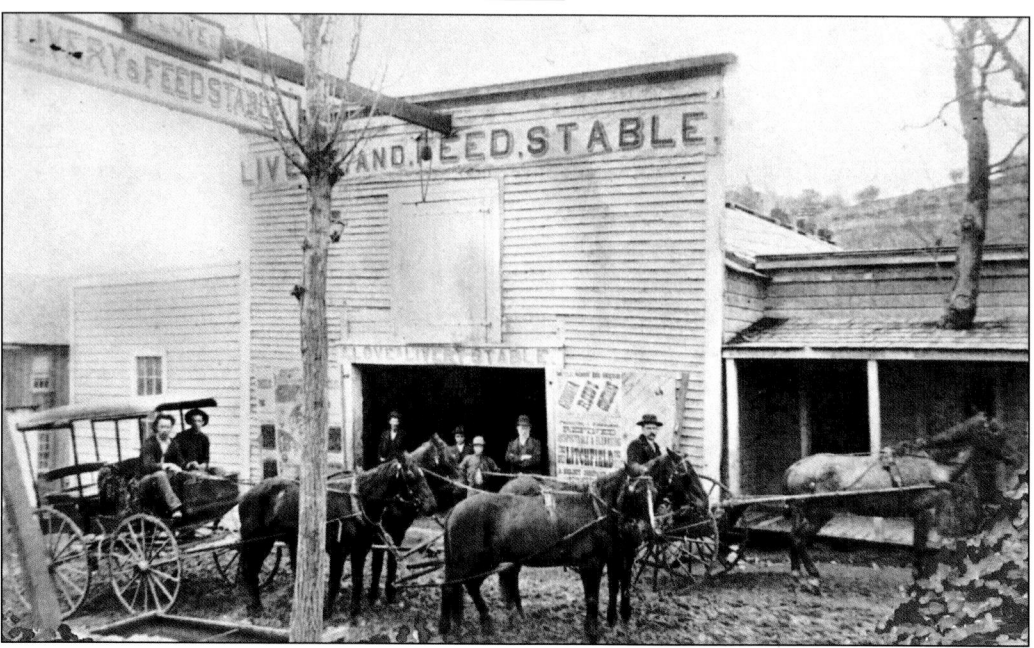

Alexander Love, a native of Scotland and stonemason by trade, and his wife, Jane, settled in Angels Camp in 1852, where his first interest was mining. Then he, with others of his family, operated a sawmill on Love Creek near Avery. He also served as county assessor for 12 years, and he eventually entered the livery stable business, maintaining the establishment until his death in 1901. (Courtesy Calaveras County Historical Society.)

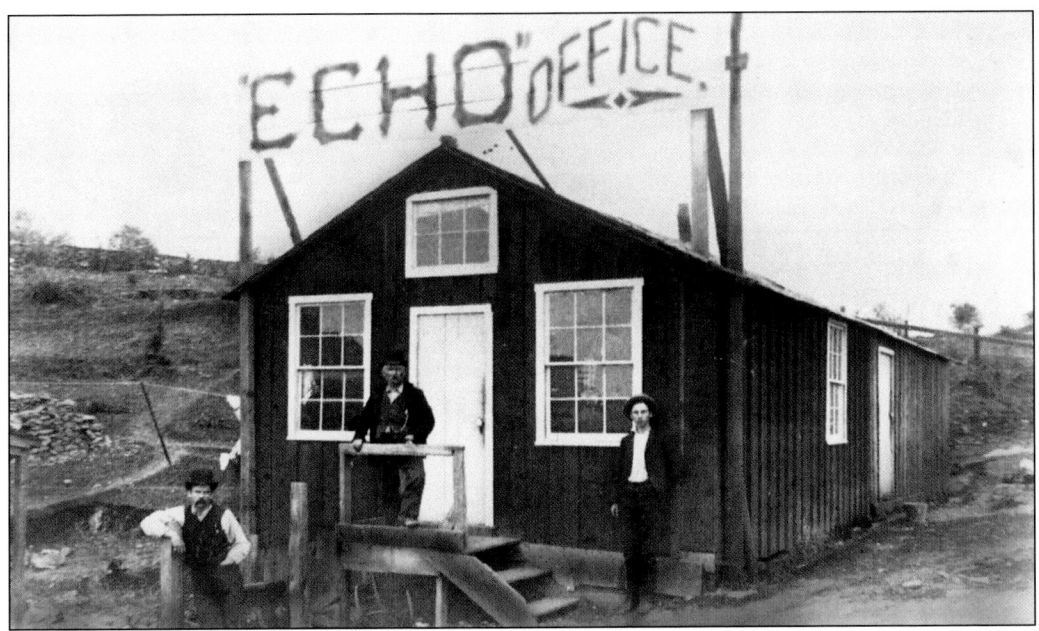

Six newspapers were published in Angels Camp between 1872 and 1923, but the longest operating was the *Mountain Echo*, produced by Myron Reed and Lewis Hutchinson from 1879 to 1885, by Reed and a Mr. Laird from 1885 to 1904, and then by Hutchinson again. Other newspapers included the *Mountaineer* (1872–1873), *Calaveras Democrat* in 1894, the *Angels Record* in 1899, and the *Calaveras Californian*, published by state senator Jesse M. Mayo for more than 23 years. (Courtesy Calaveras County Historical Society.)

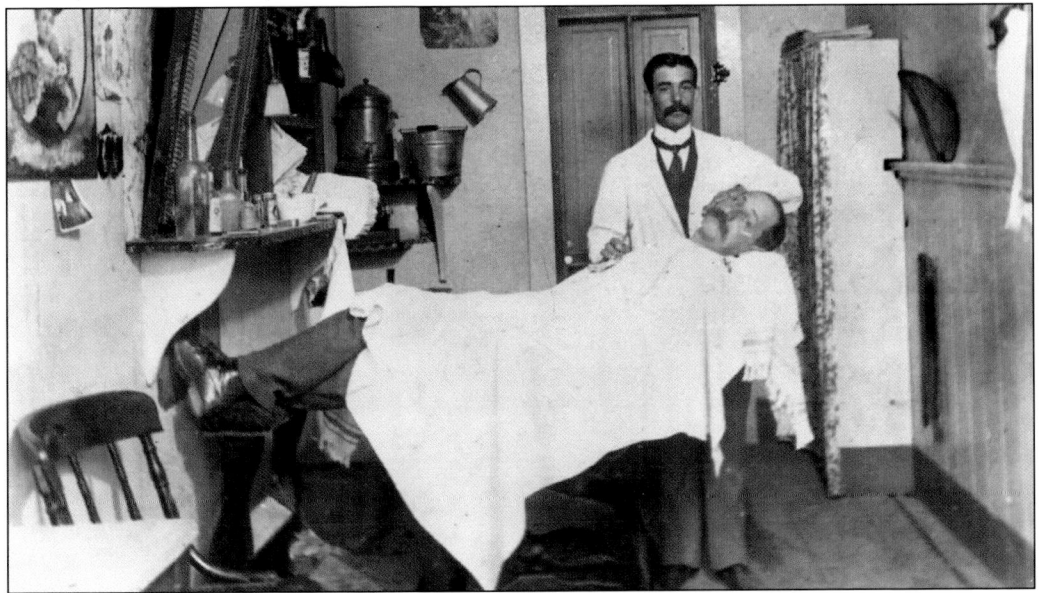

The Lemue Barber Shop provided an essential service to the men of Angels Camp. Moustaches were trimmed and waxed, hair cut, faces shaved, and other ablutions attended to. Haircuts were "two bits," and a shave was 75¢. Many barbershops were conveniently located next to saloons, so patrons could go in and out through the shop without anyone on the street knowing they had imbibed. (Courtesy Calaveras County Archives.)

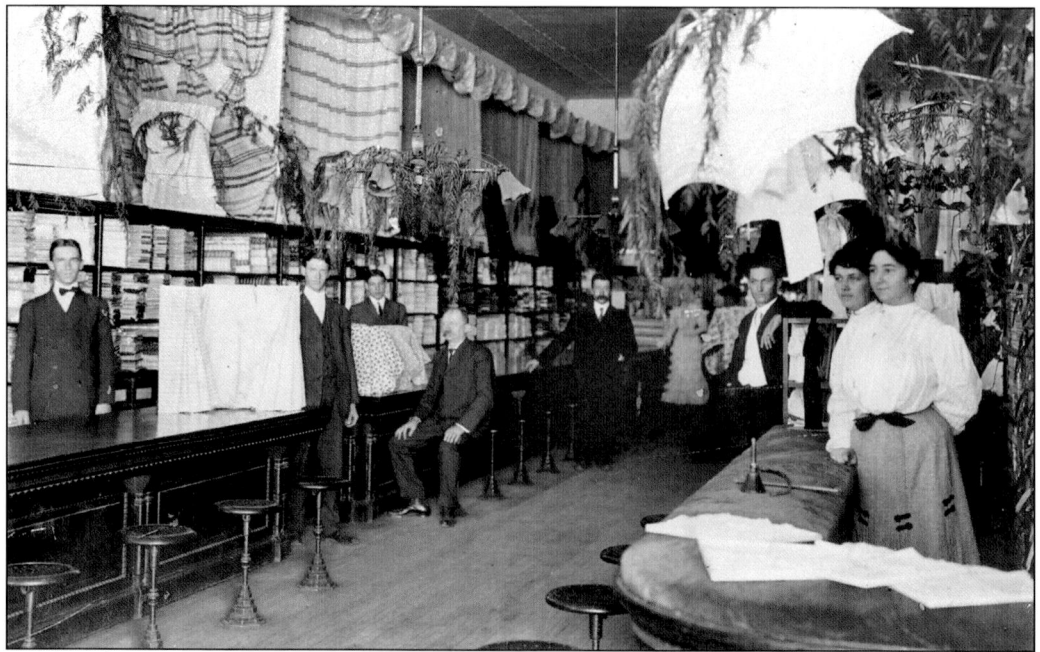

Grillo's Store sold ladies' and gentlemen's clothing and accessories on West Main Street about 1910. The stools were for customers to sit on while trying on the latest fashions in hats and while selecting gloves, shirtwaists, ties, handkerchiefs, and other articles necessary for the fashionable set. (Courtesy Calaveras County Archives.)

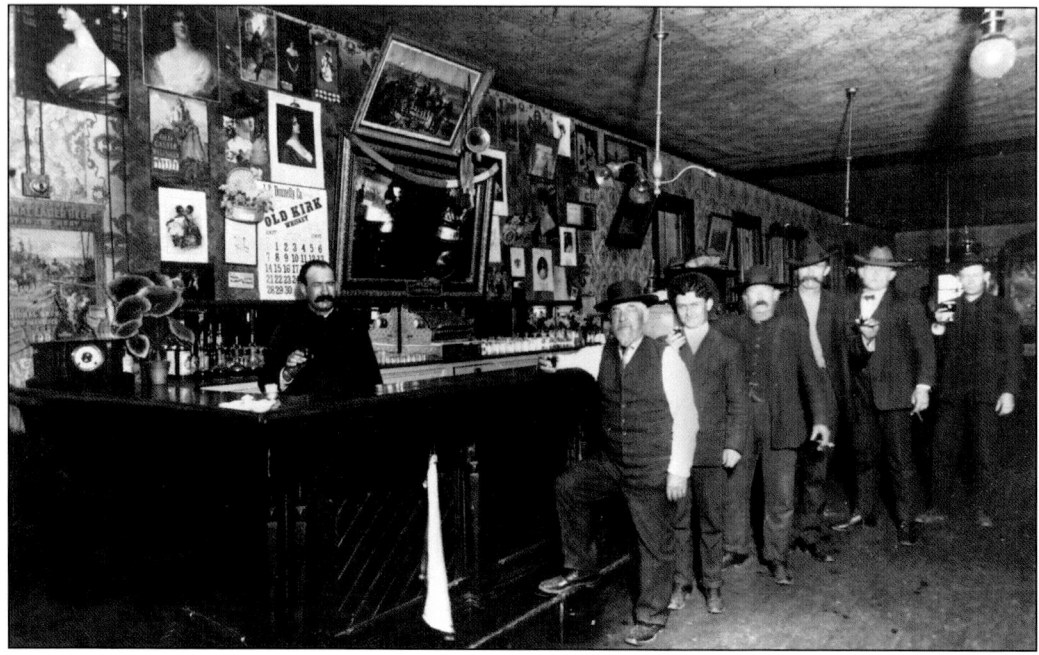

Of all the commercial establishments in Angels Camp, none were more prolific than the saloons. They were not only a place to drink, but also one where men could meet and share the camaraderie of others after working long days in the mines and commercial establishments in town. (Courtesy Calaveras County Historical Society.)

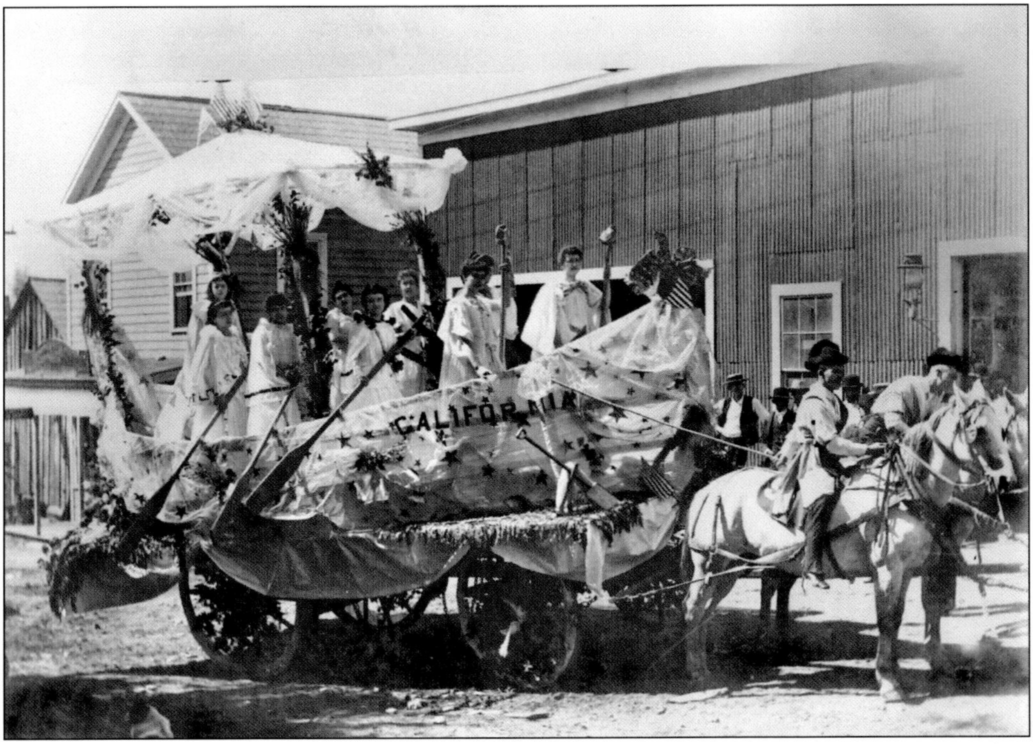

Parades were always important events in Angels Camp and throughout Calaveras County. They were held on patriotic days, especially the Fourth of July; celebrations of national identity, such as Columbus Day; and other occasions. This group of Native Daughters of the Golden West paraded through Angels Camp on the Fourth of July in the early 1900s. (Courtesy Calaveras County Historical Society.)

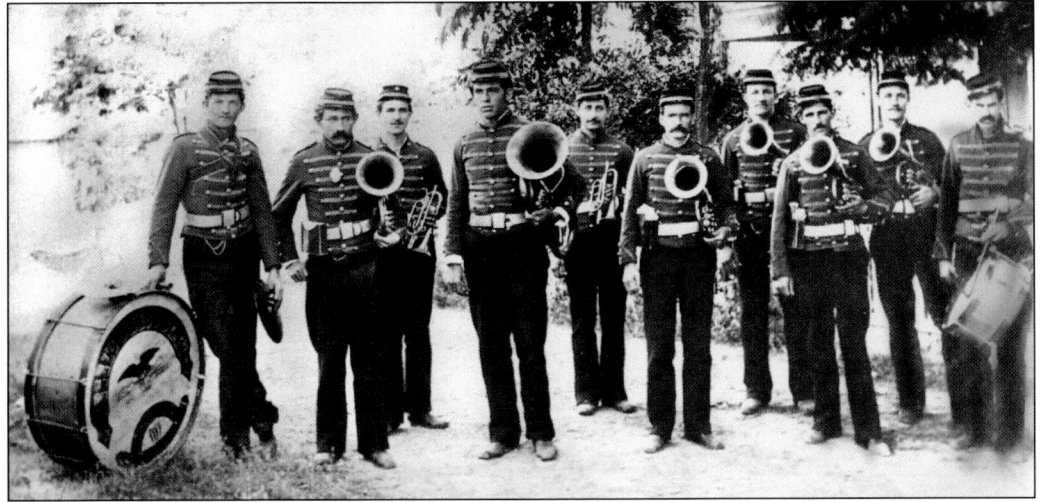

From the 1880s through the 1940s, every community in Calaveras County had a band, usually consisting of brass instruments and drums. They were in considerable demand, wearing uniforms and marching in parades and playing for funerals, celebrations, and community concerts. The Angels Brass Band poses for the photographer around the dawn of the 20th century. (Courtesy Calaveras County Historical Society.)

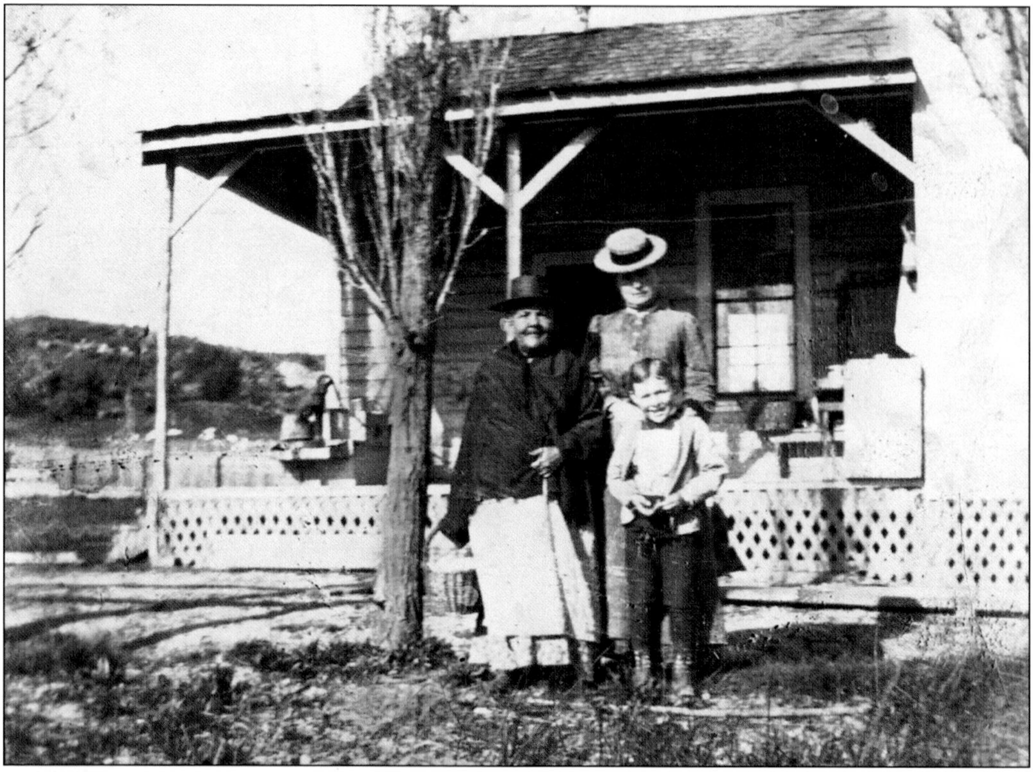

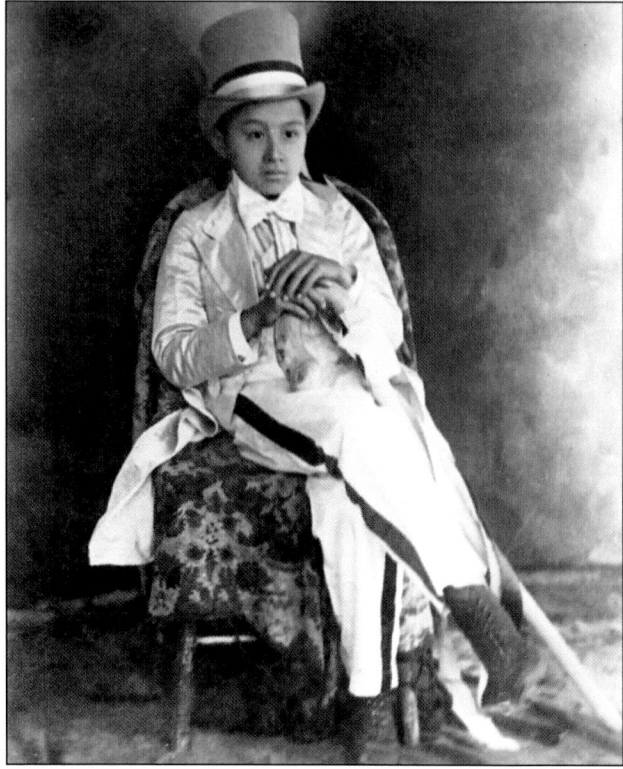

This Mexican woman (left) sold tamales in Angels Camp in the early 1900s, carrying them door to door in her woven basket. Numerous natives of Mexico settled in the Southern Mines after 1848, but most were driven out by the Euro-Americans after the Foreign Miners Tax was enacted in 1852. (Courtesy Calaveras County Archives.)

Sam Gee, the mascot of the Angels Camp baseball team around 1900, was the descendant of a Chinese family, one of many who settled in Angels Camp beginning in 1850. Most of the Chinese resided in the south end of town on both sides of Angels Creek, where Sam Choy and Lien Sing built their brick stores and where more than 20 lots were owned by Chinese in the 1870s. (Courtesy Calaveras County Historical Society.)

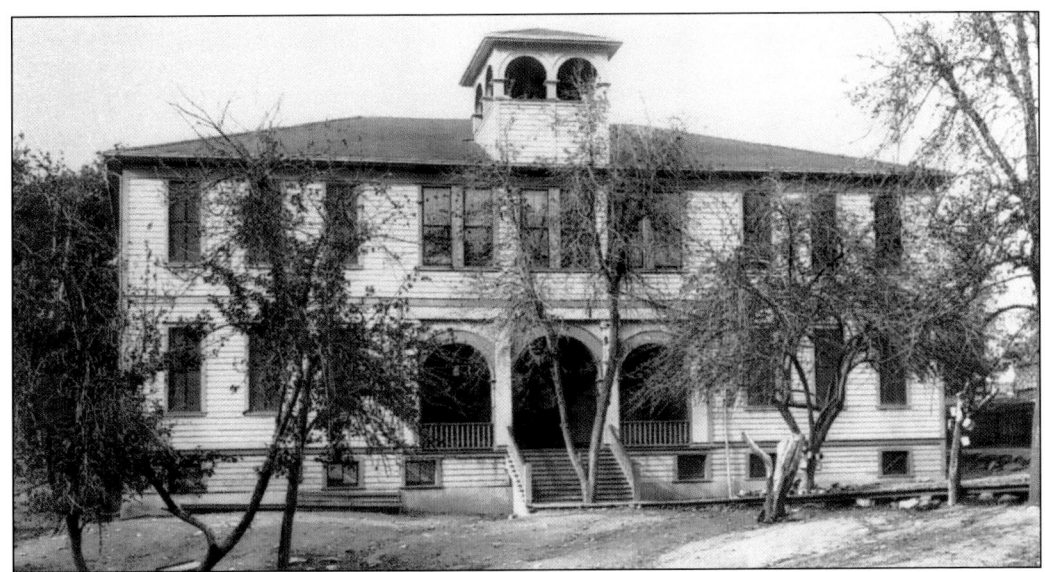

The first school was established in 1854 in a private room and was taught by John Bricknell. Shortly thereafter, a schoolhouse was built on Main Street, and by 1859, Angels Camp had 140 school-age children, a number that doubled during the hard-rock mining boom. In 1899, this two-story school building was constructed on Finnegan Lane. In 1951, several schools merged and formed the Mark Twain Union Elementary School District. (Courtesy Calaveras County Historical Society.)

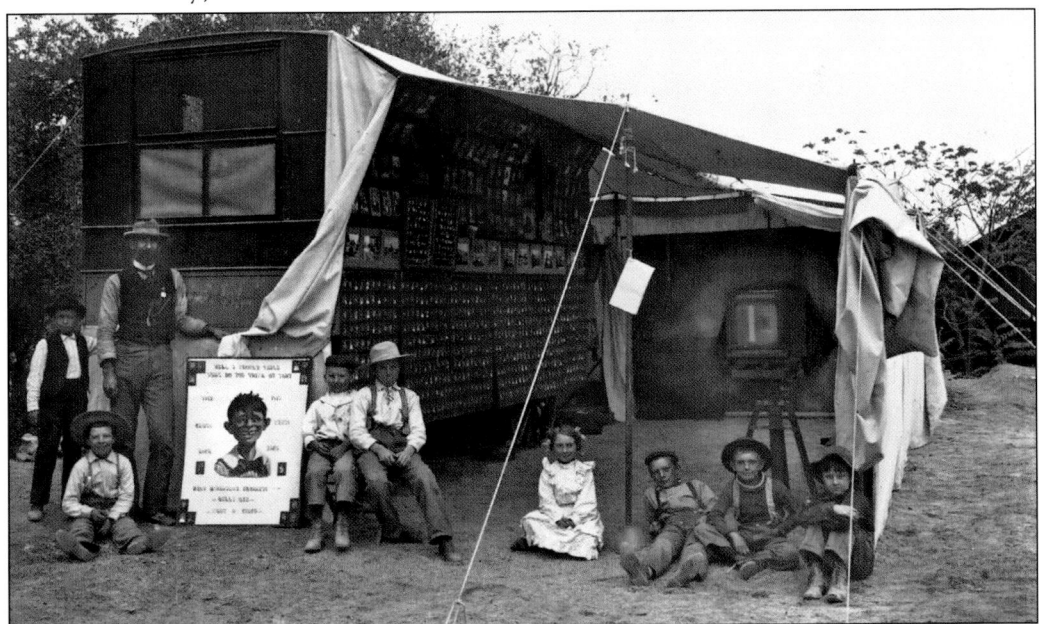

The Modern Art and Novelty Company, conducted by Wilgar Harvey Hutchins and Ralph Huddleston, operated a photography studio in Oakland. In 1902, they visited Angels Camp (above), taking pictures that sold for $1.50 a dozen for full cabinet size, $1 for one-half, and 75¢ for one-quarter. The poster image of a boy (seen here) was later popularized as Alfred E. Neuman in *Mad Magazine*. It first appeared in 1895 in Topeka, Kansas, as a dental advertisement. (Courtesy Calaveras County Archives.)

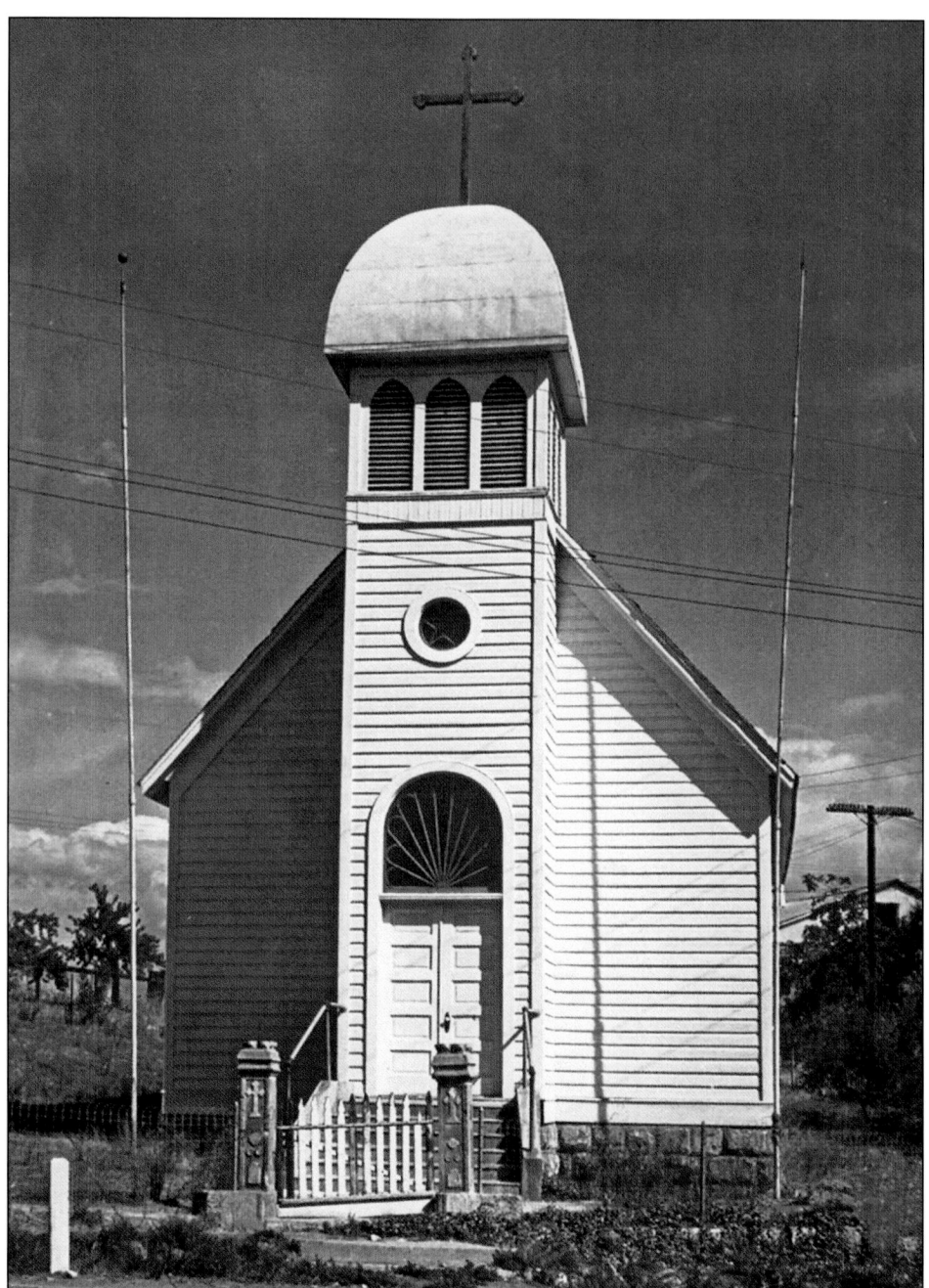

Completed in 1910, St. Vasilije (Basil) Serbian Orthodox Church is the third oldest in North America (the oldest is in Jackson, California, and the second in Texas). A member of the Orthodox communion, the denomination is based in Serbia, Montenegro, Bosnia, Herzegovina, and Croatia. Immigrants from these places arrived during the 1890s and early 1900s to work in the hard-rock mines in Angels Camp and Jackson. Slavic work crews were responsible for constructing the tortuous road from Vallecito to the powerhouse at Camp Nine in 1907 in an astounding six months. The well-laid rock walls, now more than 100 years old, are still visible along the route. (Photograph by Alma Lavenson, courtesy Bancroft Library.)

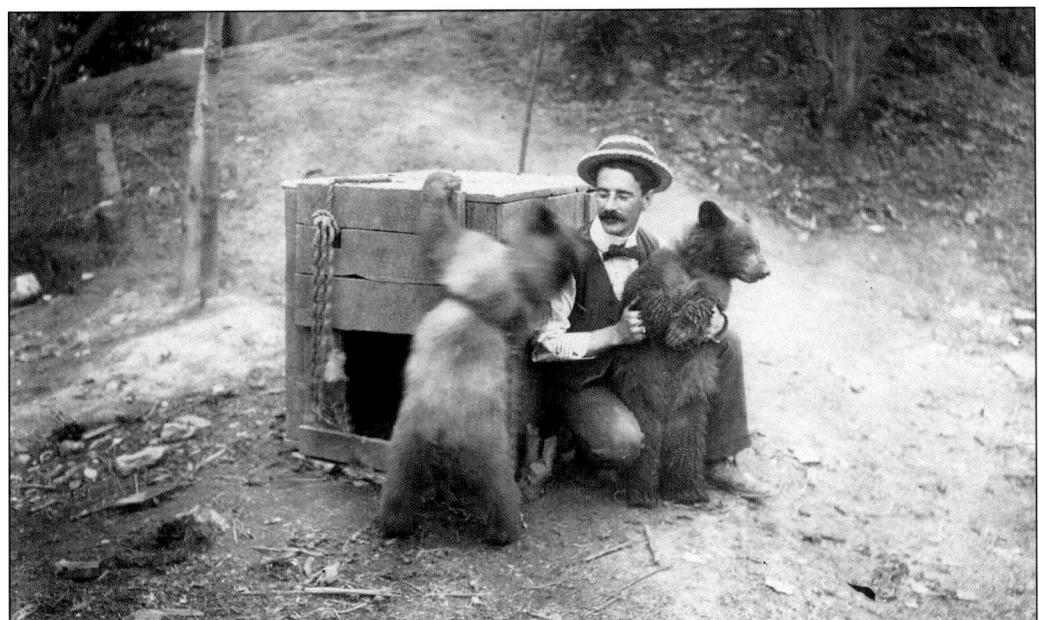

Harry Barden, who operated the Goodloe and Barden Drugstore in Angels Camp, was a civic leader, promoter of the fire department, U.S. postmaster, and instrumental in the construction of the 1926 Bret Harte High School. He rescued these two bear cubs from a tree near Mosquito Lakes and raised them until they were old enough to be given to the Stockton Zoo. (Courtesy Cornelia Barden Stevenot.)

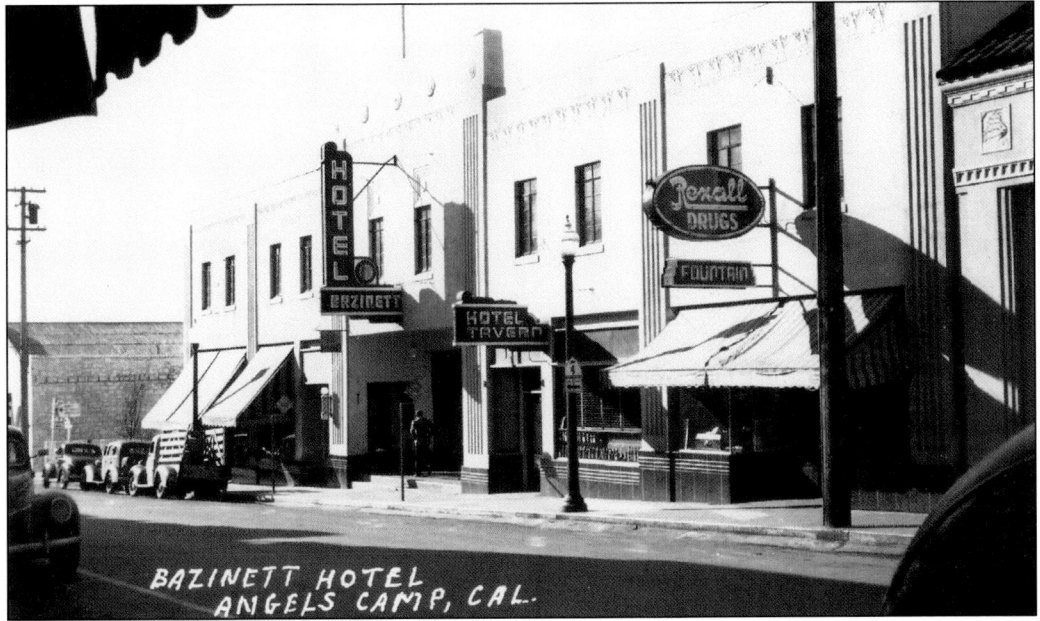

The Bazinett Hotel, built by J. H. Bazinett in 1938, was advertised as "modern in every respect" when completed. It boasted 30 rooms and one apartment, heating and air-conditioning, and hot and cold water in every room. The building also housed Giriodi's Drug Store, Nels Moller's Barber Shop, Broglio's Restaurant, a coffee shop, a saloon, and Safeway Market. Later tenants included the Angels Market and Rasberry's Bar. (Courtesy Calaveras County Historical Society.)

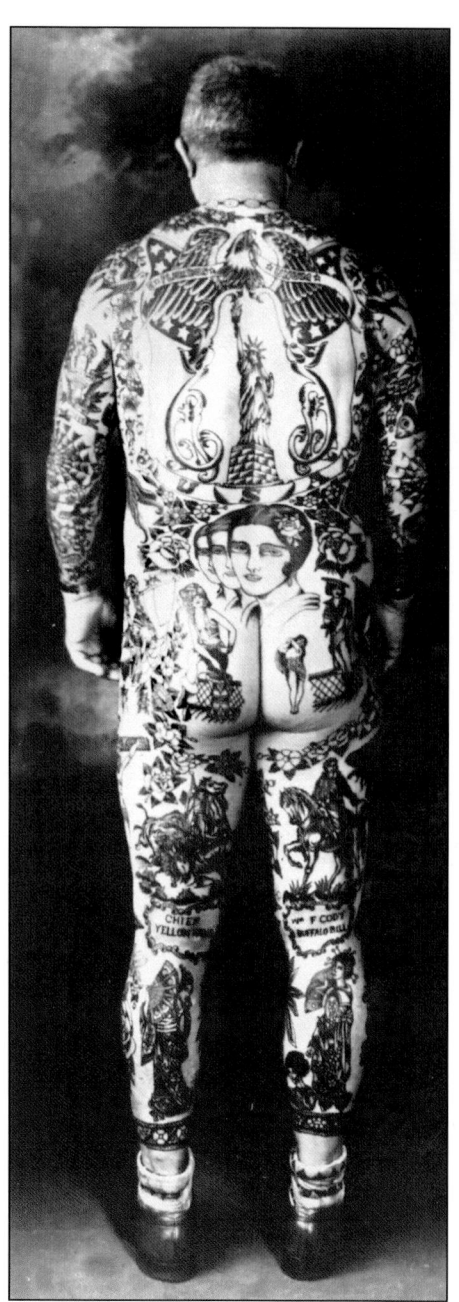 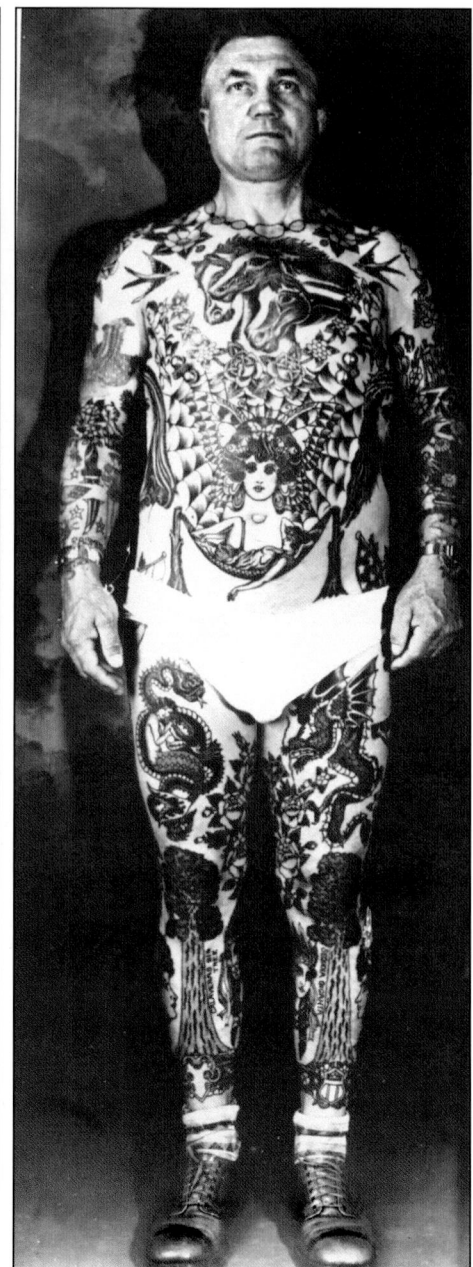

Known as "Tough Titty" for his circus act in which he lifted an anvil with his pierced nipples, Rasmus Nielsen lived in Angels Camp for many years. Born in Denmark in the early 1870s, Rasmus was originally a blacksmith but chose to enter the show business world and had his entire body tattooed, photographed here in the 1920s. Finding that there were many tattooed men in the circus field and "determined to make a freak of himself," he chose to have his nipples, nose, and tongue pierced to lift heavy objects, eventually lifting 250-pound anvils with his nipples. He came to San Francisco in 1940 for the Golden Gate Exposition and worked at Ringling Brothers, Barnum, and Bailey Circus, and, at age 65, at the New York World's Fair. He died in 1957 and was buried in Angels Camp. (Courtesy Calaveras County Archives.)

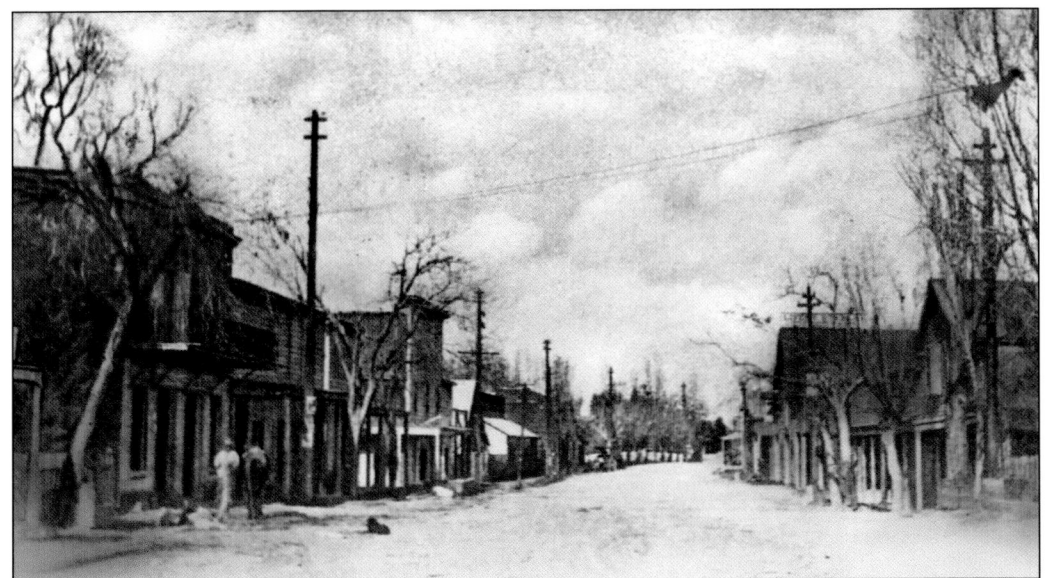

By the 1880s, Altaville boasted a hotel, a foundry, fairgrounds, a livery stable, a wagon-making shop, a blacksmith, a dance hall, stores, and saloons, as well as fine residences. In addition, several important quartz mines and mills coursed southerly down Main Street, while the Catholic, Public, and Serbian Orthodox cemeteries were established on the Stockton Road. (Courtesy Calaveras County Historical Society.)

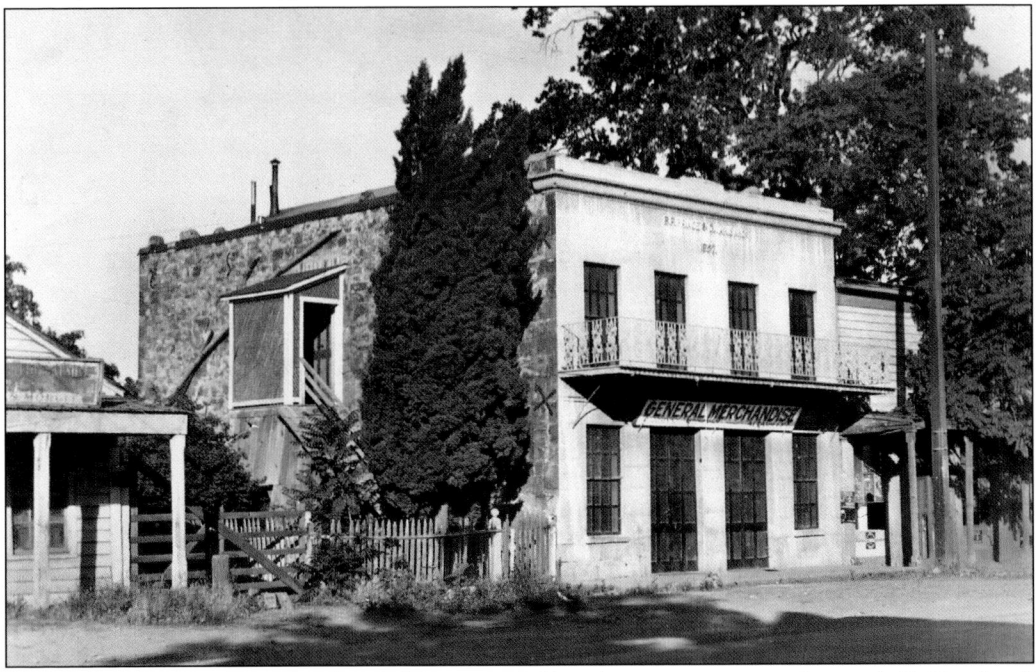

Bartolo Romaggi Prince arrived in California in 1852 and went into partnership with G. Garabardi in the dry-goods business in Altaville. In addition to this establishment, he also operated a quartz mine, a hotel, an undertaking parlor, and a silkworm business. By 1857, he had amassed enough money to contract with D. Strosberger to erect this elegant new store. (Courtesy Calaveras County Historical Society.)

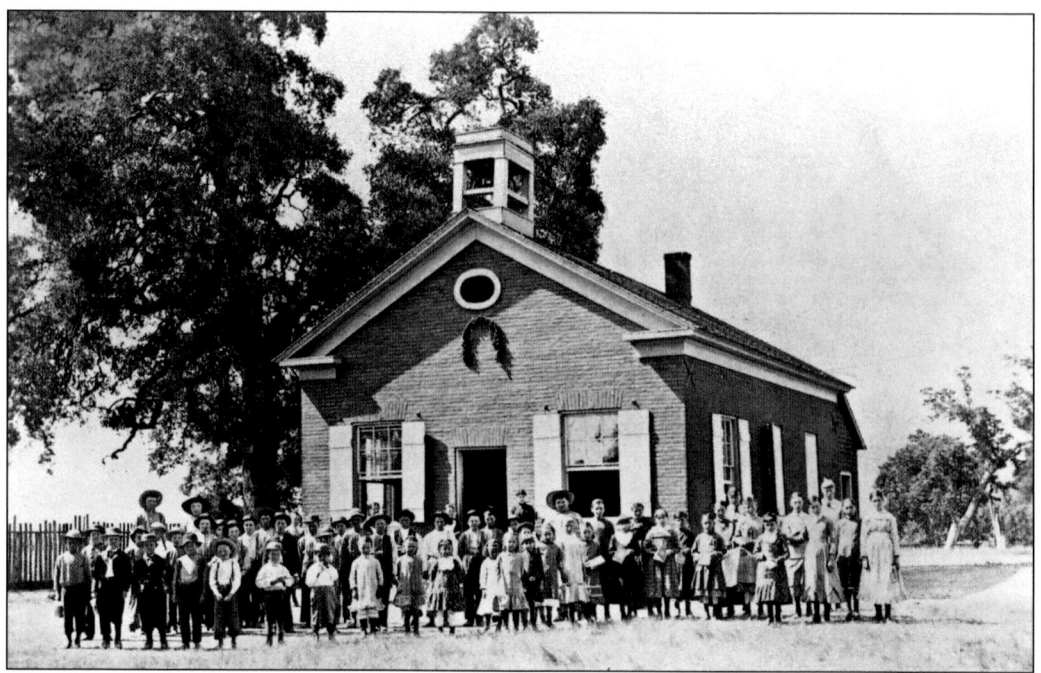

One of the oldest brick schoolhouses in California, the Altaville School was erected in 1858 and is depicted here in 1884. It served the children of town until 1950. It was restored by the California Department of Forestry and the Calaveras County Historical Society in the early 1980s and was moved from its original hilltop location a short distance to its present site. (Courtesy Calaveras County Historical Society.)

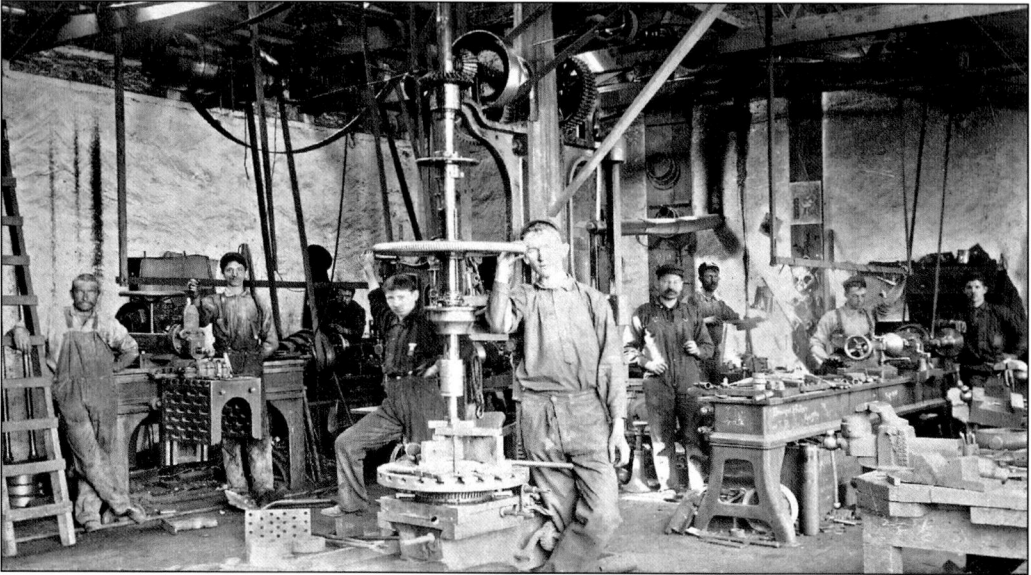

Established by Andy Gardiner and J. M. Wooster in 1854, the Altaville Foundry was purchased by David Durie Demarest in the early 1860s, operated in the 1890s by his son David Clarence, and purchased by Lawrence Monte Verda in 1928. The foundry manufactured a complete line of mining and milling machinery, shipping to other countries as well as mining regions throughout the United States. (Courtesy Calaveras County Historical Society.)

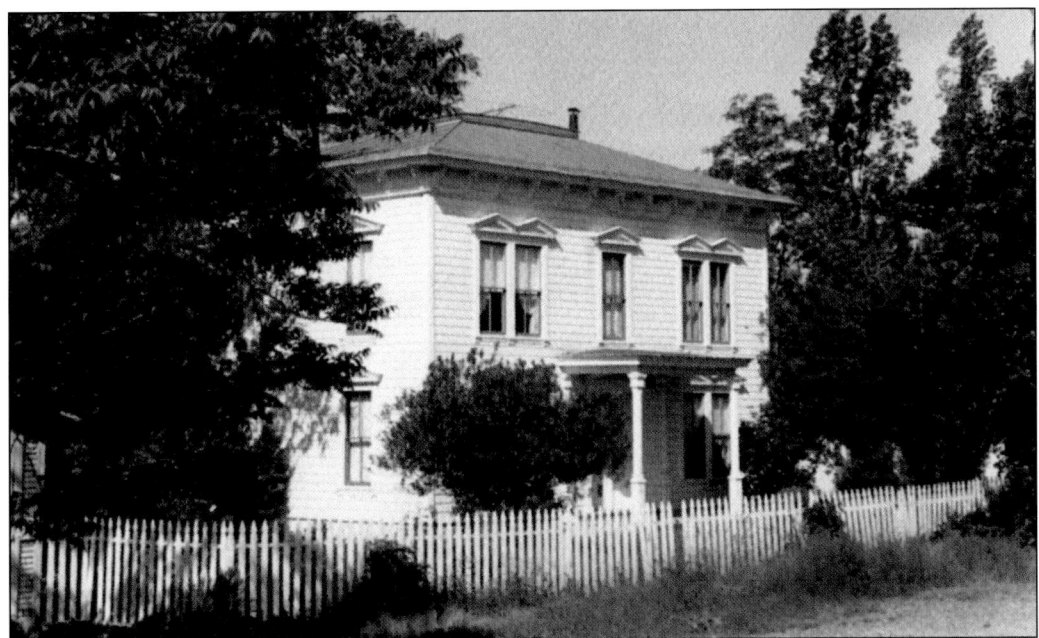

This fine Italianate home was built for the Demarest family, owners of the adjacent Altaville Foundry, by the Snow brothers in 1884. For many years, it was the home of the Monte Verda family, most recently Cyril, the last of the family to operate the old foundry. It was moved to its present site at the corner of State Route 49 and Mark Twain Road when the foundry was demolished in the mid-1980s. (Courtesy Calaveras County Historical Society.)

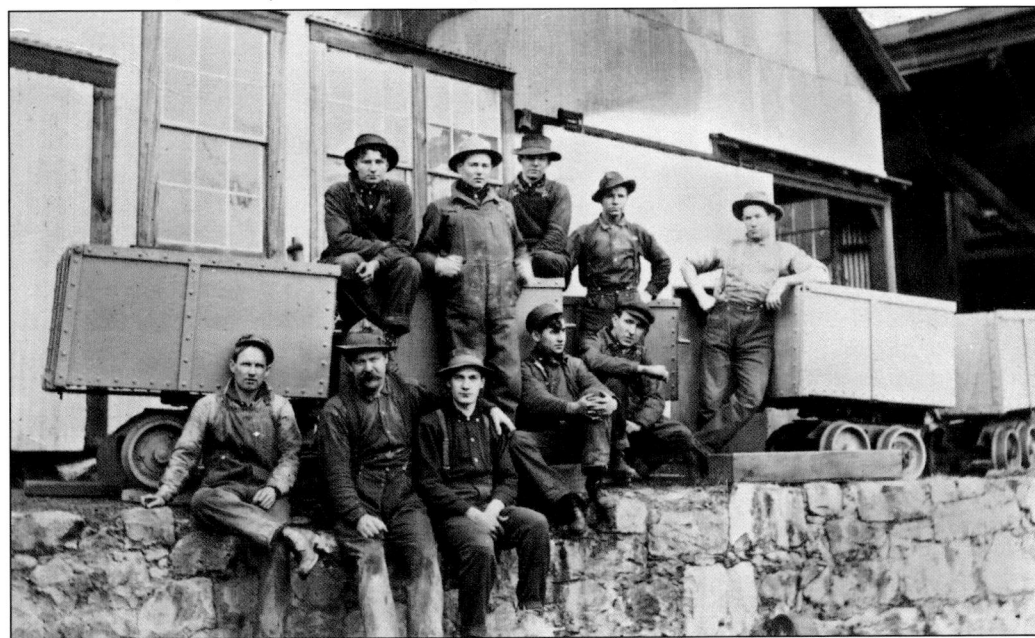

The California Electric Steel (formerly the Altaville Foundry) workers pictured in this photograph with their prototype ore cars include William Raggio, John Lamb, Dolbert Bates, Mike Marshall, Bill Nichols, Jack Daley, Frank Merdalo, and a Mr. Daverty. The site is now the location of the Angels Camp Town Center shopping mall. (Courtesy Calaveras County Historical Society.)

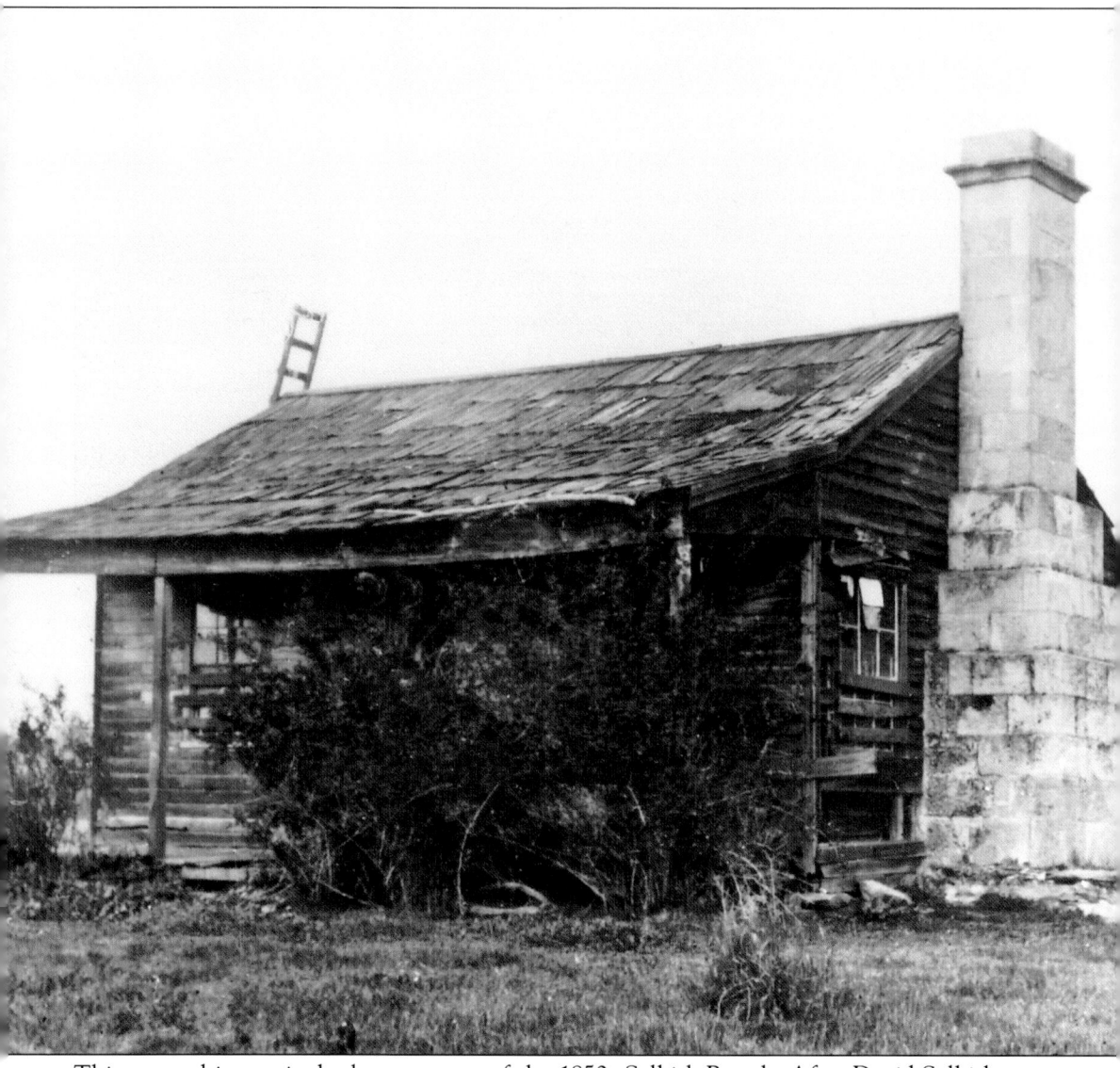

This stone chimney is the last remnant of the 1850s Selkirk Ranch. After David Selkirk was blinded by a dynamite accident, this two-room house was built for the family by the community, with a fine stone chimney constructed by Alexander Love in 1862. The dwelling, typical of many in those years, was small by modern standards for a family of six: a living room with a fireplace to cook in and a bedroom. Residents of the home included David and Perlina, their daughters, Sarah Jane (McCauley), Jennie (Lucas/Maltman), Alice (Hinkleman), and Clara (Bates); as well as boarders, usually local miners, who evidently slept in the attic. Behind the house was a storage cellar; a blacksmith shop was to the west, while a stone corral and walls delineated the yard to the south. Vegetables were grown on the hillside, with water obtained from a branch of the Gold Cliff Ditch. Nearby was the home of Ah Sun, who worked for the family all his life. This photograph was taken about 1913, before the dwelling burned. The chimney and homestead site are preserved as part of the Greenhorn Creek Golf Resort. (Courtesy Calaveras County Archives.)

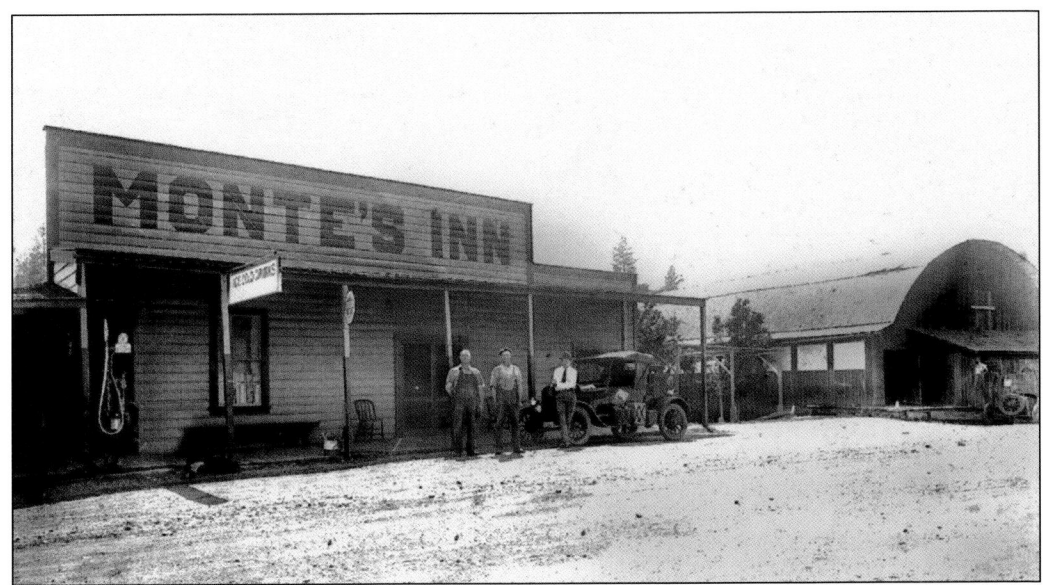

Monte's Inn, operated by the Monte Verda family on the road to San Andreas, also contained a bar and sold groceries and gasoline. Dances and events were held in the dance hall, which was also used by the Bret Harte High School girls for physical education classes in the 1920s. (Courtesy Angels Camp Museum.)

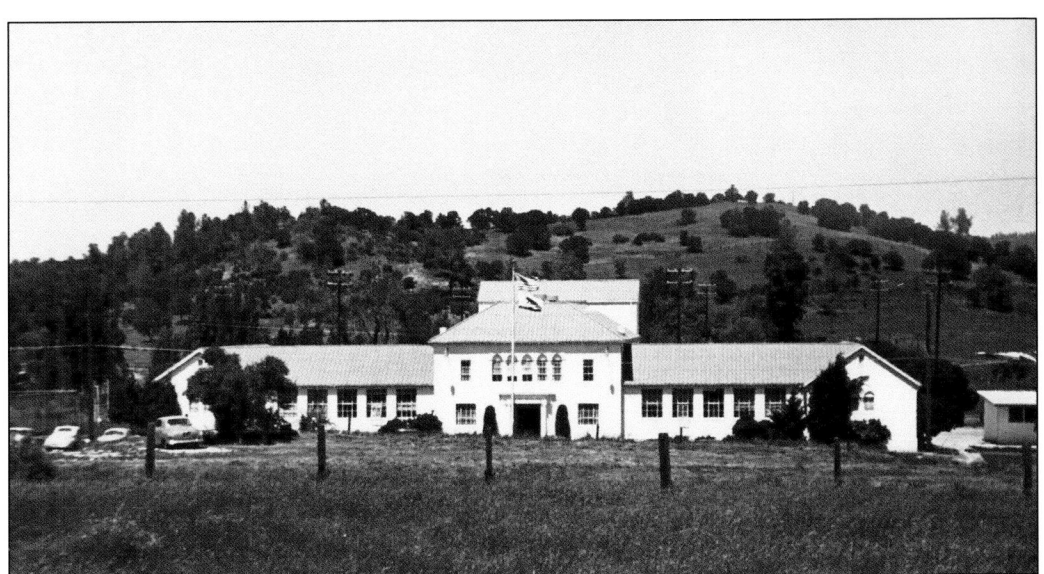

Bret Harte Union High School was founded in June 1905. It was named for the famed author and poet of the Mother Lode, whose writings include the short story *Brown of Calaveras*. By 1926, the old wood-frame school had become inadequate, and a new school was constructed, depicted here shortly after completion. It burned in 1994, and in 2002, the school's theater building opened on the site. (Courtesy Calaveras County Historical Society.)

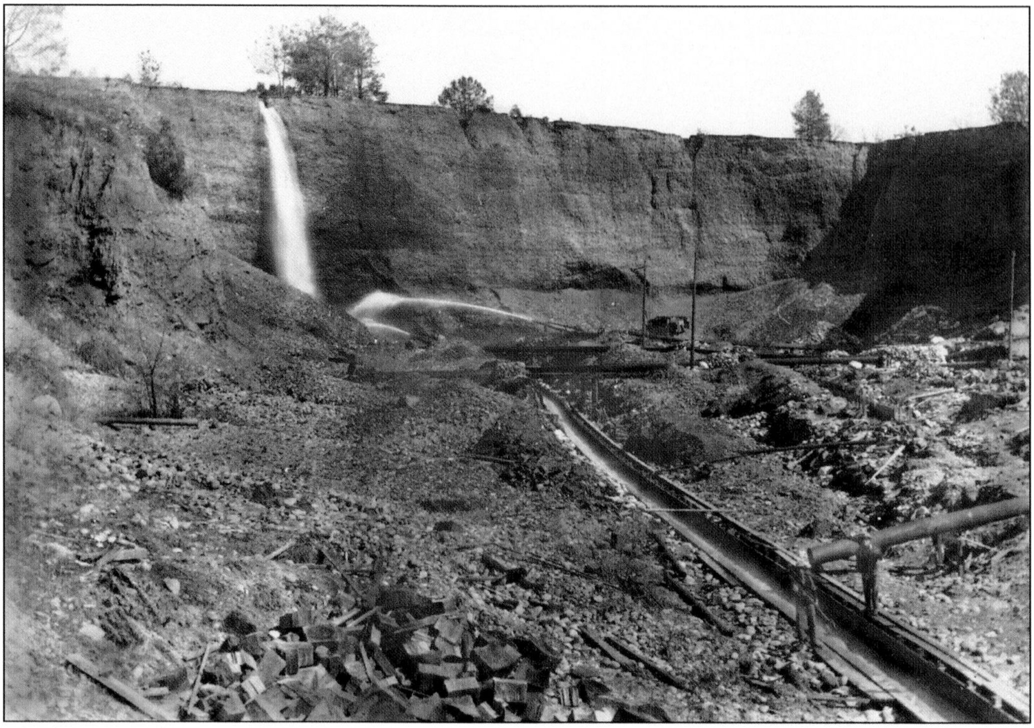

The largest and most important hydraulic mines, including the Jupiter, were located near Dogtown, north of Altaville. In the mid-1880s, Jupiter mine owner Windsor Keefer became a major stockholder in the Union Water Company, constructed Keefer Reservoir, and began extensive hydraulic mining operations. In this photograph, water from the Dogtown (or Jupiter) Ditch is ground-sluicing the bank of the ancient river while a hydraulic monitor washes tailings into the Long Tom to collect the gold in its riffles. (Courtesy Calaveras County Historical Society.)

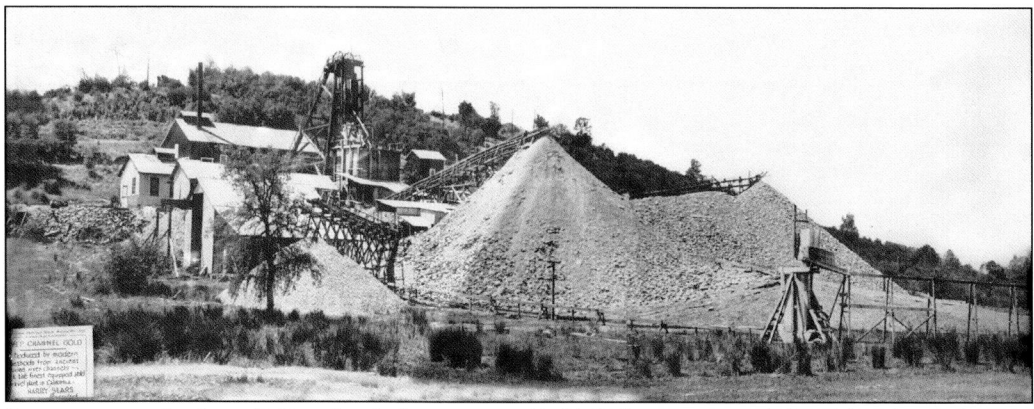

Beginning in the late 1920s, the drift mines on Bald Hill were consolidated by the Calaveras Central Gold Mining Company and were operated through the 1930s under the management of Harry Sears. After being shut down by World War II, the mine reopened in 1952, and a new steel headframe, designed by Bernard Monte Verda, was erected and now stands as a lonely sentinel along the Murphys Grade Road. (Courtesy Calaveras County Archives.)

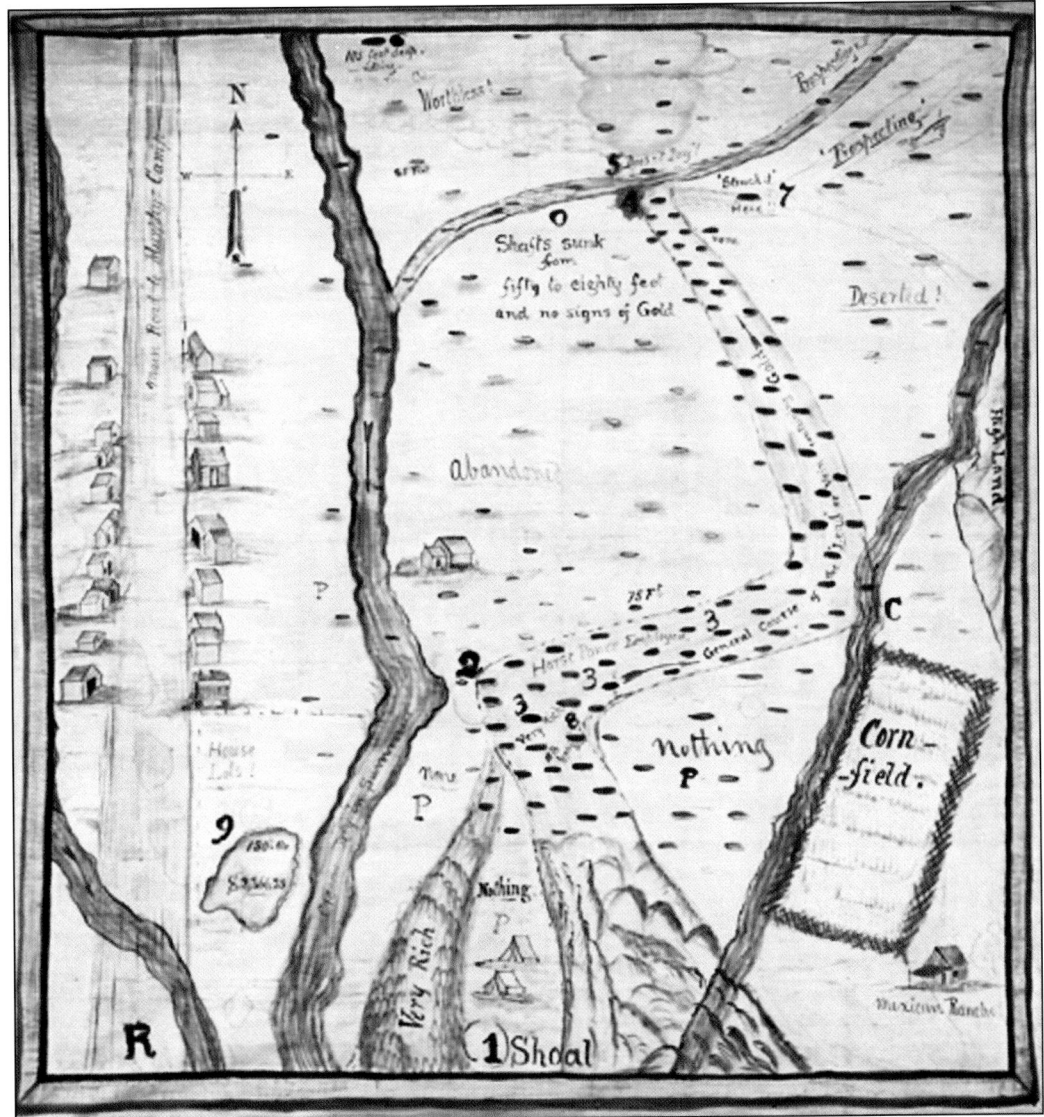

Although gold was discovered in Coyote Creek in 1848, probably by John and Daniel Murphy, who established the first trading tent in town, it was not until the spring of 1850 that Vallecito was permanently settled by a group of Mexican miners. Also known as "Murphys Old Diggings," soon there were 50 businesses supplying goods and services for the surrounding mining camps, and by 1853, it was one of the most flourishing camps in the Southern Mines. In this early map, Main Street, Coyote Creek, the rich underground channel, a cornfield, and a Mexican rancho are depicted. Like many of its neighbors, Vallecito was ravaged by fire several times, and several of the wood-frame buildings of the more prosperous merchants were rebuilt in stone, including the Vallecito Hotel, the Cuneo (French) Store, the Cohen and Levy Store, and Barney's Livery Stable, formerly a hotel. (Courtesy Bancroft Library.)

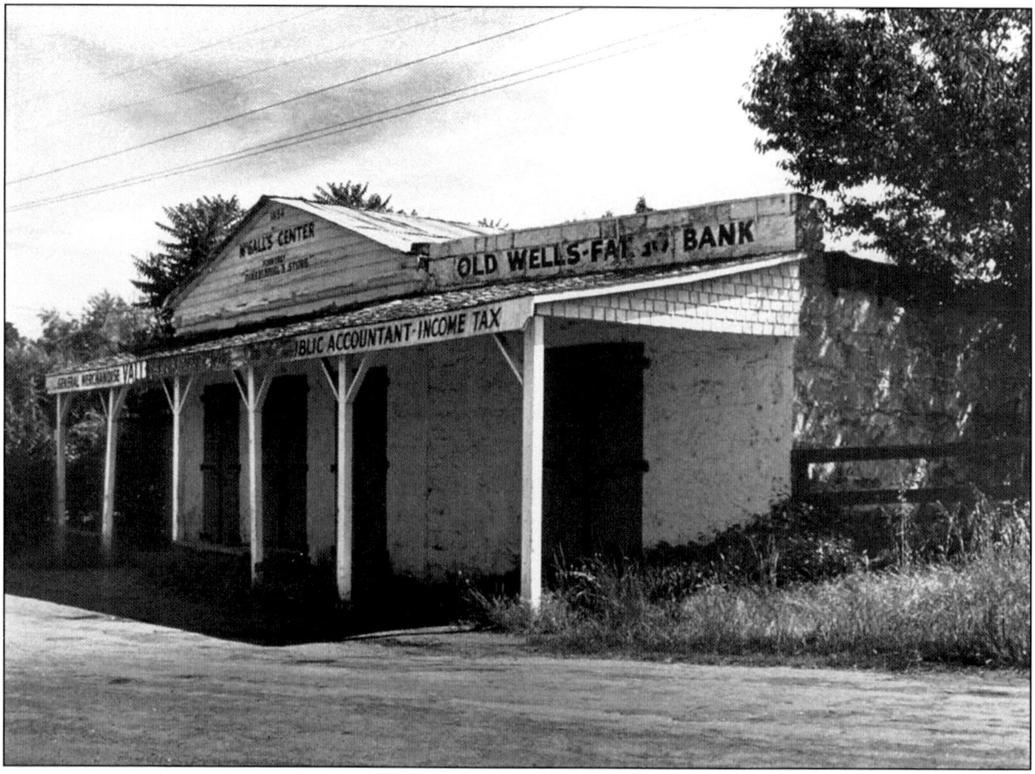

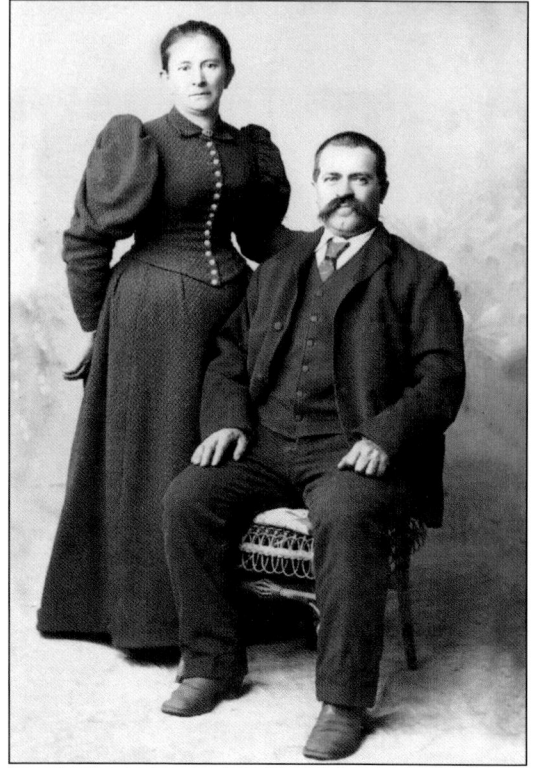

The stone Dinkelspiel Store was erected in Vallecito in 1854 by Morris Cohen and Isaac Levy, Jewish merchants from New York, who also owned the Calaveras County Water Company, which brought water from the Stanislaus River to the mines. The store was later owned by Francisco Bacigalupi and then Luke Sanguinetti. It served the community as a general merchandise store, a post office, and a Wells Fargo office. (Photograph by Alma Lavenson, courtesy Bancroft Library.)

Four other stores in Vallecito were owned by Italian families. Angelo and Mary Malatesta, pictured here around the end of the 19th century, the Cuneo, Sanguinetti, and John and Teresa Arata families also operated stores on Main Street, while Jack Solari's Saloon was the favorite watering hole. Like many of their countrymen, in addition to establishing stores, the Italians operated truck gardens and orchards while also mining seasonally. (Courtesy Calaveras County Historical Society.)

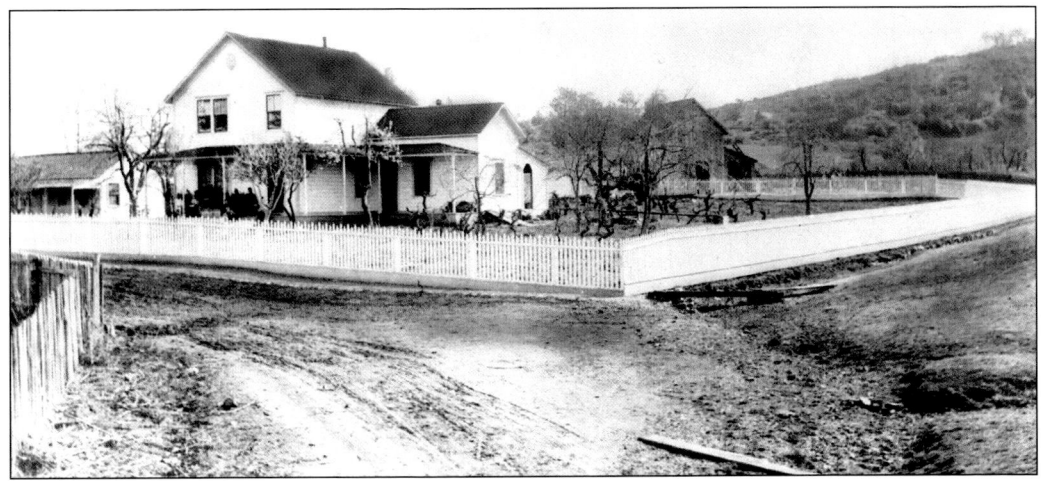

Built sometime before 1890 by the Thomas B. Bishop Logging Company, this home was later rented by the Emery family before being purchased by the Mitchell family. Other non-Italian households in Vallecito were the Isbell, Starr, Joy, Lewis, Gerlach, Copeland, Emery, Edwards, Lewis, Moeller, Wiles, Rufe, Batten, Graebe, Lundberg, Saunders, Schwoerer, Sletten, Carley, Brockway, and Meinecke families. (Courtesy Calaveras County Historical Society.)

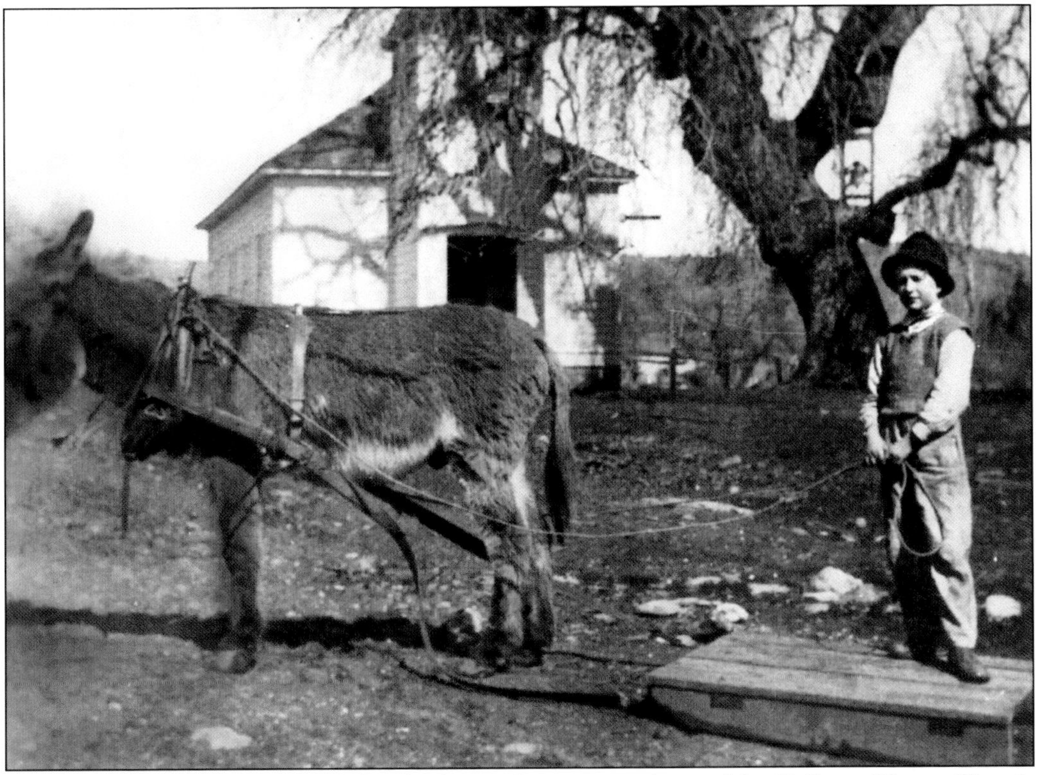

Clifton Mitchell on his sled with his donkey, Tebo, poses in front of the Vallecito Union Church in 1915. The original Vallecito Church, built in the early years, was replaced by this building in 1908. The old oak, which held a bell cast in Troy, New York, in 1853, blew down in a rainstorm in 1939. The bell now hangs in a monument adjacent to the church. (Courtesy Calaveras County Historical Society.)

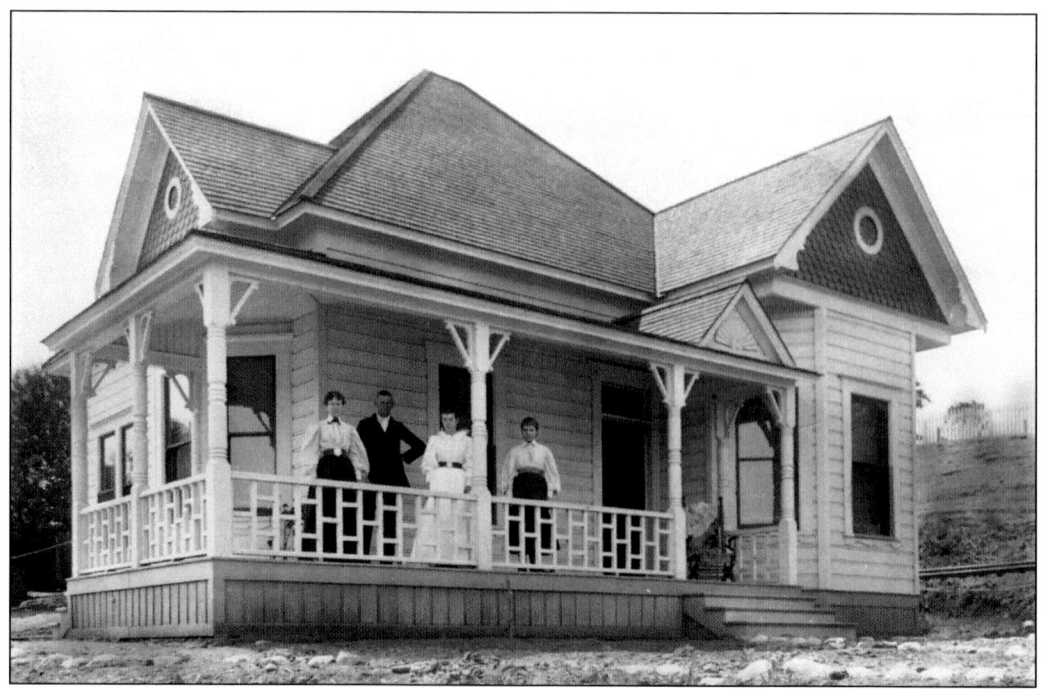

The Luke and Martha Sanguinetti home in Vallecito hosts (from left to right) Martha, Joe Carley, Kate Carley, and Anna Mitchell enjoying a day on the porch. Many of the early Vallecito families were from the vineyard areas of Italy and planted grapes and made wine in their new homeland. In addition to the Sanguinettis, other Italian households included the Canepa, Solari, Arata, Gardella, Malatesta, Sturla, and Sciaccaluga (aka Pyshon) families. (Courtesy Calaveras County Historical Society.)

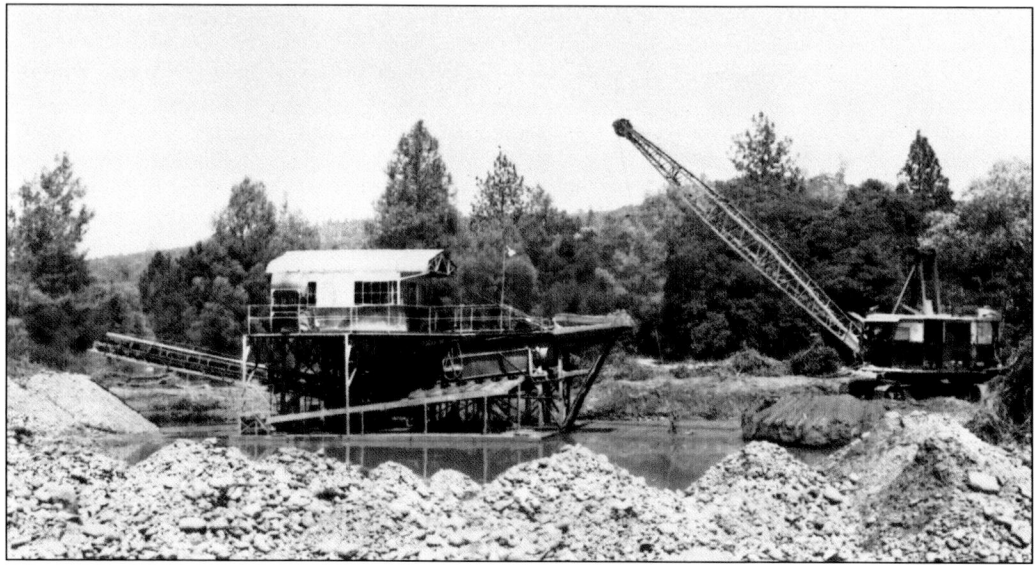

During the 1900s, 1930s, and again in the 1950s, Coyote Creek was dredged from Vallecito northerly through Douglas Flat by doodle bug dredgers, which erased much of the landscape and early placer mining activity along the creek. In this photograph, the dredge sits in a self-made pond, surrounded by its dredge tailings. (Courtesy Calaveras County Historical Society.)

Five
COPPER COUNTRY

From its beginnings in 1860 to the end of World War II, Copperopolis has been directly related to, and affected by, the extraction and production of copper ore. Copper was first discovered in the area in 1860 by Hiram Hughes on Gopher Ridge at Quail Hill and a few months later at the Napoleon Mine on Hog Hill. Shortly thereafter, a copper-bearing gossan was discovered by W. K. Reed and Thomas McCarty in the Copper Cañon Mining District on the Union Copper Claim, and a short time later, a second strike was made on the Keystone Claim. One year later, the community developing around the strikes became known as Copperopolis, the name derived from the word "copper," plus the Greek word "polis," meaning city.

From rolling hills of grazing land, the area was transformed almost overnight into a booming community because of the extraordinary need for copper for munitions and telegraph wire for the American Civil War, at which time it was the second most important copper district in the United States. The town that owed its existence to the Civil War developed around the "Plaza," with streets named for their associations with the war. The center of town was destroyed in a conflagration in 1867 and, with the cessation of the Civil War, was never completely rebuilt. It had, however, for some five or six years, reigned as the most active business and mining community in Calaveras County.

The community experienced another modest copper boom in the late 1880s, and in 1899, the Union Copper Mining Company purchased the original claims and most of the properties in town. These operations were curtailed in 1902, and it was not until 1909, when the Calaveras Copper Company purchased the Union interests, that prosperity returned. The mine was de-watered, a new smelter constructed, and thus began a long period of almost continuous operation. During this time, copper prices fluctuated, but the company continued to operate on a small scale, providing an important economic base to the local economy. At the Keystone Mine, mining commenced again briefly during World War II, but by 1945, it had shut down and has been idle ever since.

Today the headframes and mill buildings of the mines have disappeared, leaving behind large slag and mine waste piles with the distinctive rust color of copper gossan. Only basement depressions remain to show the location of the many once-booming business establishments.

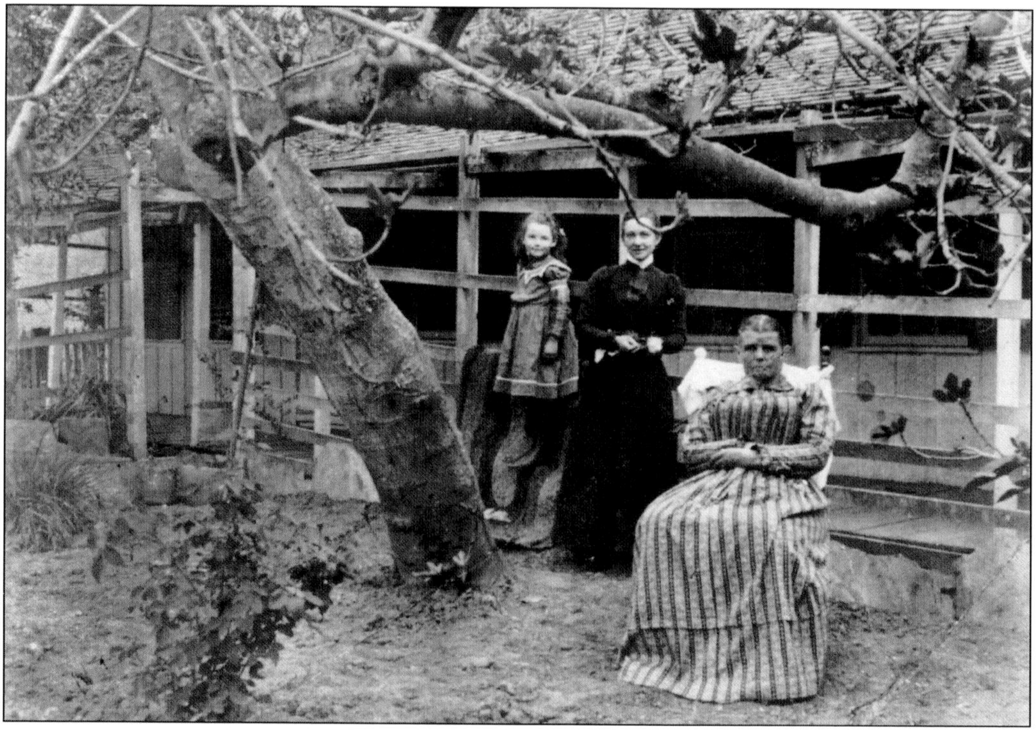

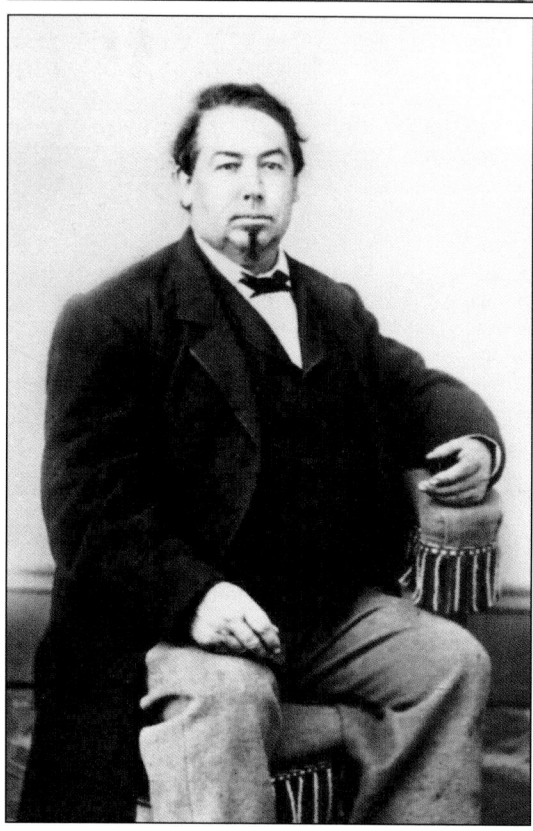

In 1852, Thomas and Agnes McCarty arrived from New York and homesteaded land on Log Cabin Creek, where they established a trading post and store, selling supplies to miners in exchange for gold dust. The family also raised horses, cows, and sheep, taking them to the mountain ranges in the summer months. Thomas and Agnes (the latter pictured above with daughter-in-law Mrs. Will (Emma) McCarty and her daughter Irene), raised nine children at the ranch. Their descendants still reside in Copperopolis. In 1860, Thomas (pictured at left) discovered some copper ore at about the same time as William K. Reed. The two men became partners in the Union Mine, genesis of the town of Copperopolis. In 1862, they sold their interest in the mine to C. T. Meader and Thomas Hardy. (Both, courtesy Ella McCarty Hiatt.)

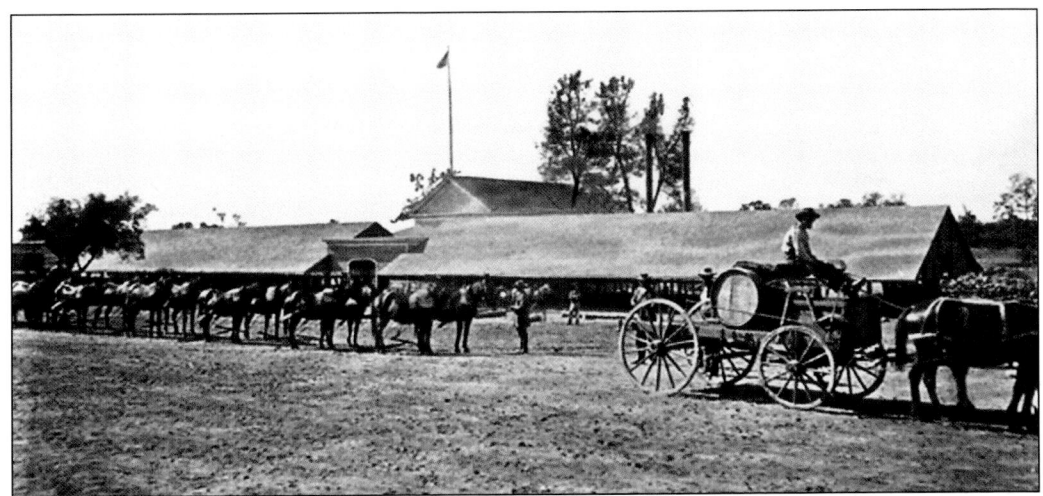

By September 1861, the Union Mine was employing 85 men at an average wage of $40 per month, including board. The shaft was 85 feet deep, producing 1,000 tons of ore, which yielded 40 percent copper. By 1866, the shaft had reached a depth of 480 feet with seven levels, and during the 1860s, the mine was the foremost producer of copper in California. (Courtesy Society of California Pioneers.)

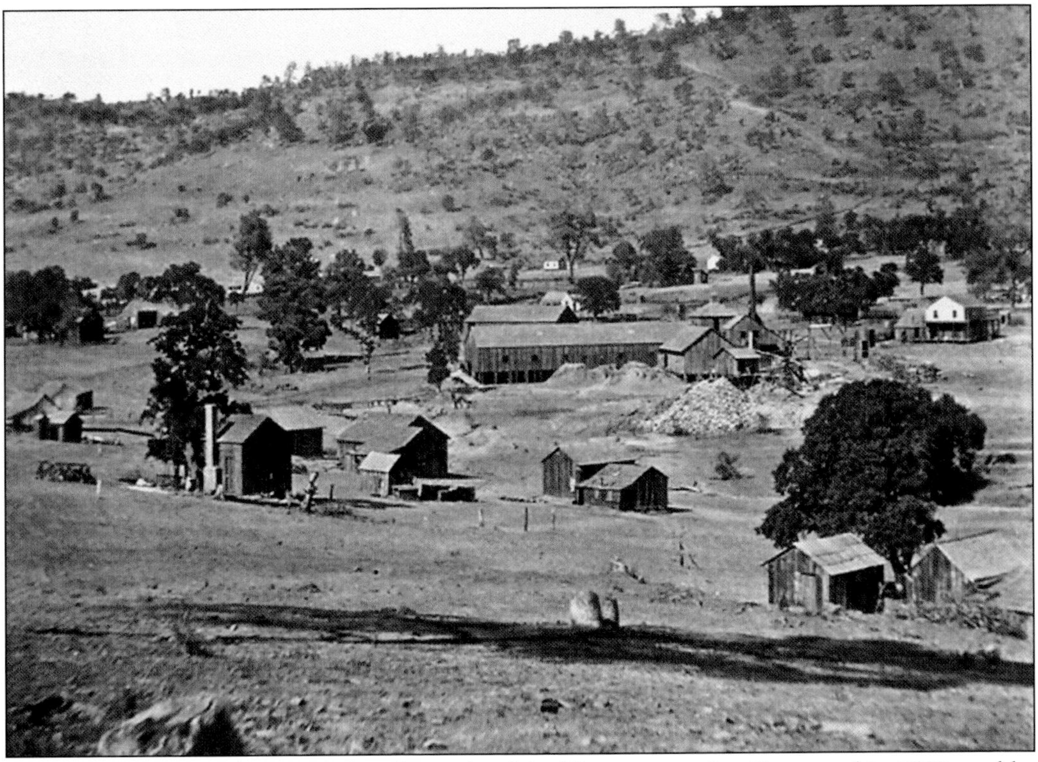

The Keystone Mine (pictured above), north of the Union, was also discovered in 1860, and by 1866, a shaft had been sunk 360 feet deep with four levels. Between 1864 and 1866, the Keystone operated a concentrating plant, which was abandoned when it proved unprofitable. The mine shut down in 1867, and beginning in 1878, the Union and Keystone mines were operated by the same owner but did not reopen until 1887. (Courtesy Society of California Pioneers.)

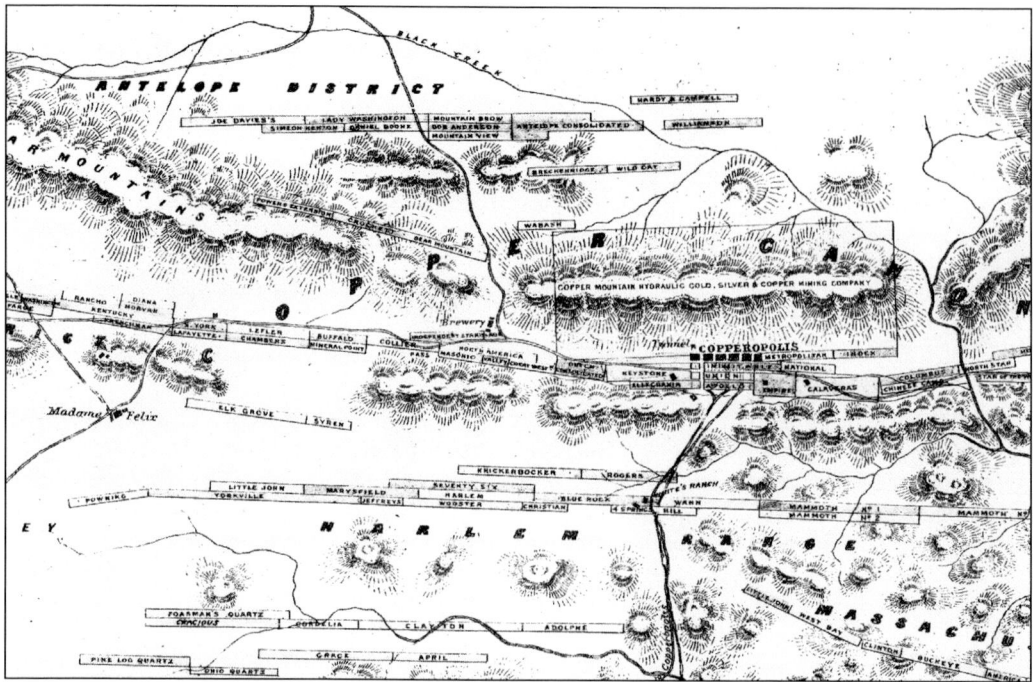

A map of the copper mines of Calaveras County (a portion of which is pictured above) was produced by engineers Handy and Wallace in 1864. Few of the 260 claims depicted ever amounted to anything, but the copper boom was of such interest that the investing public demanded more information, resulting in this detailed map. Some of the more important mines depicted included the Union, Keystone, Calaveras, Empire, and the Pine Log Quartz Mine at Hodson. (Courtesy Huntington Library.)

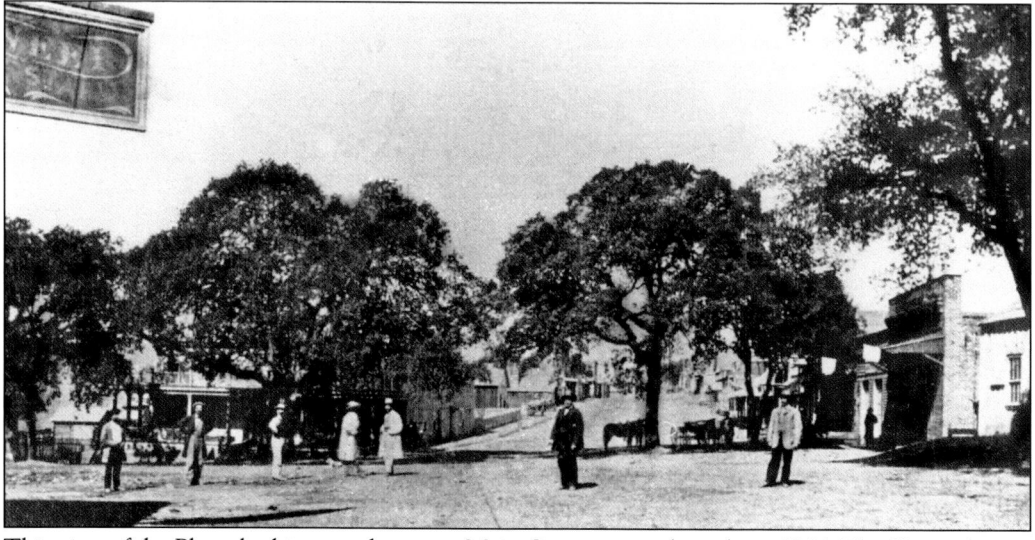

This view of the Plaza, looking northwest up Main Street, was taken about 1866. The Honigsberger Store is visible on the right, while Luke Kelly's Copperopolis Hotel is on the left. The fire of August 28, 1867, started in Kelly's sumptuous hotel and spread with amazing rapidity to the adjoining properties, burning most of the establishments on both sides of the street. (Courtesy Society of California Pioneers.)

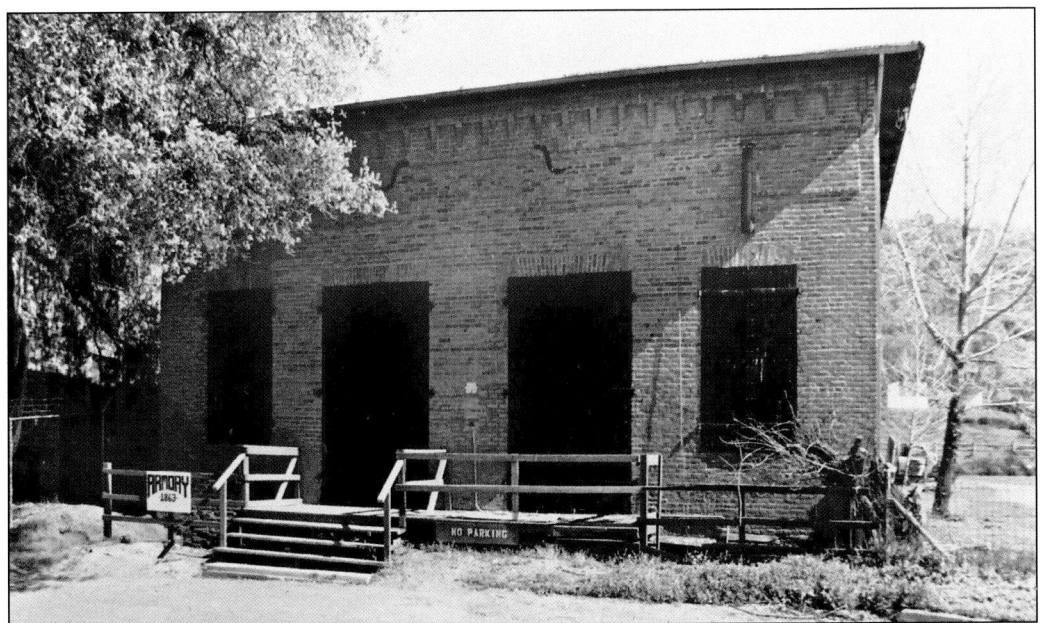

Built by public conscription in 1864, the Armory Hall was completed at a cost of $8,000 for the Union Guard militia, which was comprised of volunteers, mostly miners. Under Capt. James Oliphant, they trained with weapons, wore uniforms, practiced marching and basic infantry tactics and military order, and performed ceremonial functions, but they never fought anywhere. (Courtesy Calaveras County Historical Society.)

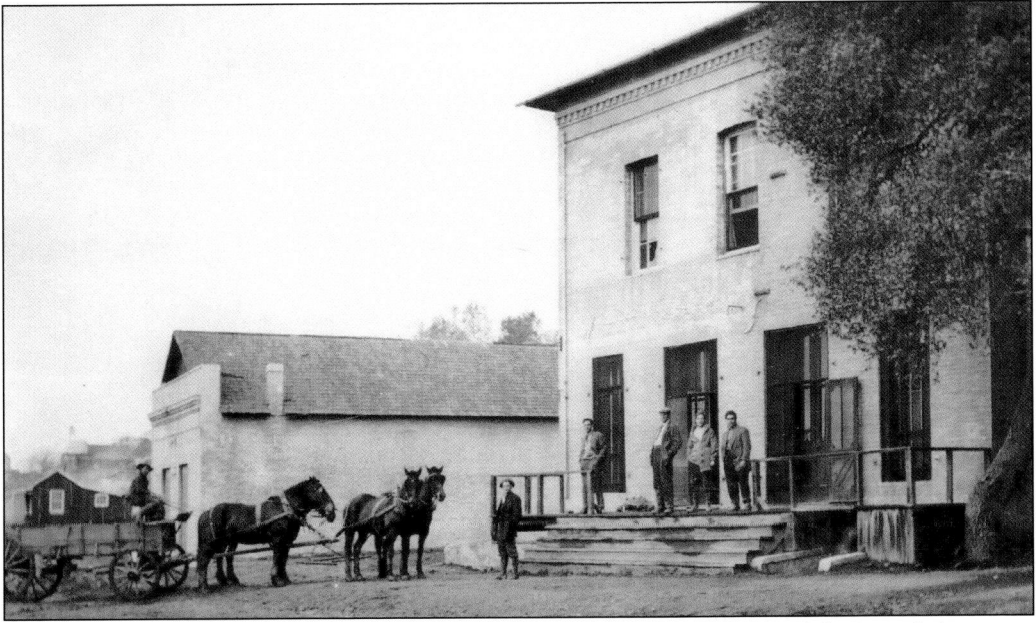

The brick stores built by L. Honigsberger (1865, left) and William K. Reed (1861, right) are two of the oldest buildings in Copperopolis. Operated by a succession of renters over the years, both buildings were purchased by the Union Copper Company about 1905 for use as company offices and a warehouse. They were restored by Howard Tower in the late 1980s. (Courtesy Calaveras County Historical Society.)

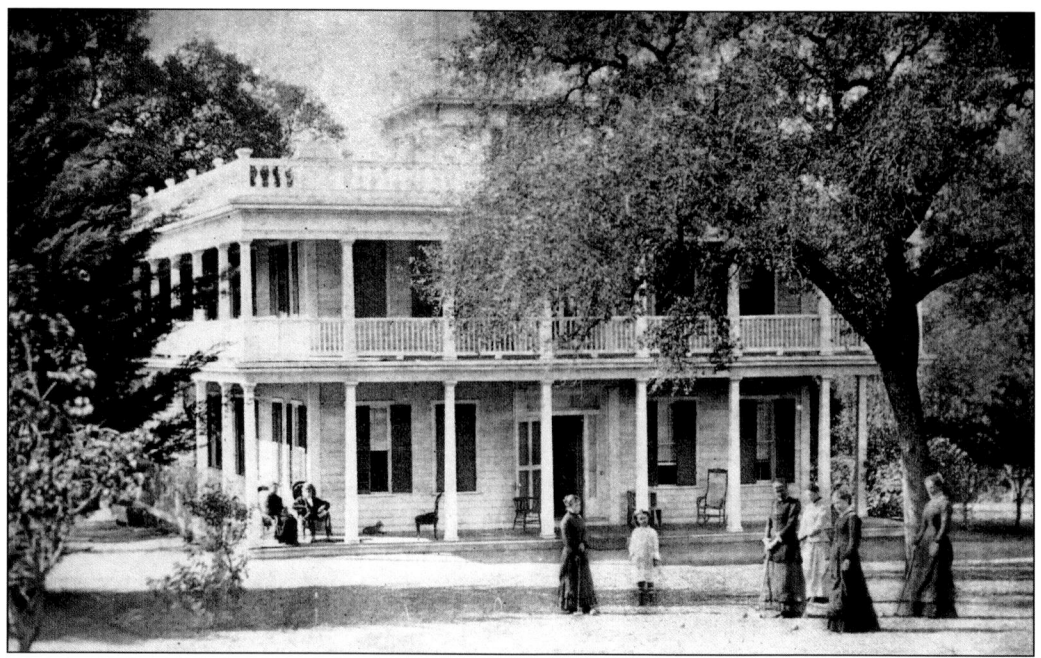

Capt. Thomas B. Meader reached California in 1849, settling in Copperopolis in the early boom years. There he built a fine hotel known as Meader's Resort, surrounded by a garden, vineyard, and orchard, where these ladies played croquet one day in the 1860s. (Courtesy Calaveras County Historical Society.)

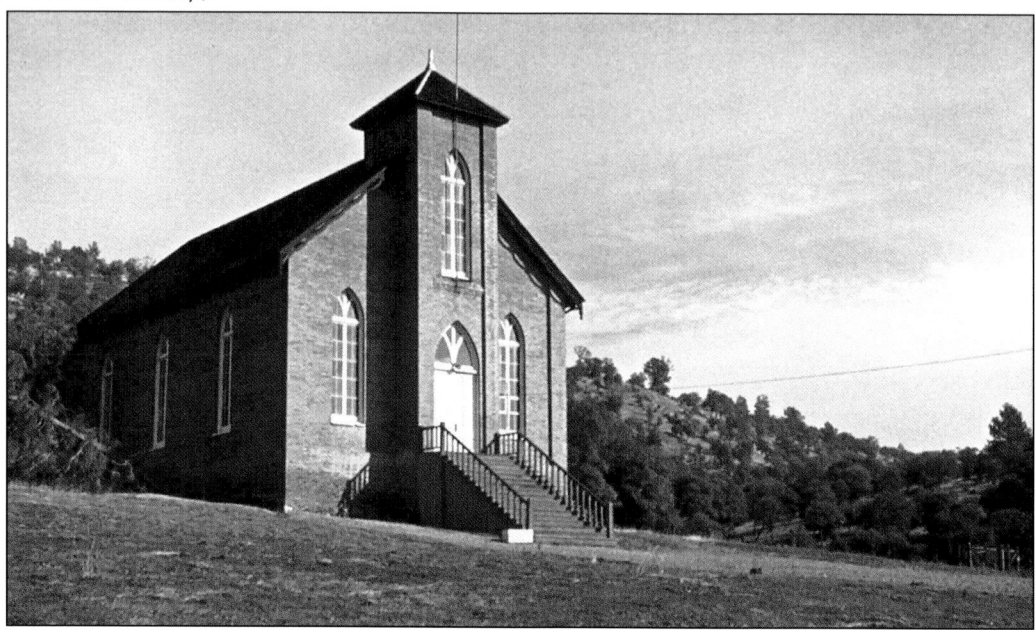

In 1865, mine owner C. T. Meader purchased land for the Congregational church, with construction completed in June the following year under the Reverend M. B. Starr at a cost of $12,000. It has also been used as a Presbyterian church. In 1903, it was purchased by the Mineral Lodge, the Independent Order of Odd Fellows, and, in 1939, by the Copperopolis Community Center. (Photograph by Alma Lavenson, courtesy Bancroft Library.)

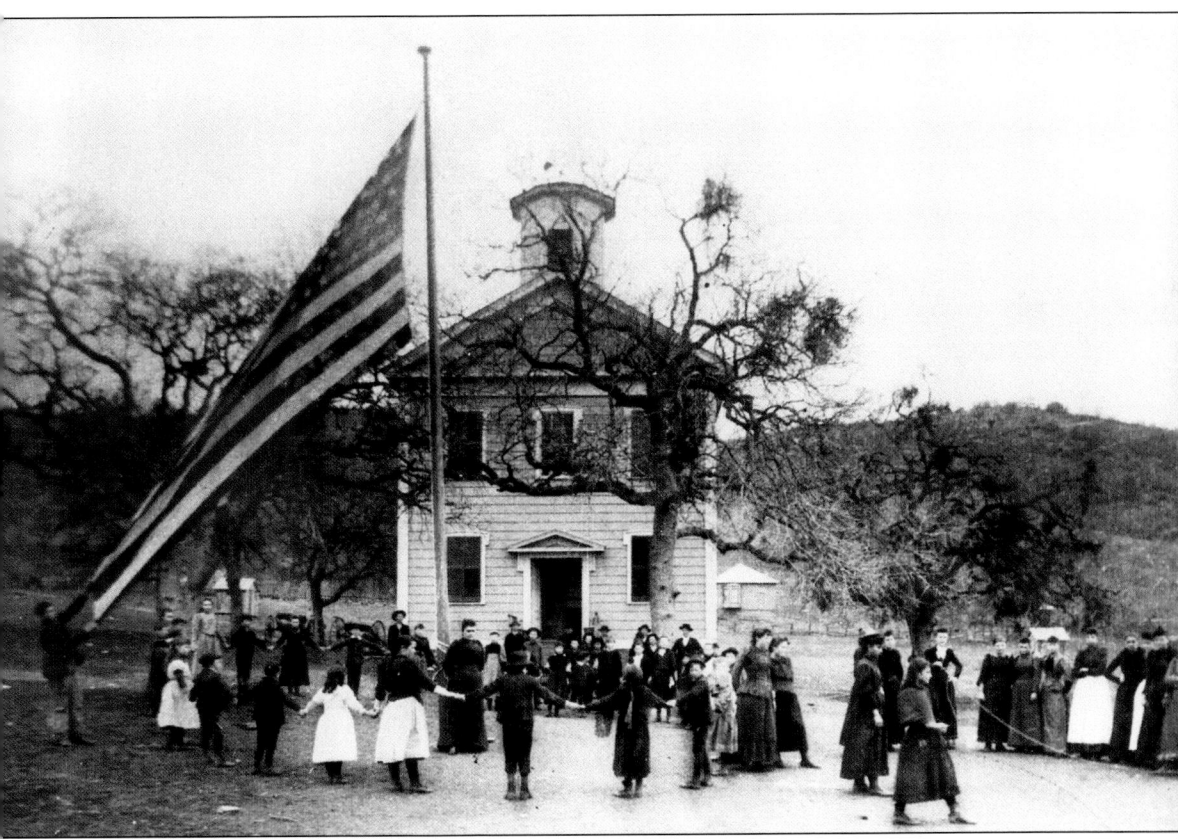

The Copperopolis School District was established on September 27, 1862, but it was not until 1865 that this school building was erected. An election was held in April of that year, and a tax of $1,000 was approved for the purposes of furnishing school facilities. The contract for the construction was awarded to the firm of Angell and Chaloner, who also built the interior of the Congregational church. A new three-room school was erected in 1908 after this school was consumed in a fire. In that year, about 90 students were in attendance. The second school was occupied until it was torn down in 1967, when the new school was erected. (Courtesy Ella McCarty Hiatt.)

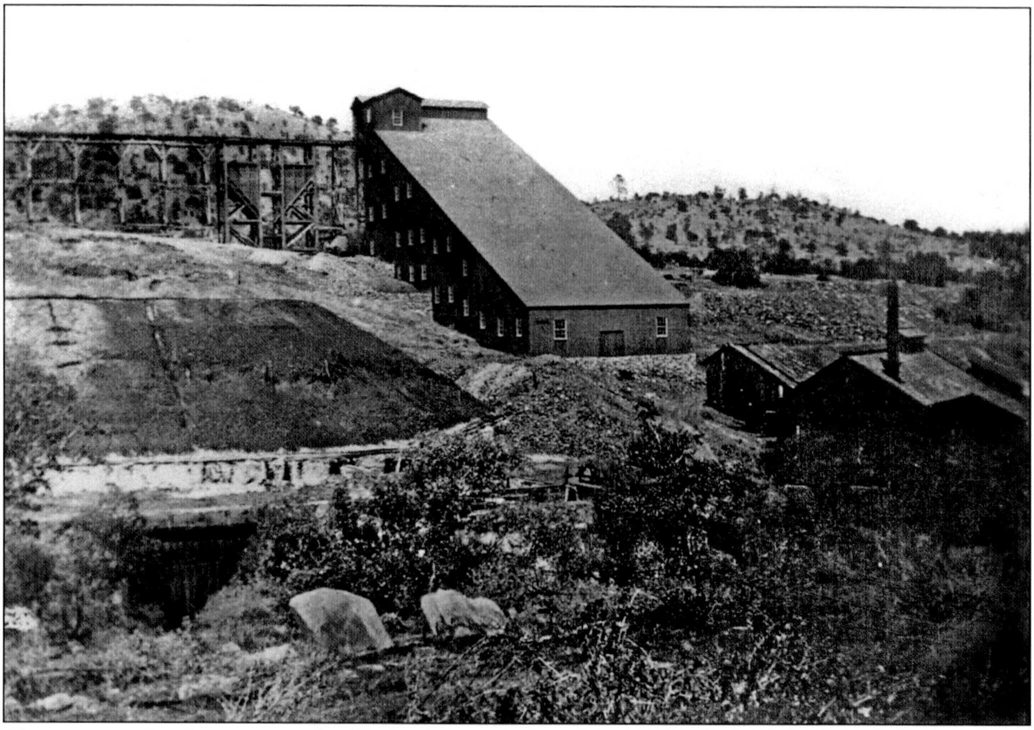

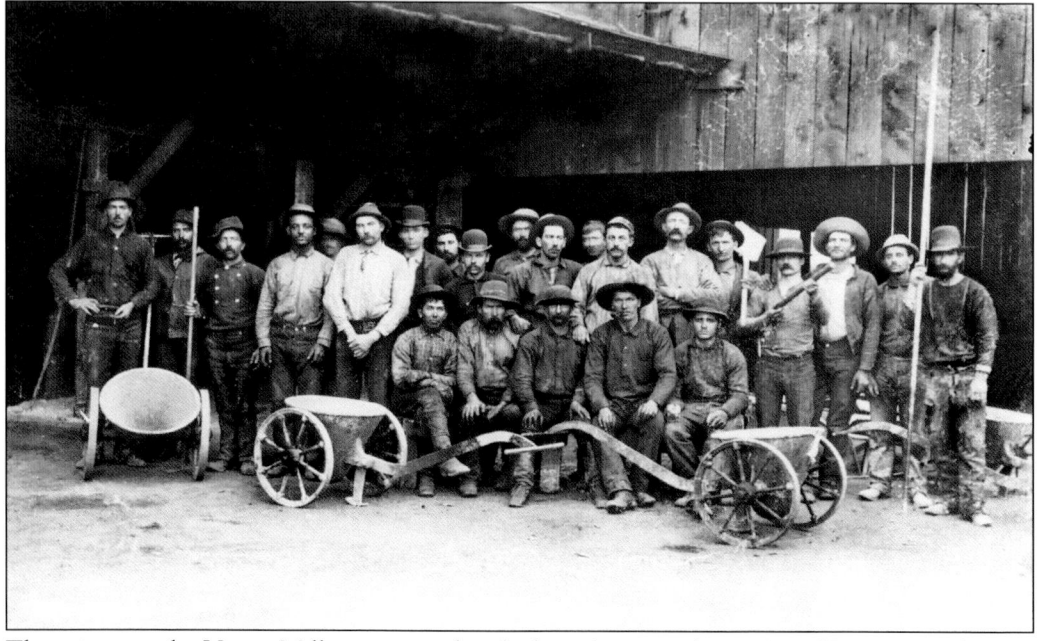

The greatest development at the Union Mine occurred under the direction of G. McMillan Ross, one of the most important California mining engineers, between 1900 and 1907. The headframe, hoist, compressor, mill, smelter, and trestle were all erected, and the mine reached full production under his tenure. It finally closed in 1930. (Courtesy Calaveras County Historical Society.)

The miners at the Union Mill are pictured with their slag pots about 1900. (Courtesy Calaveras County Historical Society.)

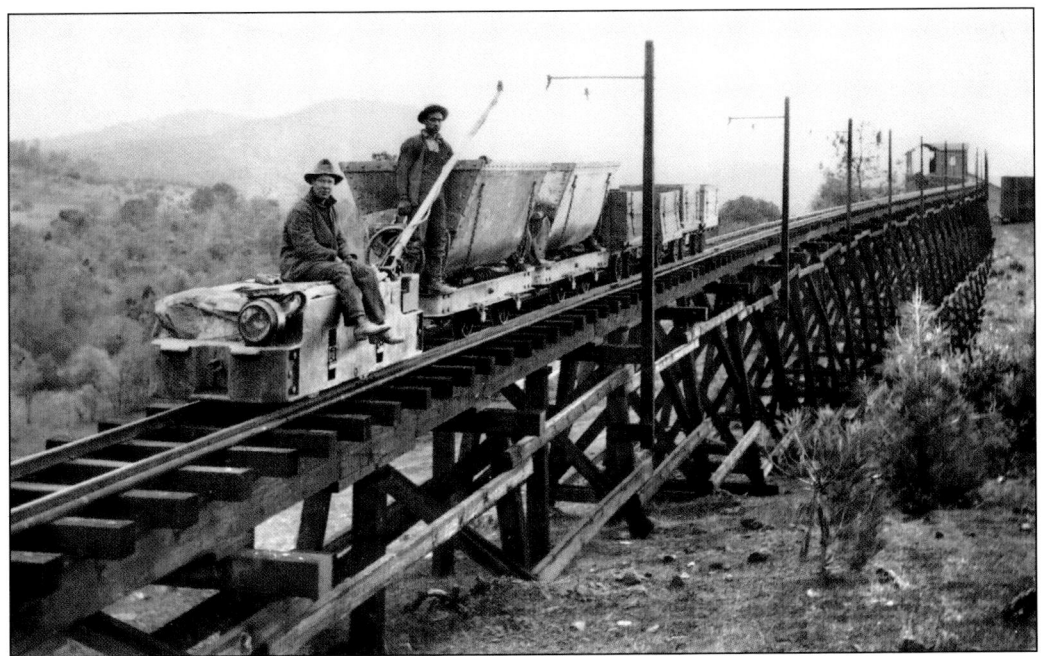

Constructed about 1900, the 4,000-foot-long electric tram and trestle carried ore from the Union and Keystone mines over the fills to the crushing plant. The crushed ore was then conveyed to the concentrator at the mill southeast of town, from where it was later fed to the adjacent smelter. (Courtesy Calaveras County Historical Society.)

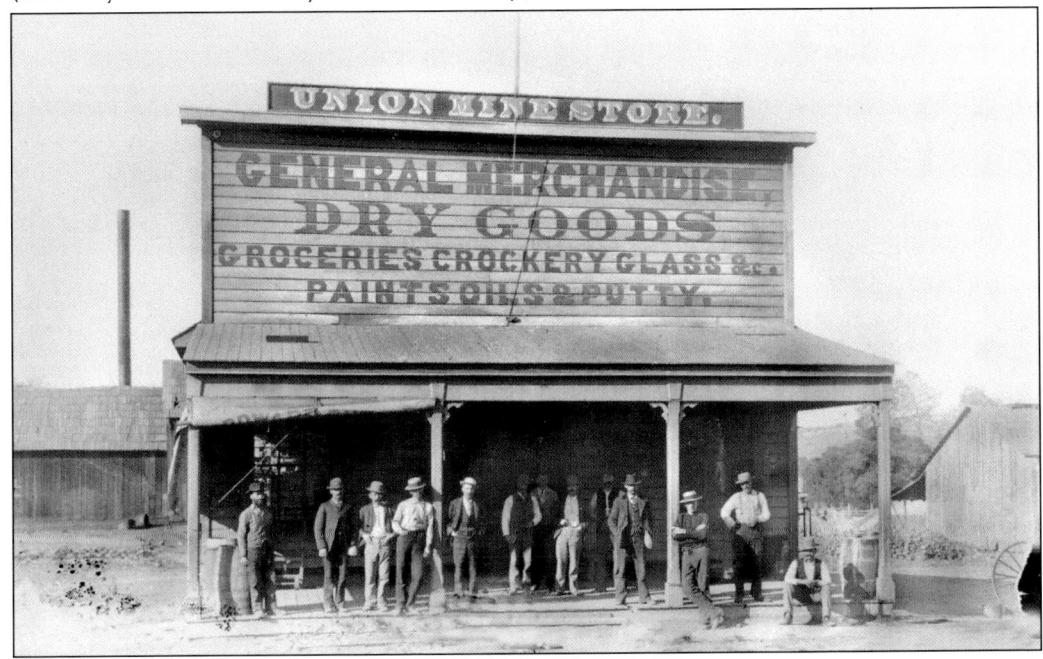

From 1909 to 1930, the Calaveras Copper Company operated almost continuously, running their own store, boardinghouses, electric plant, and stables, and providing company housing for their workers. In this early-1900s view, the Union Mine Store advertises the wide variety of merchandise available to the miners and townsfolk. (Courtesy Calaveras County Historical Society.)

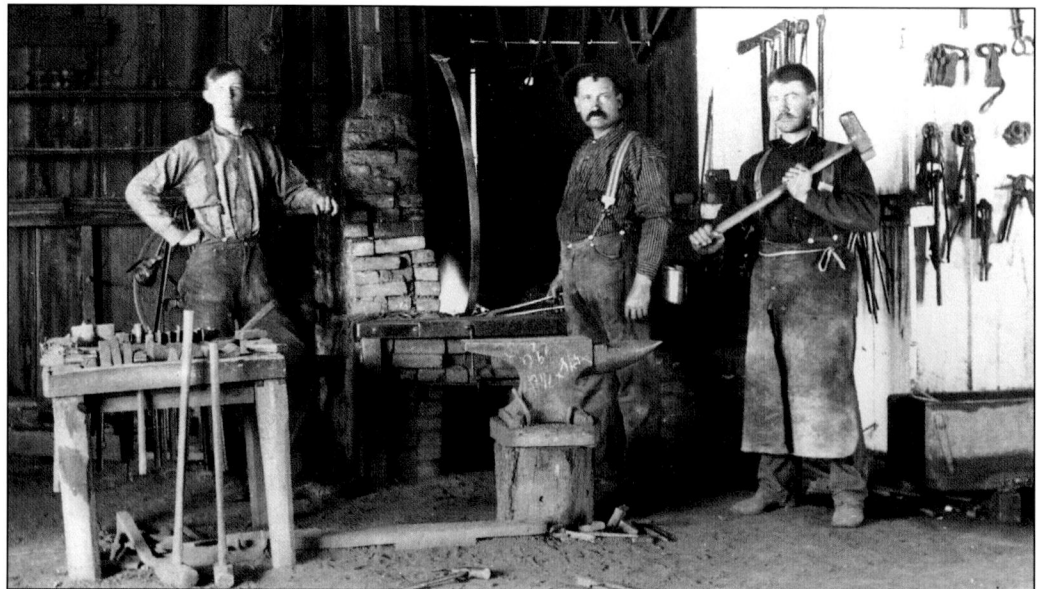

James M. Stone married Rose O'Hara of Sonora, and in 1890, they moved to Copperopolis, where he purchased the blacksmith shop of Charles Hartsook. Two of James's three sons, Frank, Charles, and James Jr., worked in the shop. In this photograph, (from left to right) Frank Reddick, James M. Stone, and George Madison Copeland are working in the shop. In 1915, however, realizing the horse-and-buggy days were disappearing, James Jr. replaced the blacksmithy with the Stone Garage. (Courtesy Charles A. Stone.)

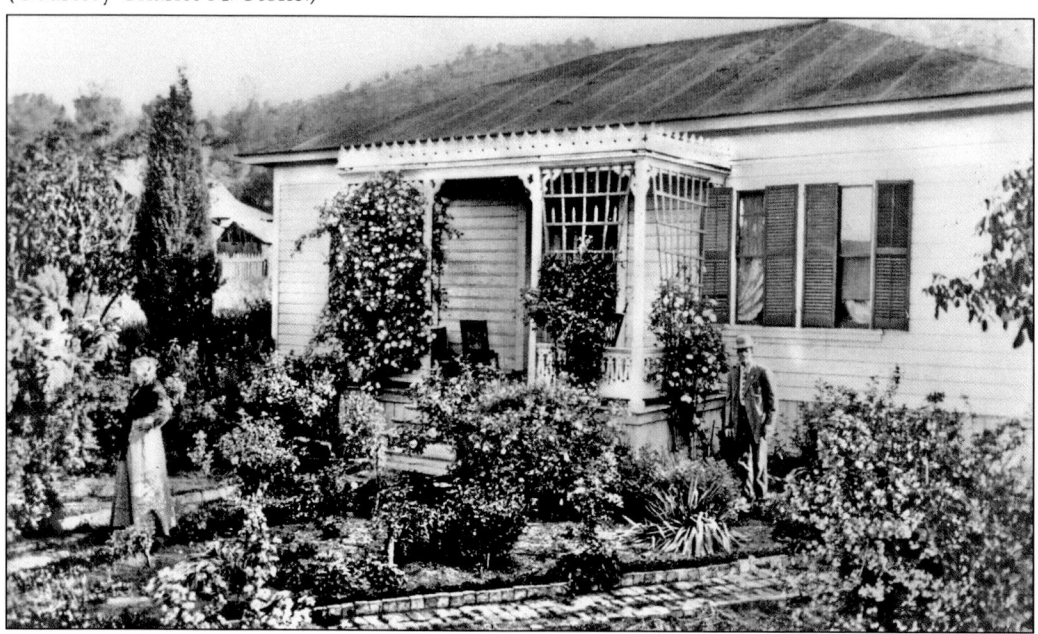

Built in the late 1880s, the Hendsch home still stands on the south end of Main Street. In 1861, German Charles Hendsch set up a tailor shop on Main Street. After the death of Charles in 1871, his widow, Augusta, continued to reside in Copperopolis with her eight children. Her sons, involved in mining and blacksmithing enterprises, built this home for her. (Courtesy Calaveras County Historical Society.)

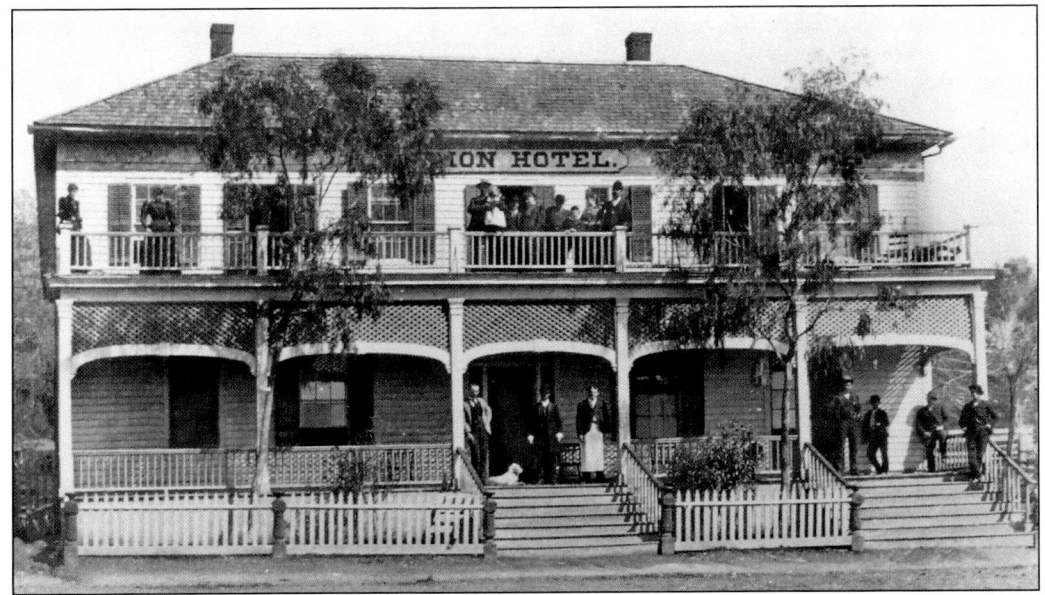

Copperopolis slumbered during the last decades of the 19th century, but with the reopening of the mines, it was once again a bustling community with stores, hotels, liveries, saloons, and dwellings lining Main Street. One of the most prosperous new enterprises was the Union Hotel, operated by George W. Hayes. (Courtesy Calaveras County Historical Society.)

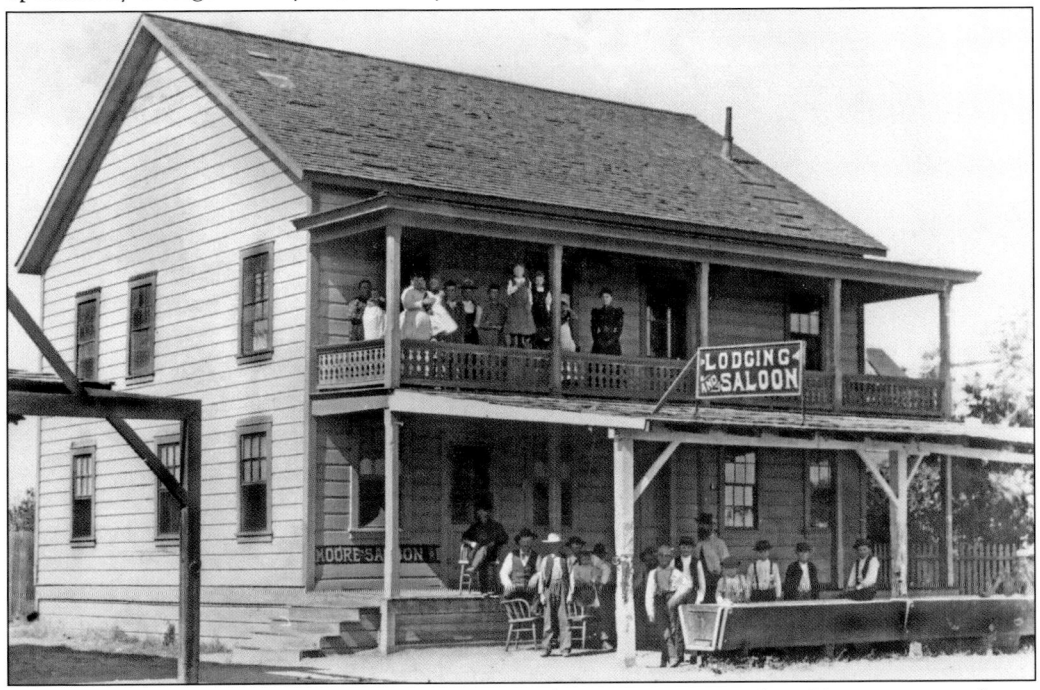

The Old Corner Saloon, constructed in 1889 as the Copper Inn, is the oldest surviving frame commercial building in the community. Operated by E. B. Moore, it served as a rooming and boardinghouse for the miners who labored in the adjacent Union Mine. Historian Charlie Stone remembered when there were nine saloons in town, noting, "Copperopolis didn't have a town drunk, they all took turns." (Courtesy Calaveras County Historical Society.)

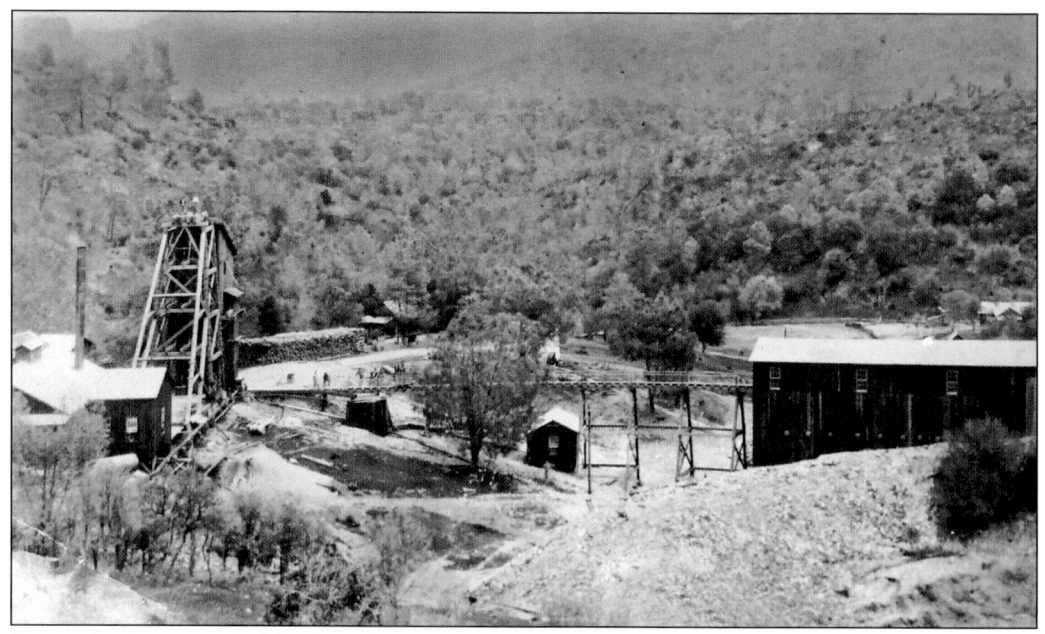

Located at Scorpion Gulch, the Alto Mine was the site of the only significant gold mining activity in that area. Mining commenced in the 1850s, but it was not until the early 1900s that a 40-stamp mill, a headframe, a tramway, a boardinghouse, dwellings, sheds, and other support facilities were erected. The mine operated with moderate success until it burned in 1907. (Courtesy Calaveras County Historical Society.)

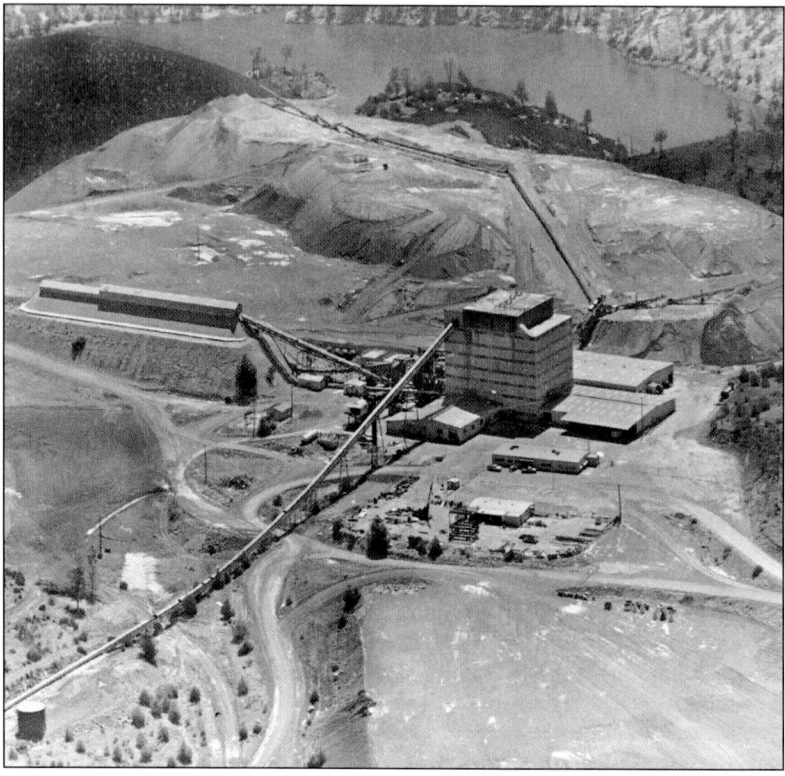

Long after the copper mines played out, a new and different type of ore was wrested from the earth. Asbestos had been discovered on the Bowie Ranch on Central Ferry Road as early as 1868. It was not until the early 1960s, however, that production began in earnest on a 480-acre site, where ore was extracted by the open-pit method, shown at the height of production in 1975. (Courtesy Calaveras County Historical Society.)

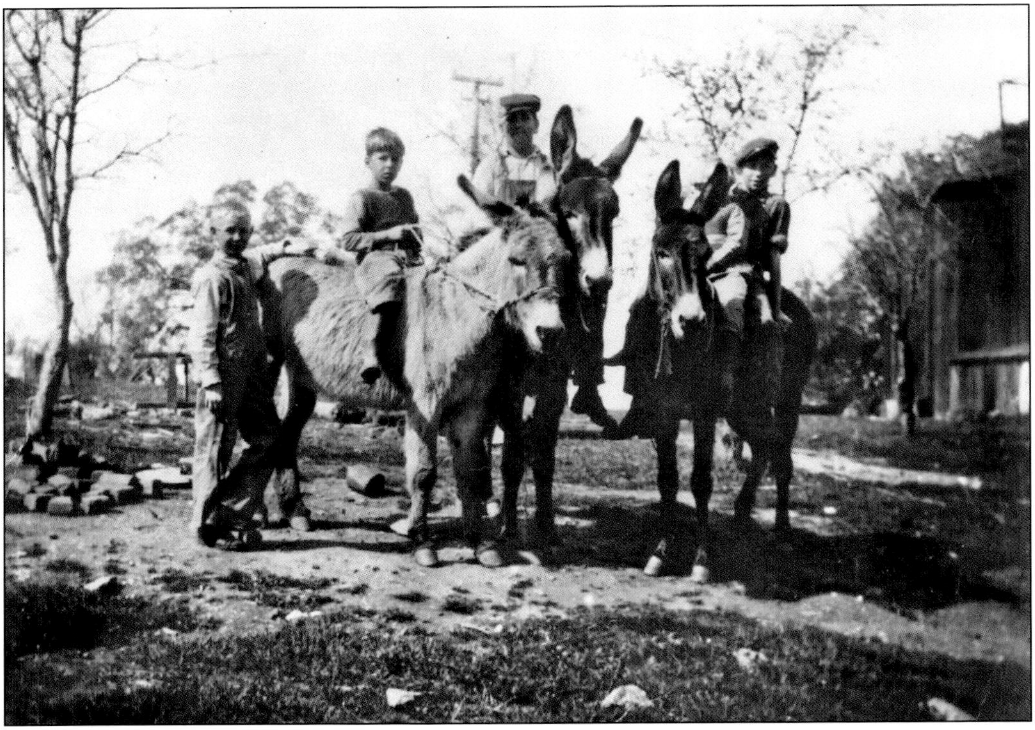

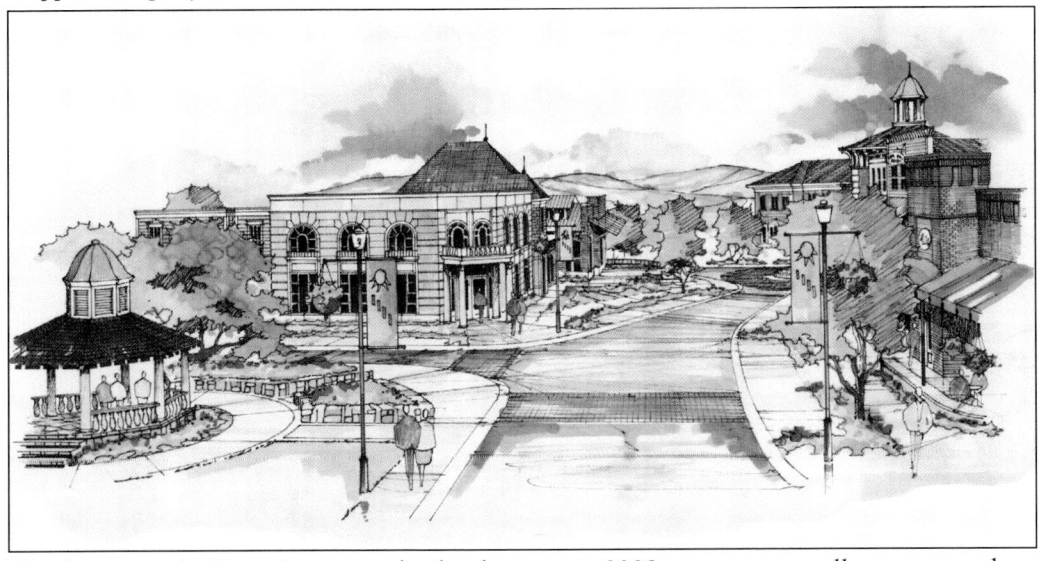

In this 1921 photograph, Frank Riggs and his friends pose for the photographer with their "wild" burros. In 1916, during the World War I boom, Edgar Leon Riggs, his wife, Dara, son Frank, and the rest of his family moved to Copperopolis, where he worked as mine foreman for the Calaveras Copper Company. (Courtesy Calaveras County Historical Society.)

The Copperopolis Town Square, under development in 2008, promotes a small-town atmosphere enhanced by a central plaza. In an effort to reflect the town's rich history, streets in the new town center—which includes retail businesses, offices, and residences—are named after pioneers such as Stone, Tower, Egan, and McCarty. Nearby recreation includes Saddle Creek, one of the top golf resorts in the western United States. (Courtesy Rudolph Ortega.)

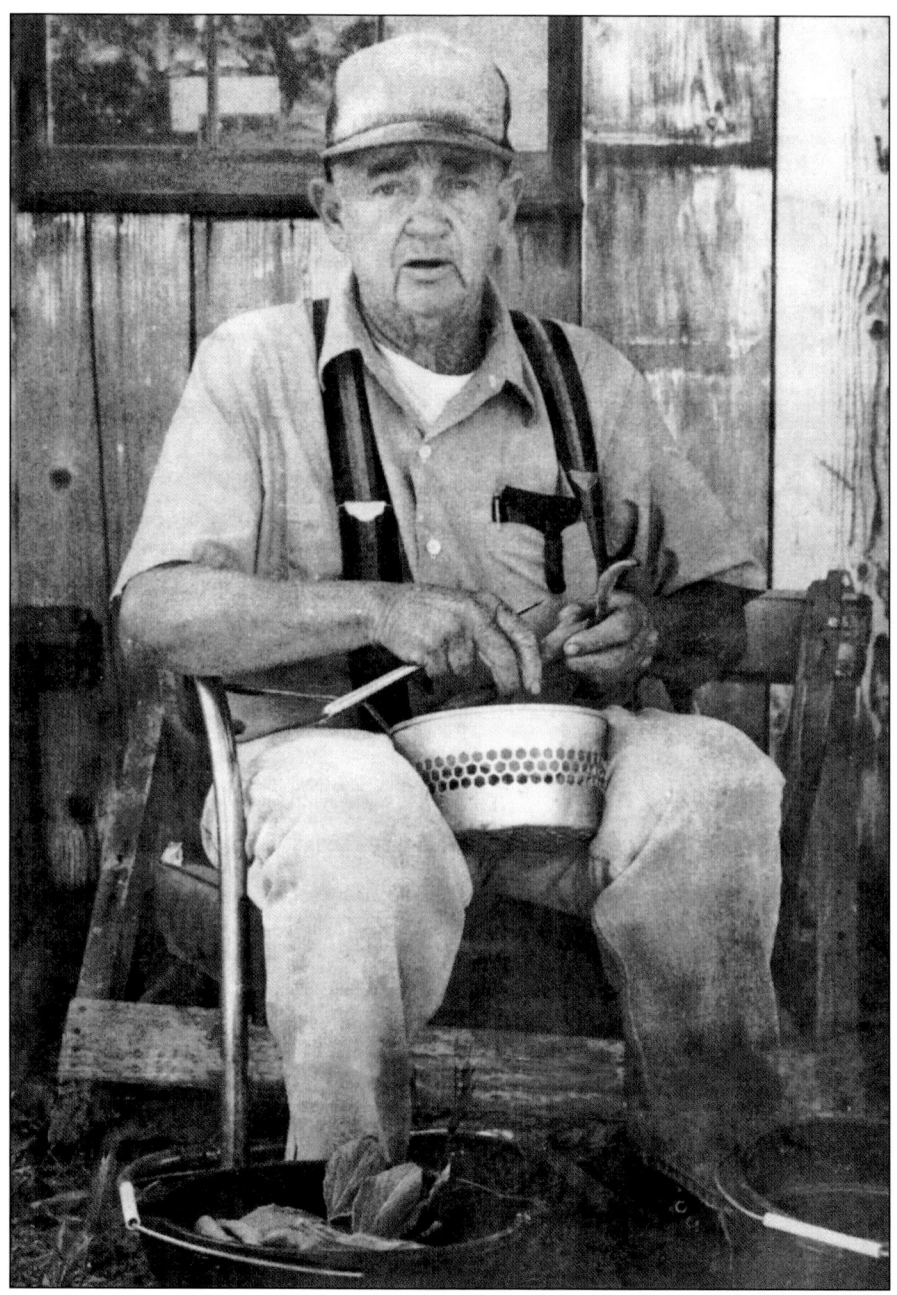

Vice mayor (the mayor of vice) and storyteller Charles Stone (son of Charles and Catherine Stone and grandson of James and Rose Stone) and his wife, Rhoda, were longtime residents and were devoted to the history of Copperopolis. They were instrumental in preserving its brick buildings and produced its story, *The Tools are on the Bar*. The title indicated that the mining days were over for Copperopolis. Charlie traveled to Swansea, Wales, to study the connection between the two communities, discovering that, in the 1880s, Swansea was known as the "Copperopolis of the World." As he was fond of saying, "If you've spent a summer in Copperopolis, you're not afraid of hell," but for those newcomers who have settled on the old ranches surrounding the town, it appears to be more like heaven. (Courtesy Calaveras County Historical Society.)

Six

MINES OF MADAM FELIX

The small Madam Felix mining district, located in Salt Spring Valley on the West Belt of the Mother Lode, is a typical problem district where the gold was not easy to find and, once found, difficult to extract from the parent rock. The district is undistinguished by big strikes or celebrated nuggets. However, it does have a tenacious mining history reaching from the present back to the late 1850s. Prospectors first followed the trail of placer gold up to the quartz veins, where it was mined by sporadic surface ventures through the 19th century. The turn-of-the-20th-century boom that invigorated most of the Mother Lode saw an enormous 120-stamp mill built for the Royal Mine. The ore body, however, proved smaller than expected, and the venture rapidly failed.

The district settled back into intermittent small-scale operations through World War II and until the 1980s, when the Madam Felix mining district was resurrected by the Meridian Gold Company. Using modern open-pit, conventional mill, and cyanide leach operations, it achieved much success in solving problems associated with recovering the district's low-grade ore. The ore bodies exhausted, the land recontoured and reclaimed, Salt Spring Valley is once again an agricultural landscape.

The history of a mining district, however, can be richer than the value of its ore. The characteristics of the local population can profoundly affect development, especially in a long-lived district like Madam Felix. The land attracted modest ranching and farming operations, and from the earliest years, these ranchers and their employees and retainers all dabbled in mining. They prospected, proved up claims, formed ventures, and milled ore. The lives of several generations of families like the McCartys, Towers, Blazers, and Wombles are interwoven with the more transient prospectors, promoters, and miners. The history of Madam Felix's gold—achievements and failures—is typical of the numerous similar districts that once covered the Mother Lode.

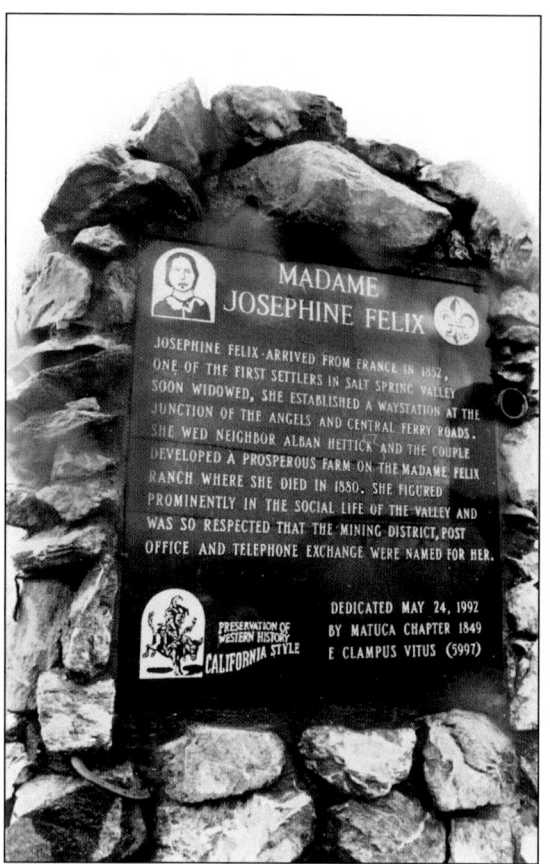

Frenchman Sylvester Felix died at age 30 in Salt Spring Valley, leaving his widow, Josephine, to fend for herself. Converting their home into a way station for travelers, she became the center of the valley's social life. Although Josephine soon married neighbor Alban Hettick, her ranch was always called "the Madam's," the mining district was "Madam Felix," and the later post office and telephone exchange were both named "Felix."(Photograph by Judith Marvin.)

Hopeful prospecting in Salt Spring Valley in the 1850s turned over soil in every gulch and gully, and hoists like the one pictured below were common. Although the source of gold was located in the Hodson Hills, these new diggings were not productive. The activity did result in a ditch being dug to bring water to the mines from Tule Lake. Hopes and prospecting increased in the 1860s with the nearby discovery of copper, and the small settlement at Pine Log briefly bloomed. (Courtesy Julia Costello.)

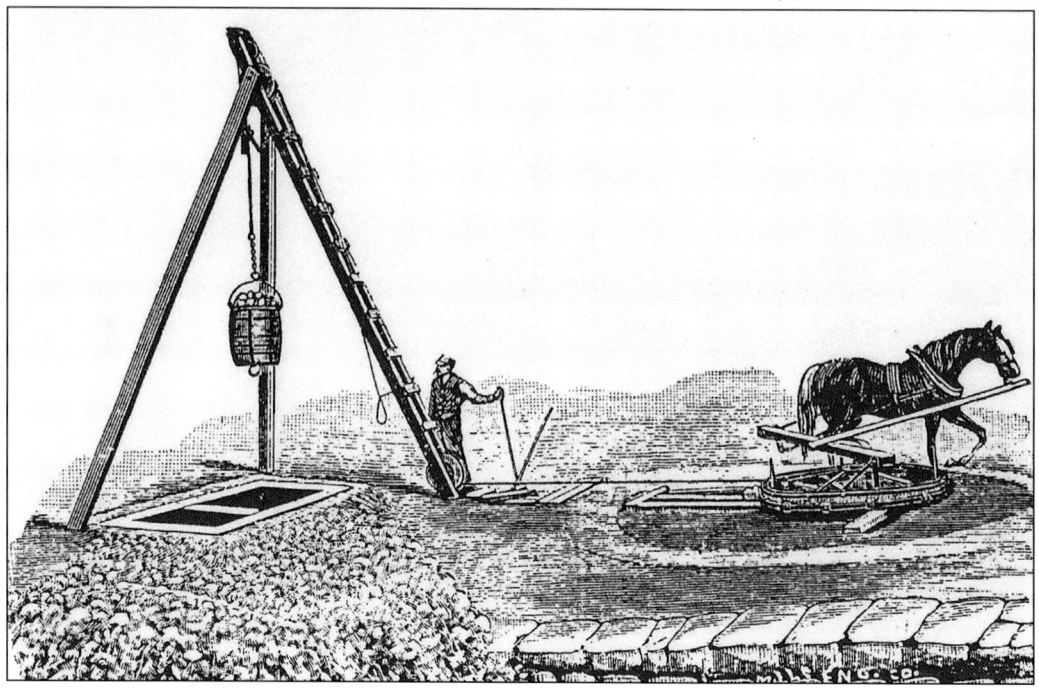

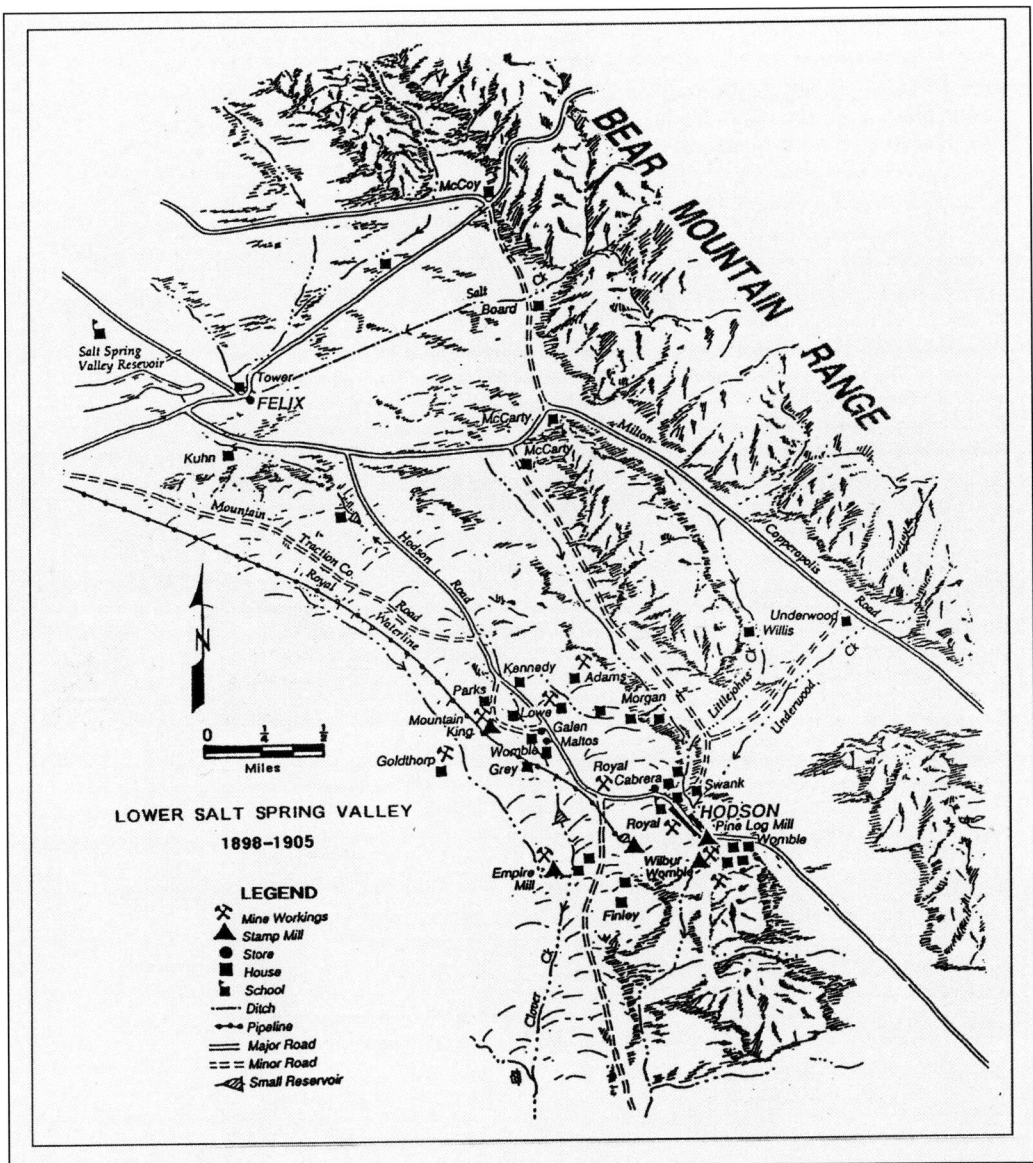

Mining activity lagged in the district until 1876, when local ranchers Francis Jetzer, Jacob Tower, and Alban Hettick filed on the Pine Log claim and convinced San Francisco investors to purchase and develop it. With this endeavor, serious hard-rock mining began, and by the end of the century, more than a dozen small mines and two mills—the Empire and the Pine Log—were in operation. The high point of the district's social and economic life was between 1898 and 1905, following development by the Royal Consolidated Mining Company, which bought out the Pine Log, built an enormous 120-stamp mill, and established the company town of Hodson. Locals joined the excitement by developing other claims and constructing the Mountain King and Wilber-Womble mills. Ranching families like McCarty, Tower, and Kuhn also kept their hands in the mining activities. (Courtesy Foothill Resources, Ltd.)

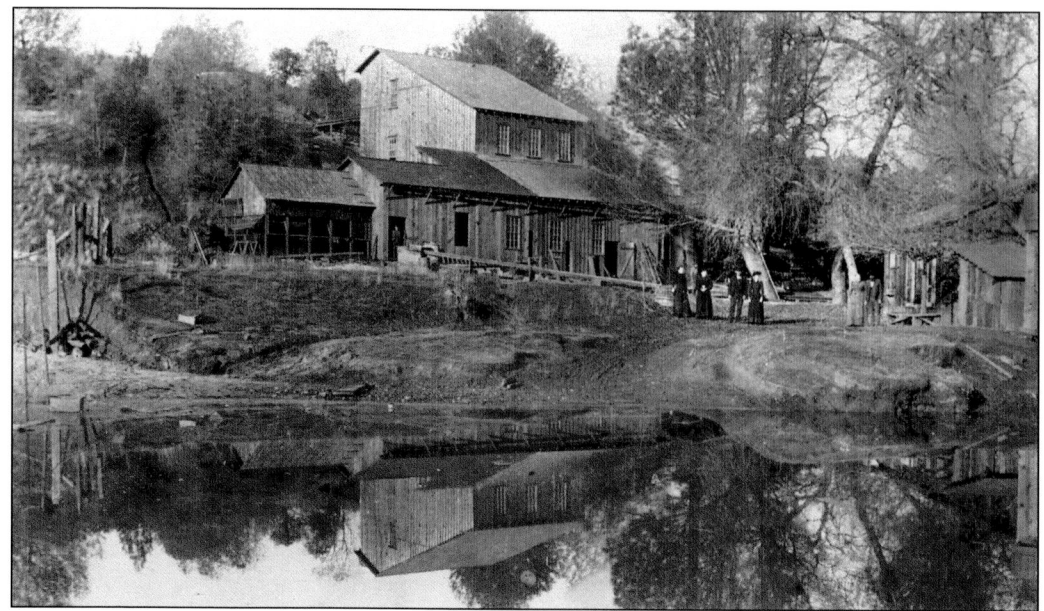

Tulloch's mill on Littlejohns Creek, built in 1870, was revamped in 1877 as the Pine Log. In 1890, it was torn down and replaced by a 10-stamp mill (pictured here) as part of the new development by the Royal Consolidated Mining Company. Enough gold was found under the floor of the old mill to pay for all the lumber in the new structure. (Courtesy Calaveras County Historical Society.)

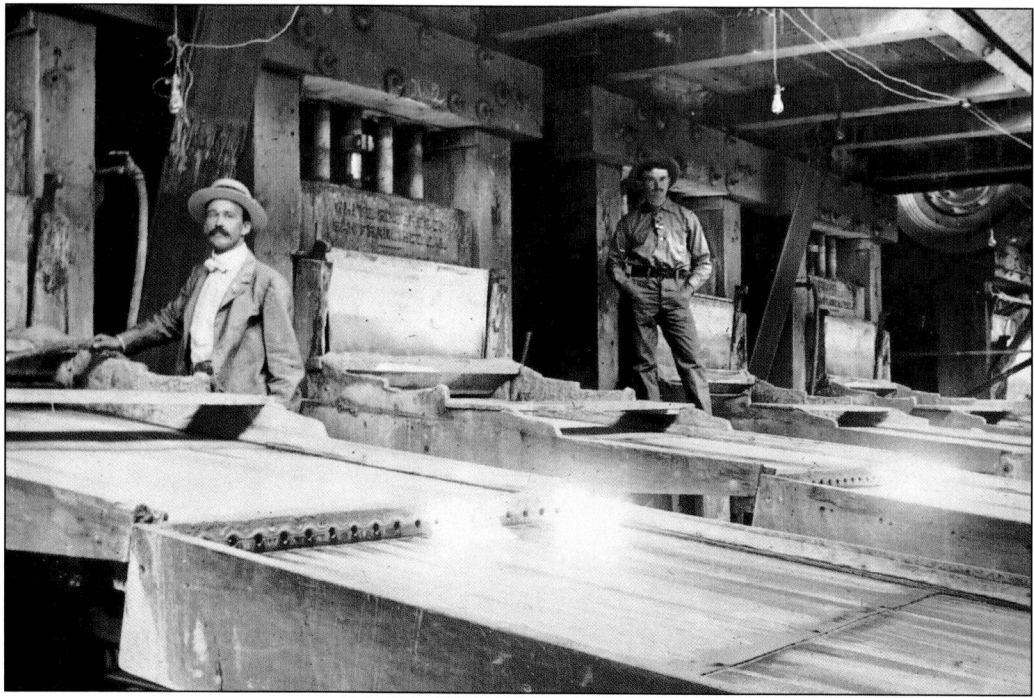

In 1898, the Royal Consolidated Mining Company was in full swing, and the Pine Log mill was increased to handle 40 stamps. This photograph shows the batteries of five stamps feeding pulverized ore to the separating tables. Will Dennis, the mine's electrical engineer, is at far left. (Courtesy Calaveras County Historical Society.)

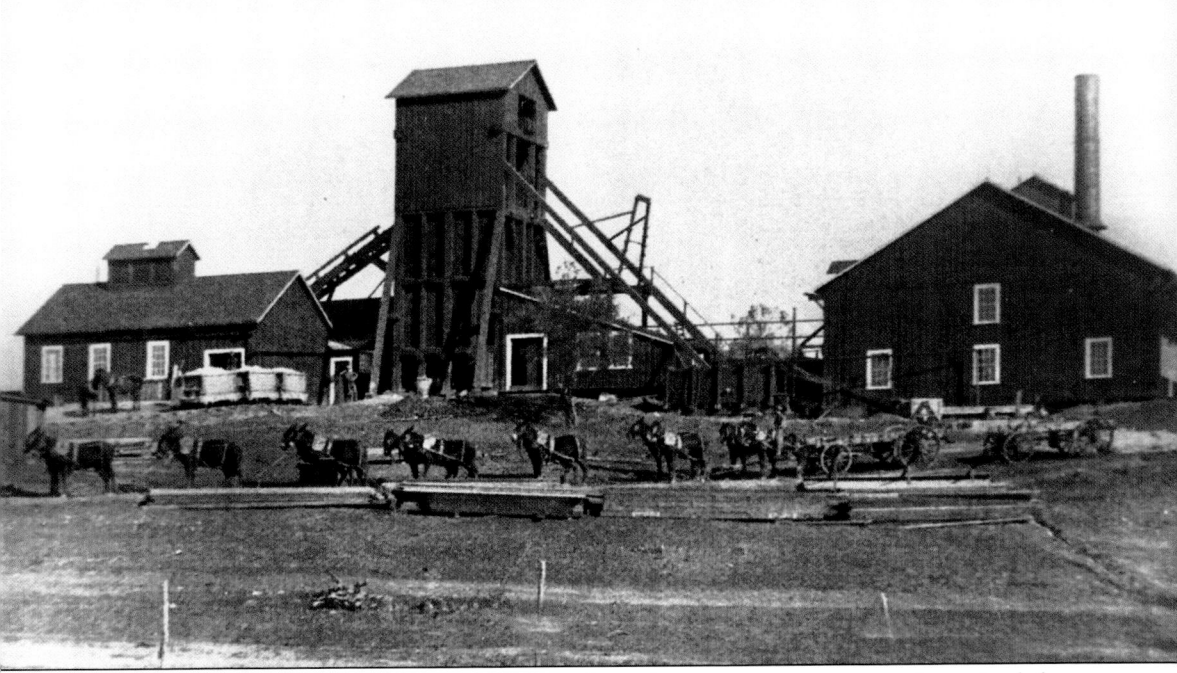

By 1899, the surface plant at the Royal featured two hoisting compartments that raised the ore and waste rock up the 900-foot-deep Jutton main shaft. A crushing plant was added to reduce the ore, and electricity was brought to the site in 1902 from Lane and Tulloch's new hydroelectric plant at Knights Ferry. At this time, ore was still being processed at the Pine Log mill down on Littlejohns Creek, transported there along a surface tramway. The horses or mules would follow the loaded three-car train down, knowing that feed awaited them at the mill, and then haul the empty cars back up to the mine. (Courtesy Blazer family, Calaveras County Historical Society.)

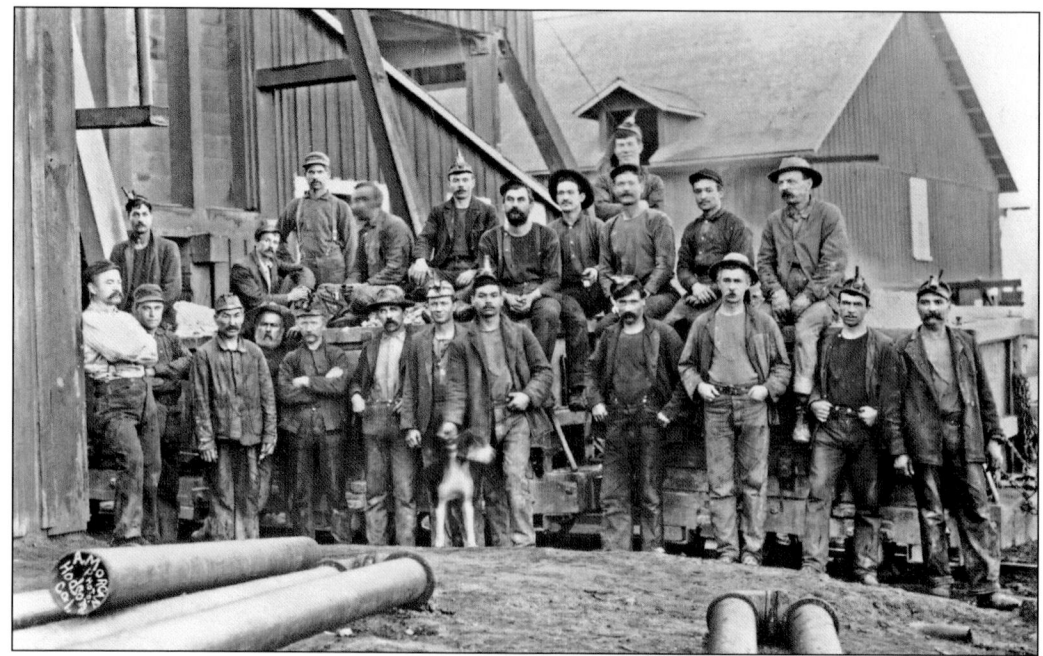

By the end of 1899, there were 100 men at work at the Royal. Among the crew were numerous members of local ranching families, most of whom had been part-time mining all their lives. This photograph in 1900 captured a shift near the main shaft. (Photograph by Arthur Morgan, courtesy Calaveras County Historical Society.)

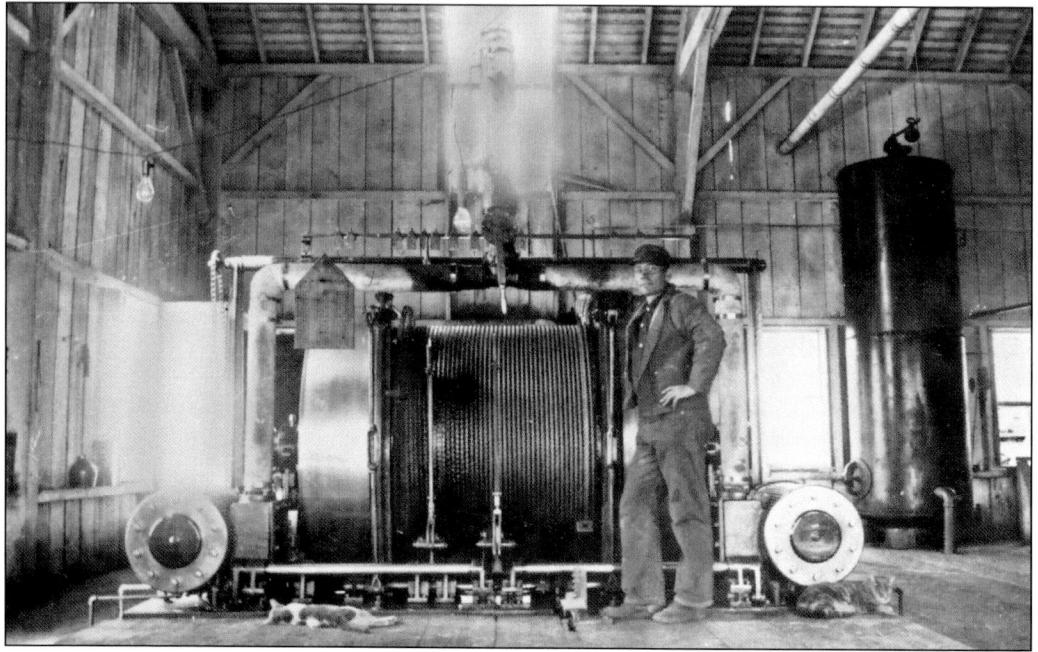

This single-drum steam-powered hoist was used at the Royal's Jutton shaft. A steam cylinder can be seen at each side. The hoist was converted to electric power in 1902 and was replaced with a double-drum hoist in 1903. (Photograph by Will Dennis, courtesy Calaveras County Historical Society.)

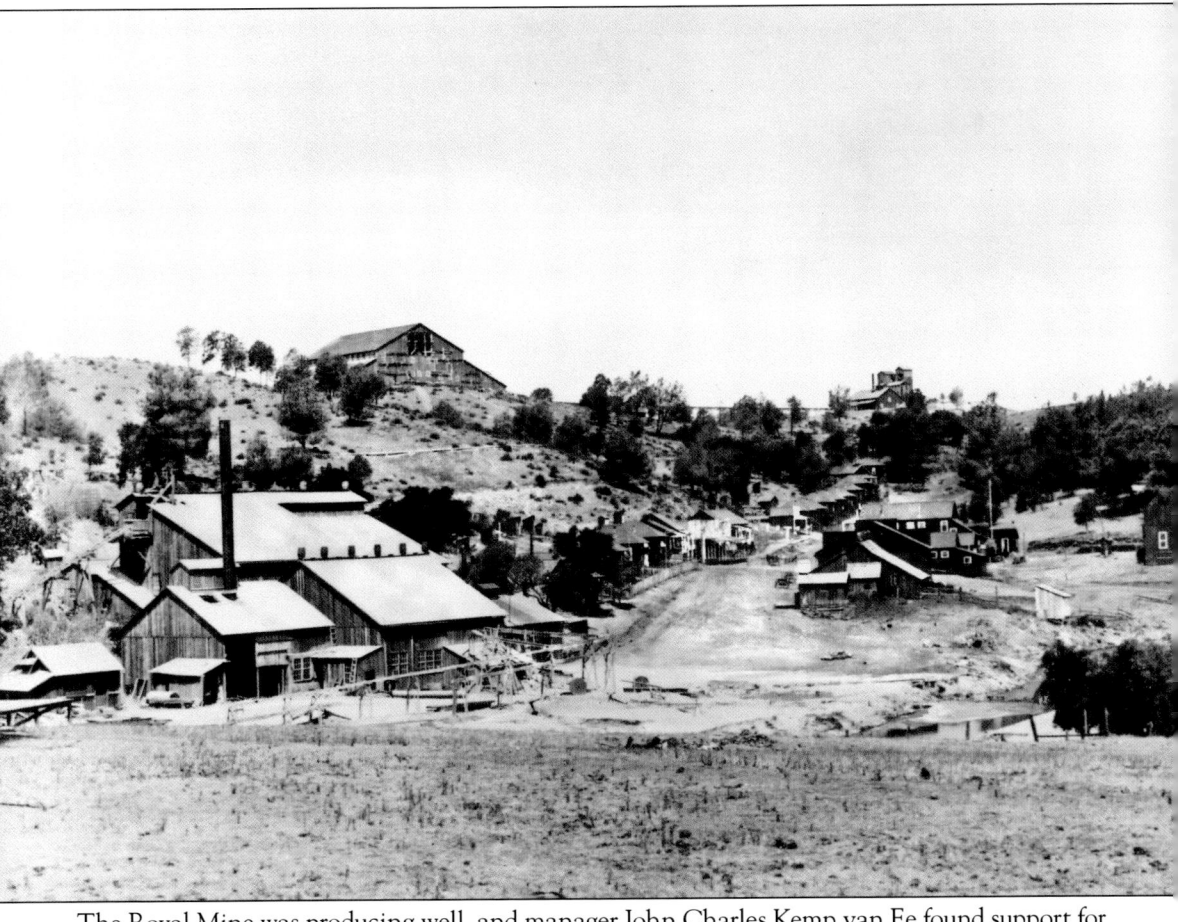

The Royal Mine was producing well, and manager John Charles Kemp van Ee found support for building a new mill, seen on the skyline in this 1903 photograph. Its unusual design had six stamp batteries mounted on each side of the mill, with each battery consisting of two five-stamp units, for a total of 120 stamps. This larger facility required 1,000 pounds of ore per day to be kept busy, and the mine shaft was therefore enlarged to accommodate a second hoist. A 1,600-foot-long elevated trestle was constructed to carry ore from the hoist and surface plant (on the skyline to the right) to the mill. The town, named after Thomas Hodson, the firm's London backer, featured cottages for key employees, a post office, a general store, a school, a company office, a boardinghouse, and a hotel. In 1903, its population reached 300 persons. It was said that Herbert Hoover, then a well-known mining engineer, visited the Royal on his way to the Gwin mine in Paloma. The old Pine Log mill, seen at lower left, was then abandoned. (Photograph by Arthur Morgan, courtesy Calaveras County Historical Society.)

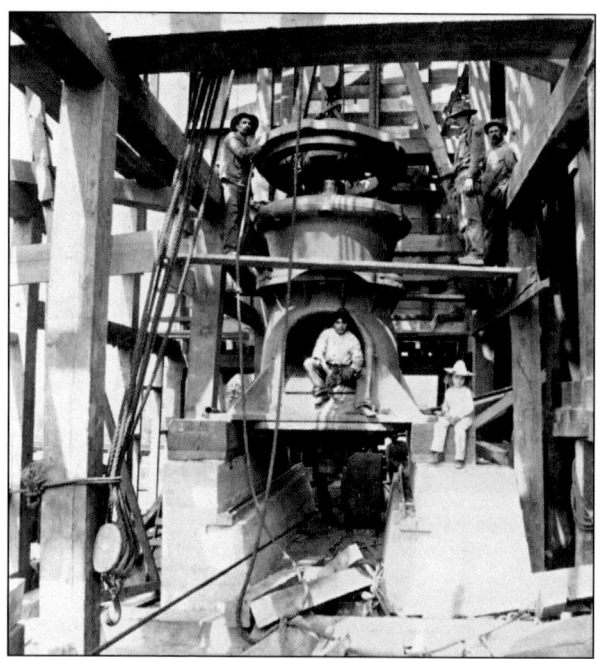

This massive gyratory crusher was installed in 1903 to reduce ore before it was trammed to the mill. The workmen and two children pose for photographer Arthur Morgan, a miner/photographer who lived near the old Felix Ranch with his wife, Sarah. (Photograph by Arthur Morgan, courtesy Calaveras County Historical Society.)

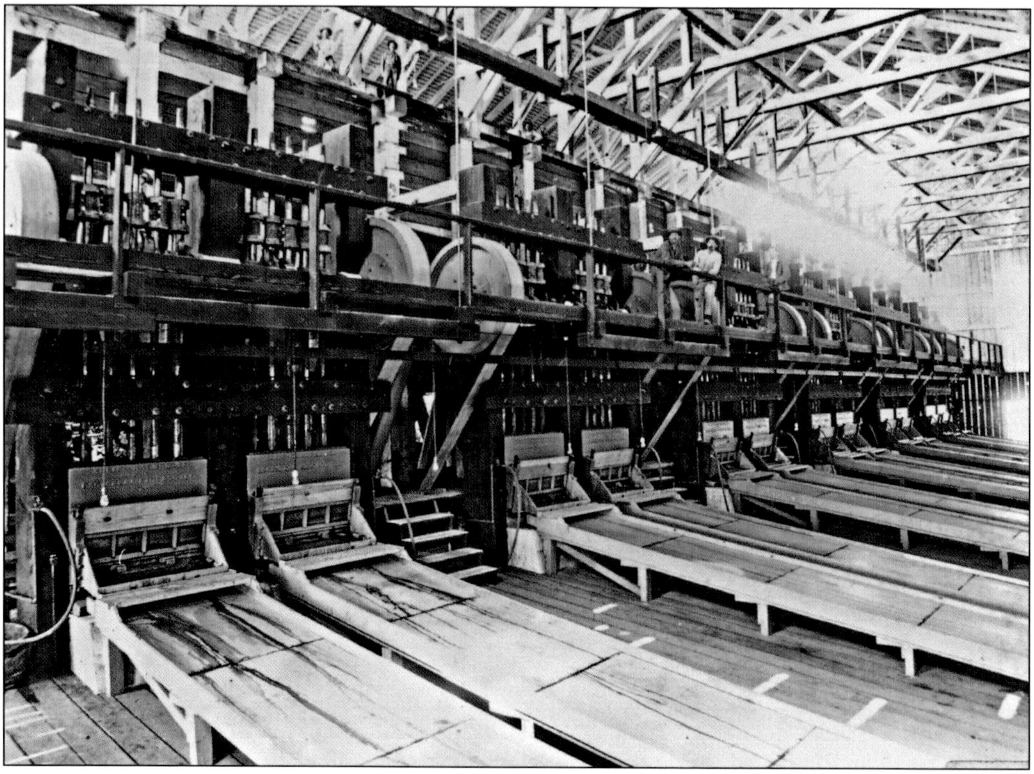

This 1903 view shows the new mill's five-stamp batteries discharging onto amalgamation tables. From here, the pulp dropped down onto Standard concentrator tables, and the "middlings" from these were cleaned on Johnson vanners. Tailings were slurried into a retaining pond in the ravine below. (Photograph by Will Dennis, courtesy Calaveras County Historical Society.)

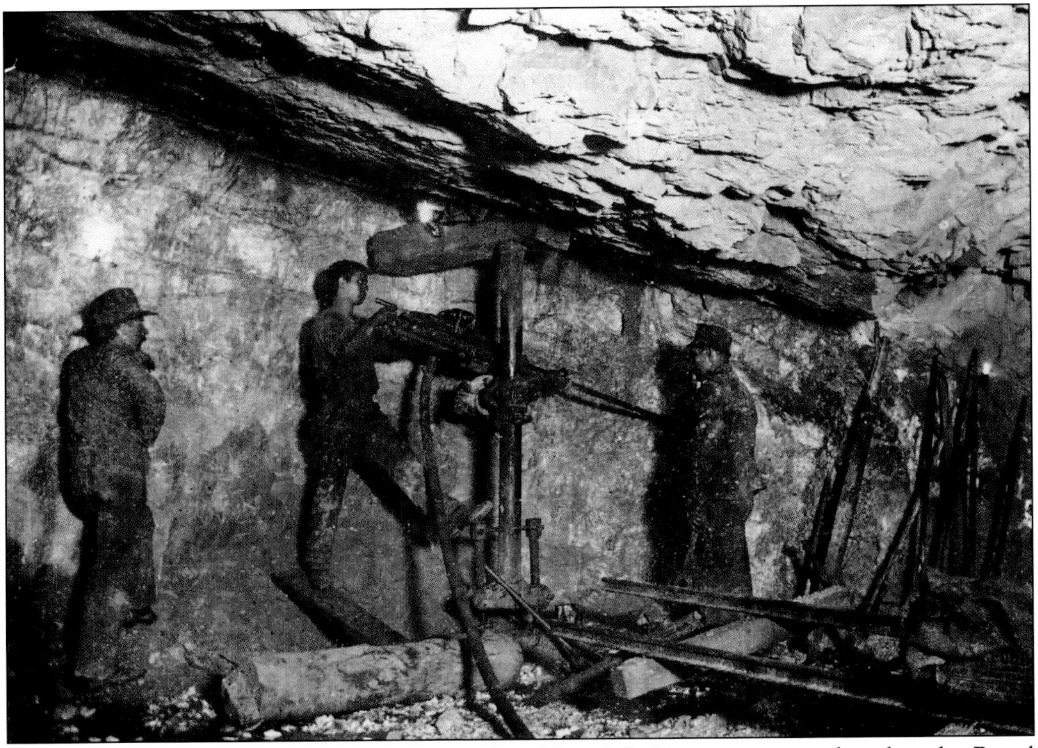

Air-powered Ingersoll rock drills, which replaced hand drilling, were introduced at the Royal Mine about 1900. These cumbersome machines gave many miners deadly silicosis before later models were equipped with water to quiet the quartz dust. (Photograph by Will Dennis, courtesy Calaveras County Historical Society.)

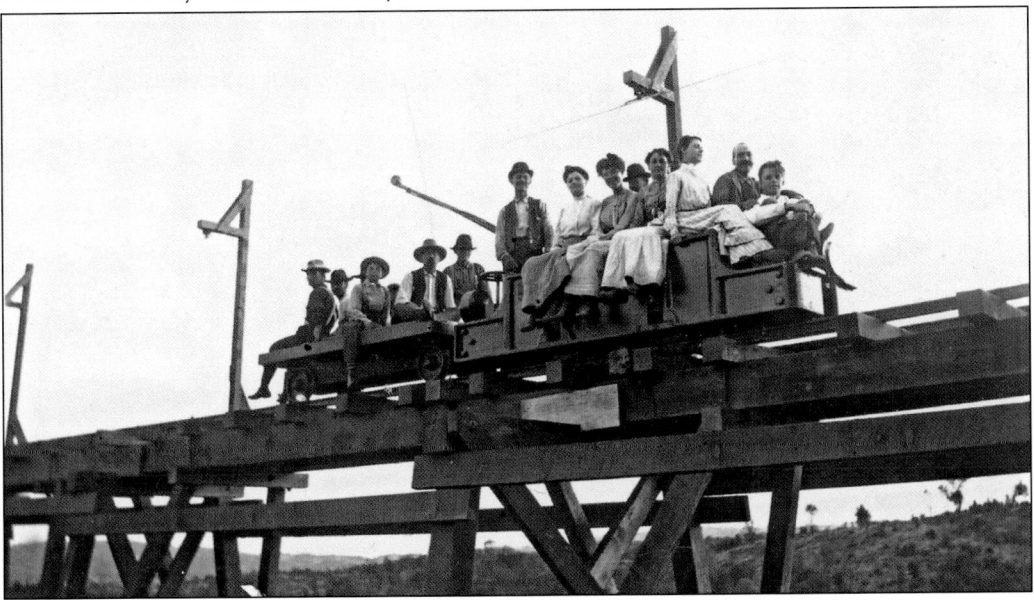

Visitors to the Royal mill are enjoying a ride on the ore cars that ran between the surface plant and the mill. These folks often stayed at the hotel in Hodson. (Courtesy Calaveras County Historical Society.)

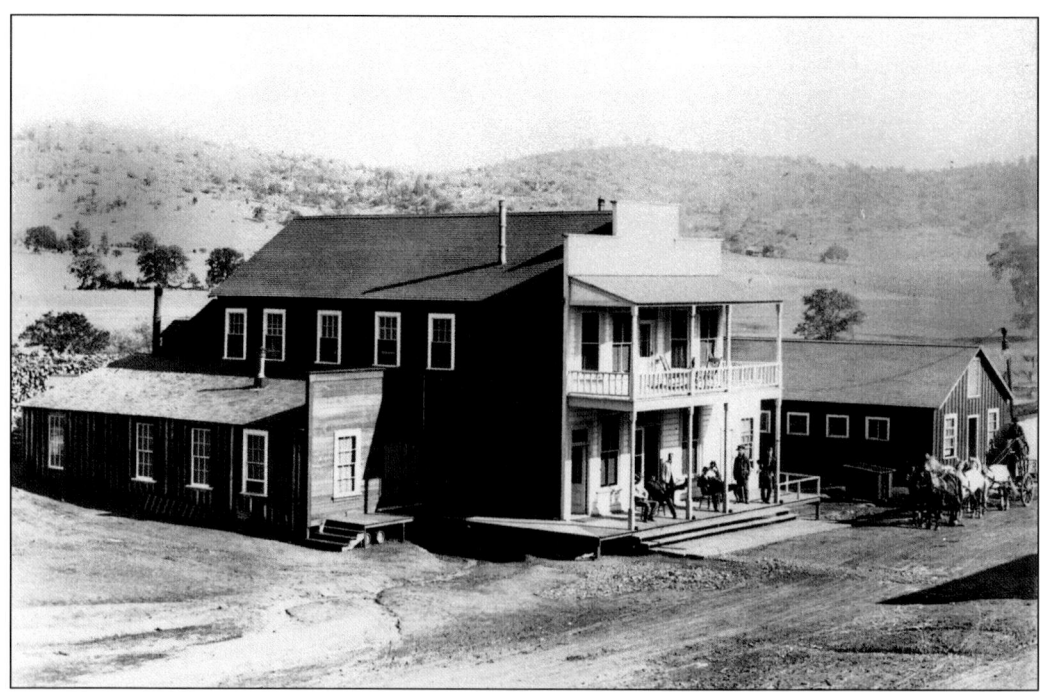

The hotel in Hodson, as with all other buildings, was owned by the Royal Consolidated Mining Company. It continued to be used until 1910. The shed-roofed extension on the left housed the dining room. (Courtesy Calaveras County Historical Society.)

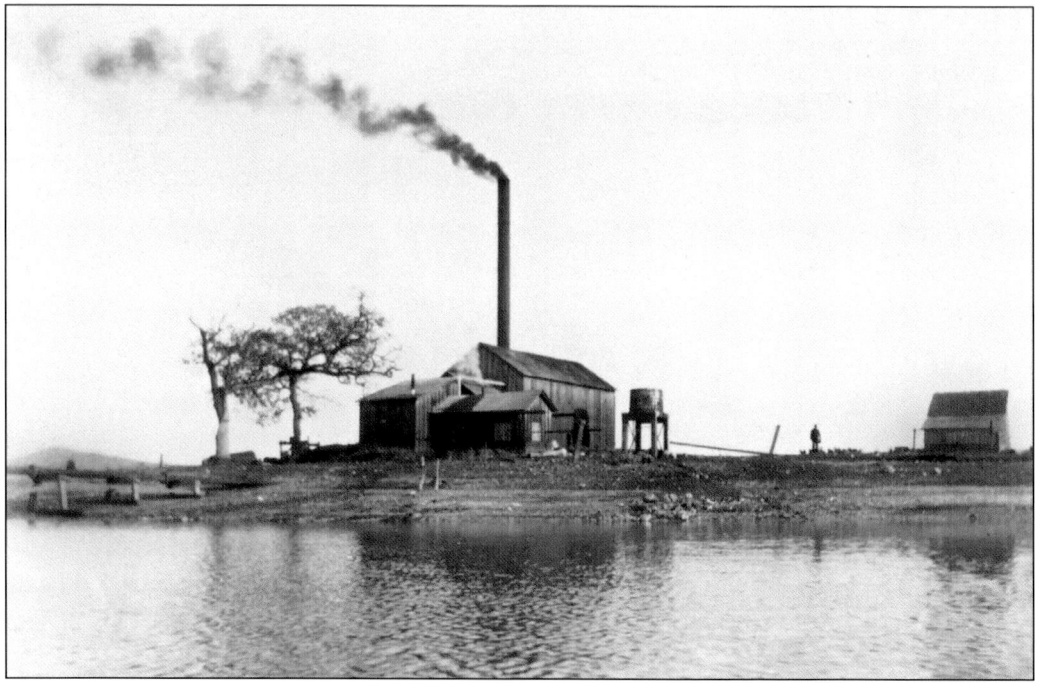

Salt Spring Reservoir, completed in 1858, provided water for the Royal operations. This steam-powered pumping plant was installed in 1899 with an 8-inch pipeline running the four miles to Hodson. (Courtesy Calaveras County Historical Society.)

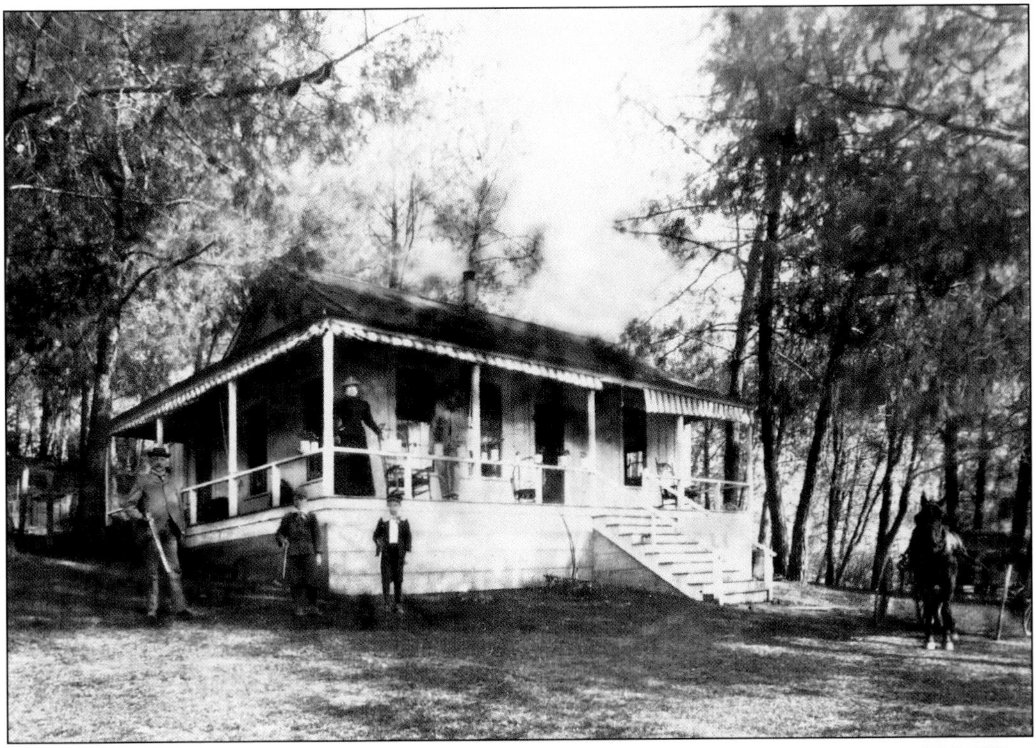

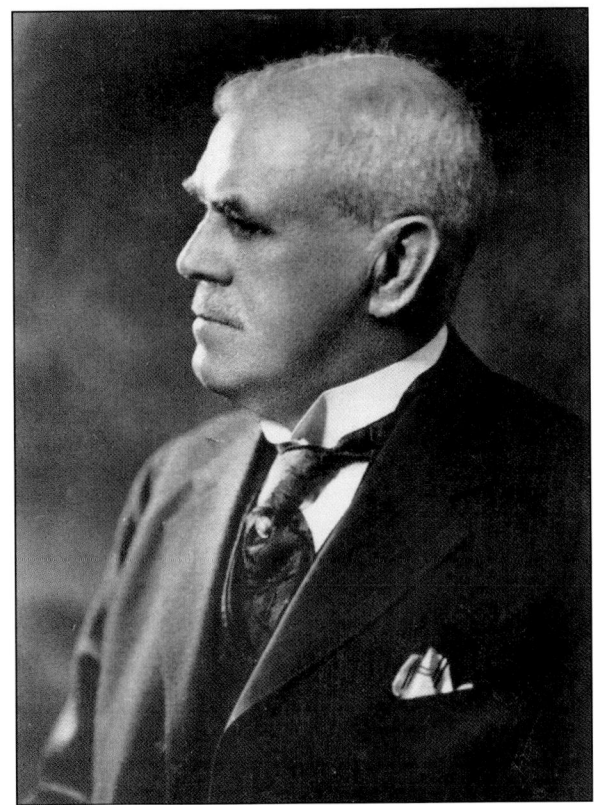

As a young man, John Charles Kemp van Ee (pictured at right) mined in Tuolumne County and eastern Nevada before setting up a photography studio in the roaring town of Bodie. He then distinguished himself as superintendent of operations at the famous Sheepherder vein in Mono County, completing the Tioga Road as a side project. He moved on to Mexico, Idaho, and then London, where he promoted projects such as the roll film camera, which he sold to George Eastman, who perfected it as the Kodak. Kemp van Ee spent eight years developing the Royal, moving his family to this company house in Hodson (the building was later moved to the McCarty Ranch). Seen on the porch in the photograph above are John and his wife, Hattie, while in the yard (from left to right) guest Gustaf Baumann, Carl Shepherd, and Charlie (John and Hattie's son) prepare to go hunting. (Both, courtesy Calaveras County Historical Society.)

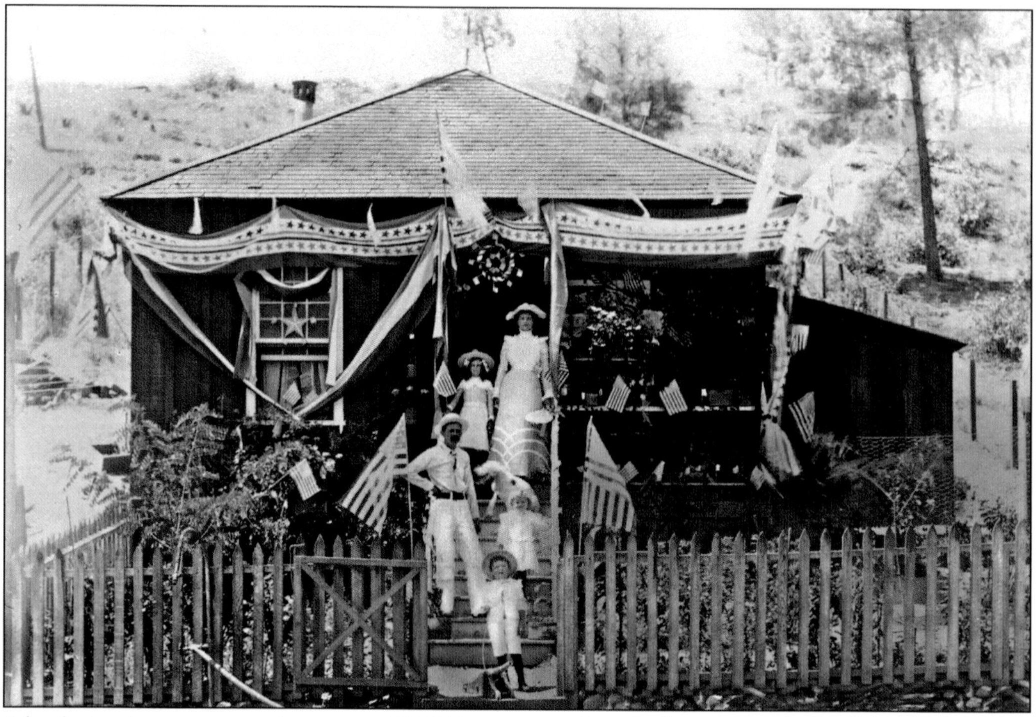

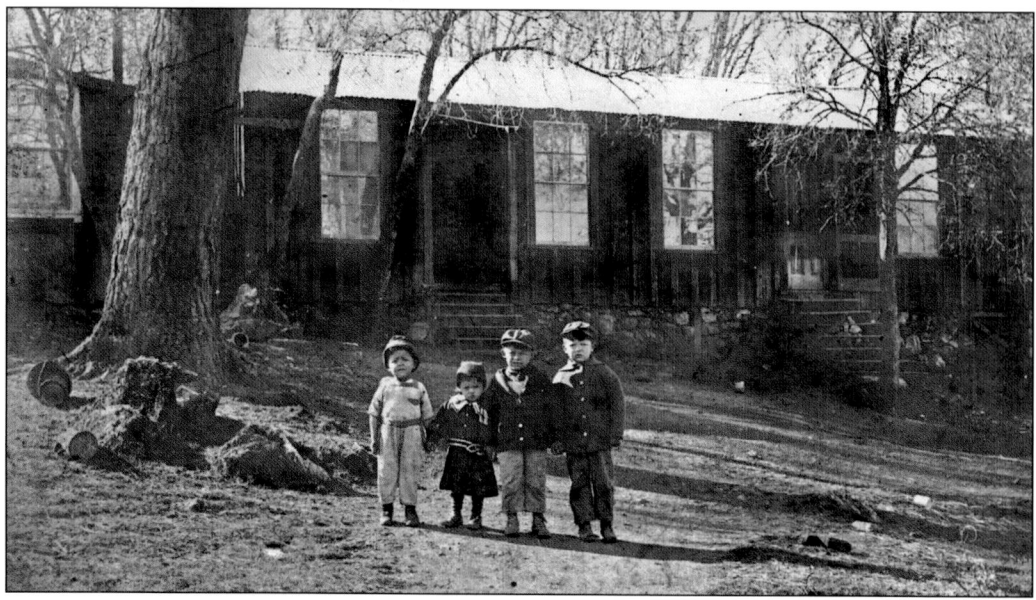

Also living in a company house was Will Dennis, an electrical engineer for the Royal, seen here with his wife and three children on July 4, 1903. Dennis was an excellent photographer and took many fine photographs while living at Hodson. (Photograph by Arthur Morgan, courtesy Calaveras County Historical Society.)

Across Littlejohns Creek from the Pine Log mill was the Womble property, where this bunkhouse was built for workers at the Wilber-Womble Mine. It was later home to numerous families, including the Frank Covarrubias family, whose children are posing for the camera in 1917. (Courtesy Calaveras County Historical Society.)

Helen Hunt McCarty is pictured here in 1902, shortly after her marriage to Jackson Dean McCarty. Neighbor Howard Tower described J. D. as "one who had made many fortunes in ranching and put many more fortunes into mining." Helen and J. D. had 10 children. Helen tragically died in childbirth in 1917, and J. D. never remarried. (Courtesy Calaveras County Historical Society.)

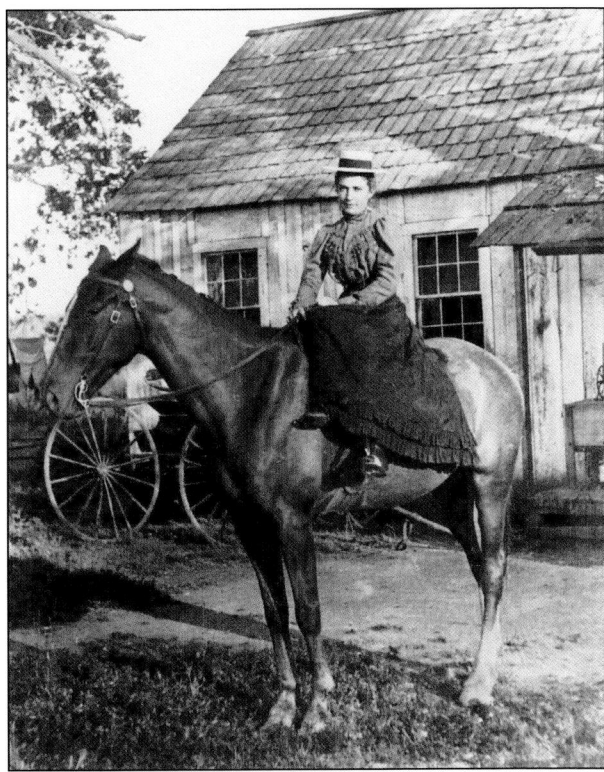

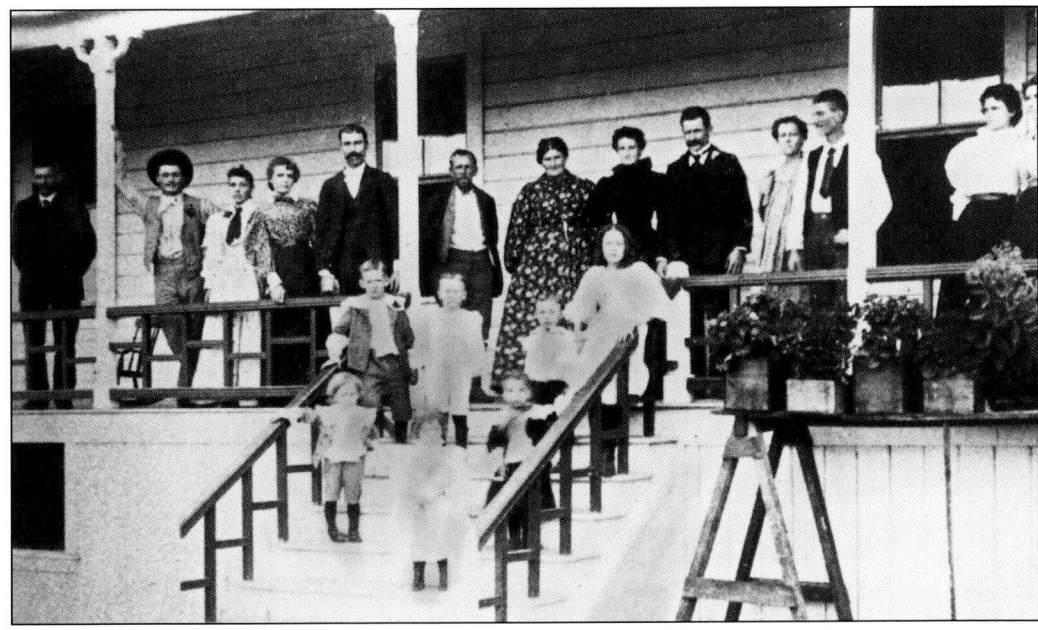

John T. and Mary Womble acquired their ranch at the edge of Hodson in 1883, where they raised their four children: Willis, Clayburn, Martin, and Mamie, among those shown in this c. 1900 photograph. The family turned its interests to mining and developed the Gold Knoll and Wilbur-Womble mines. Willis, Clayburn, and Mamie married into local families, while Martin remained a single miner. (Courtesy Calaveras County Historical Society.)

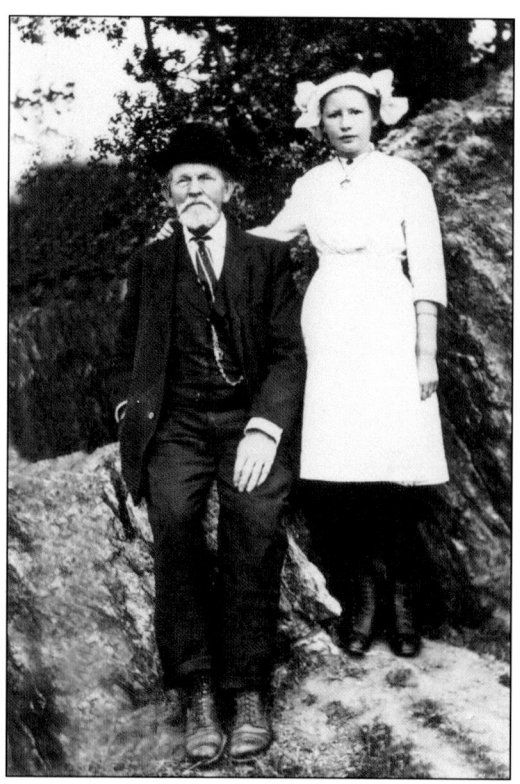

John T. Womble is pictured here with his granddaughter Elsie Womble (daughter of Willis and Kate Womble) in about 1914. Kate cooked for the miners at the Mountain King boardinghouse. Elsie married Earl Blazer, from another local family of miners and ranchers. (Courtesy Calaveras County Historical Society.)

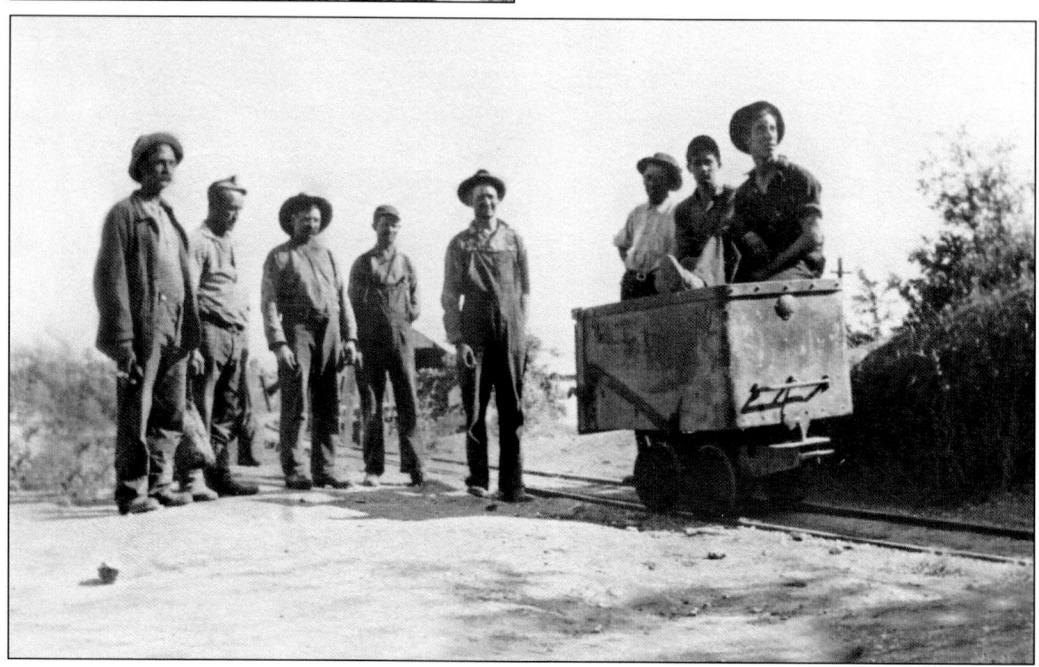

In 1901, Isaac R. Wilber and partner E. I. Braddock leased mineral rights from the Wombles and opened the Wilber-Womble Mine. Returns were poor, however, and the mine closed in 1904. The Wombles lost the land, but Willis leased the mine back for another disappointing attempt. This photograph is from the mid-1910s. (Courtesy Calaveras County Historical Society.)

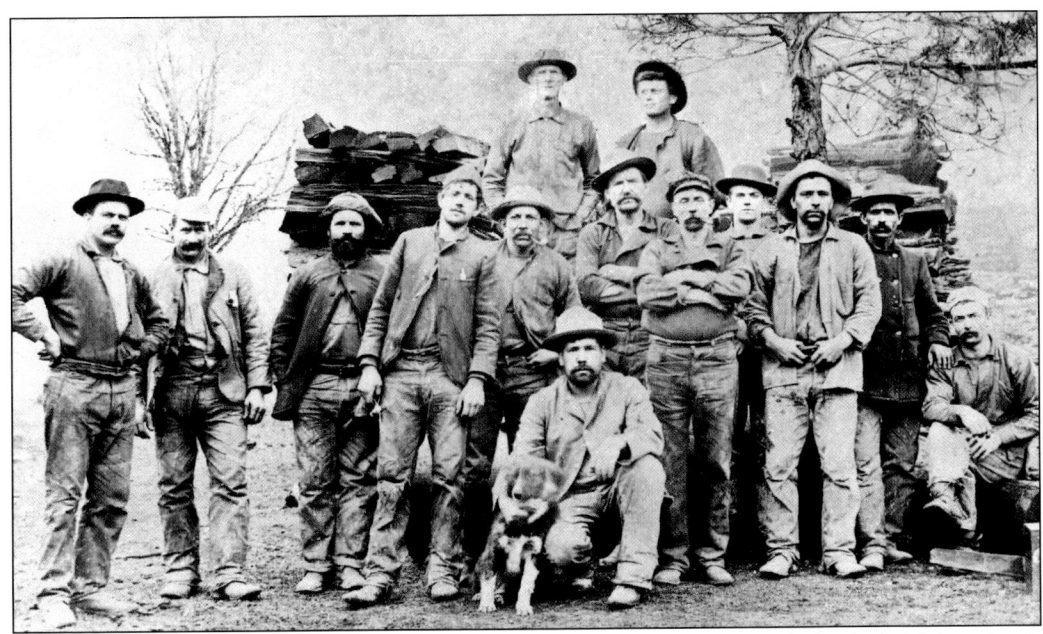

Clay Womble's (far left) woodcutting crew, photographed in 1900, includes Jack Maltos (with his dog), Dave Cabrera, Phil Swank, Joe Huber, Ed Olsen, and Juan Paredes. Until 1902, all of the district mills were powered by steam, requiring massive amounts of wood for the boilers. The hills were denuded of oaks for miles around. At the Royal alone, 5,000 cords were consumed each year. (Courtesy Calaveras County Historical Society.)

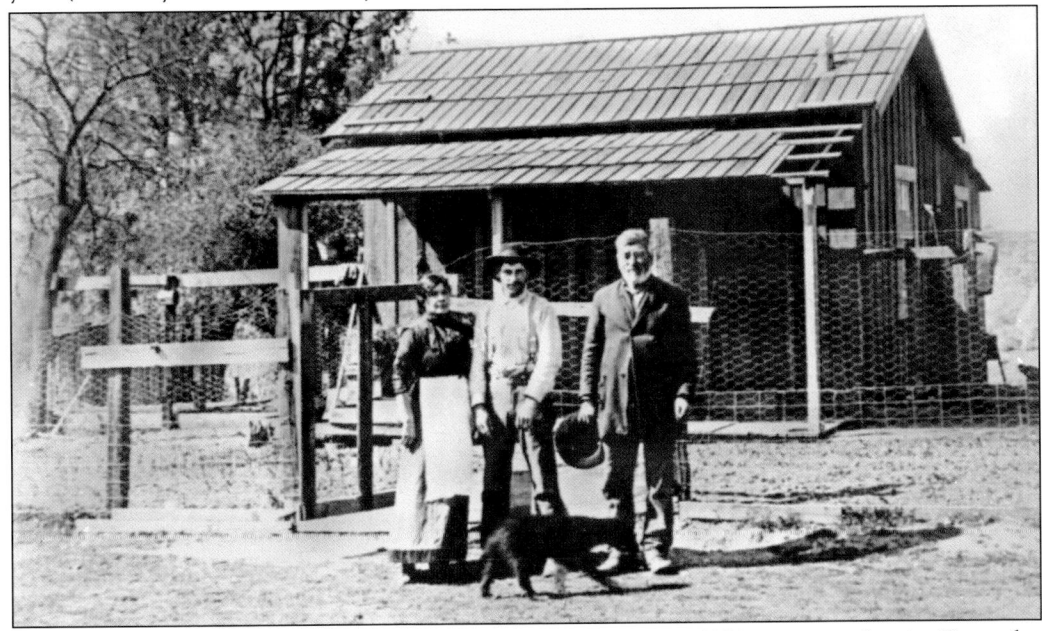

Camillo Dutil (right) homesteaded land in Calaveras County in 1880, marrying Louise Granados that same year. Camillo became a teamster for the Pine Log in the 1890s, beginning an association with the Madam Felix district that would last three generations. Son Augustine "Gus" is in this 1920 photograph with his wife, Josephine; Camillo's other children were Virginia, Adolph, Lena, Lorenzo, John, and Andrew. (Courtesy Calaveras County Historical Society.)

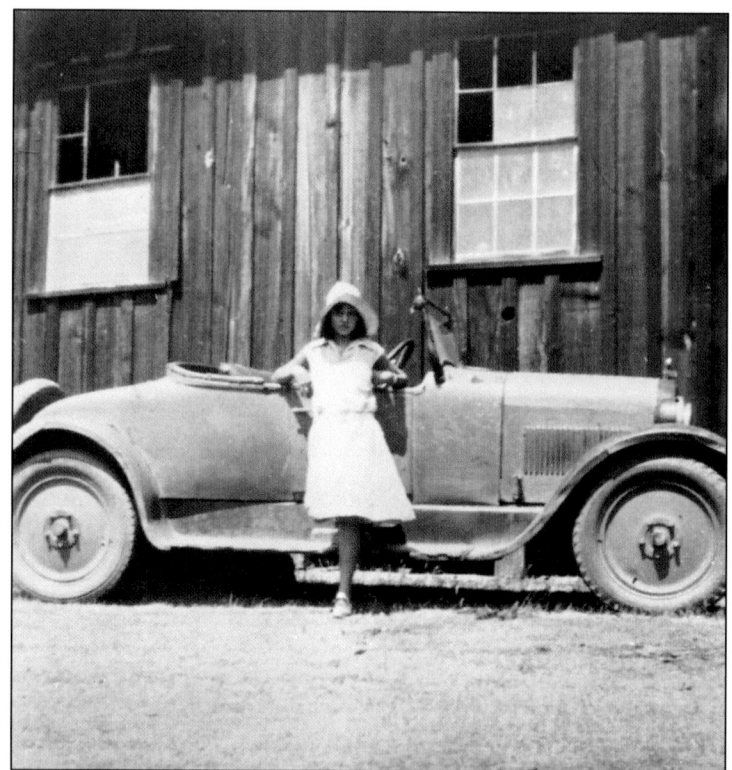

Josephine and Gus Dutil's daughter Mary poses in front of John Canada's roadster in the early 1930s. She and her brothers Tony and Frank became intimately involved in almost all aspects of the district's mining and social life until the mills closed in the 1940s. (Courtesy Calaveras County Historical Society.)

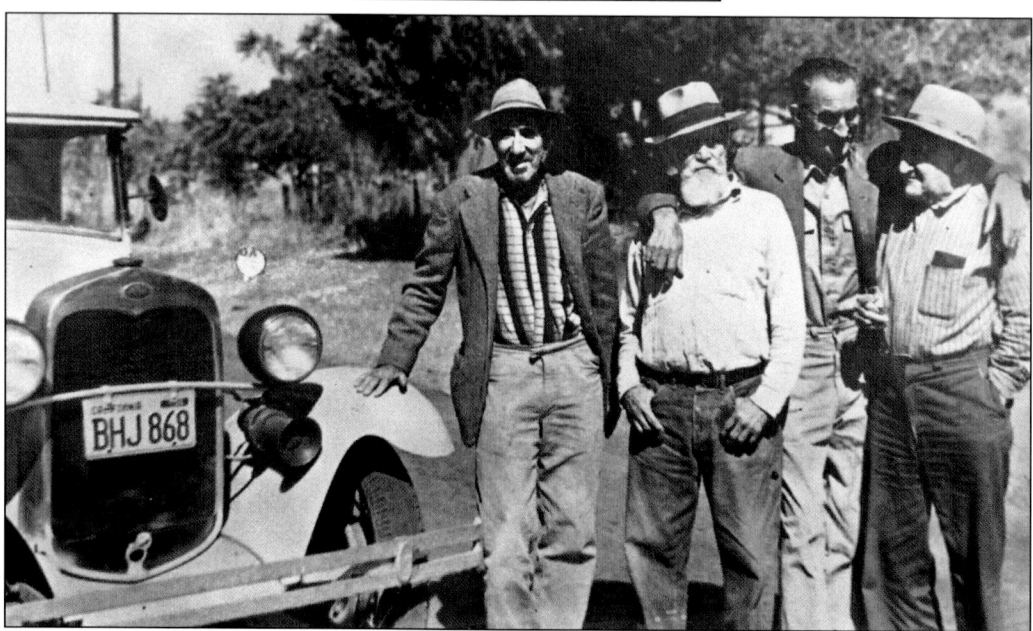

Dick Ford (far right) takes his friends (from left to right) Joe Paltor, George Brewer, and Frank Cardin on a trip in his Model A. At one time, Ford worked with the Felix Mining Company and later lived in the old Womble house. In the early 1940s, Ford resided in the old Wilber-Womble mine office when it was the last building standing in Hodson. (Courtesy Calaveras County Historical Society.)

Seven

RANCH FAMILIES

The earliest Euro-Americans to settle in present-day Calaveras County were Francisco Rico and José Antonio Castro, who were granted the Rancho del Rio Estanislao by the Mexican governor Pio Pico in 1843. The grant included 11 square leagues of land "bounded on the east by the Sierra Nevada, north by the low hills, and south by the Stanislaus River." Extending into Stanislaus County, 10,000 acres of the land was patented to William Hicks, Abraham Schell, and James Stubbins in 1863, and the northern portion to George Wright.

Following the decline of placer deposits in the Mother Lode after about 1860, agriculture gained importance as a family enterprise, which helped to establish more permanence and stability in the society. Settlers established large farms in the area, where they grew hay, alfalfa, and wheat, and planted orchards. Most families practiced a mixed agricultural economy, raising cattle, sheep, hogs, and poultry, which ensured them a steady supply of foodstuffs augmented by vegetable gardens and orchards. Some families established vineyards and made wines and brandies for personal use and for sale, while others bottled the clear, fresh waters of local springs and sold it commercially. Hops were grown and baked in kilns for breweries that produced local beers and ales. Local farming never developed beyond a subsistence level and gradually gave way to livestock operations.

Many of the lands were taken up in the 1850s and 1860s with farms and dwellings located on the existing roads and along the rivers and streams, and where springs abounded. Schools were centrally established so children would not have to walk more than three miles to attend. Stores, churches, and other commercial enterprises tended to congregate in the towns, so farmers and ranchers had to travel to obtain the necessities (such as sugar, flour, salt, and coffee) not produced at home. Some ranches also served as way stations with stores if they were located along traveled roads, providing goods for travelers and neighbors alike.

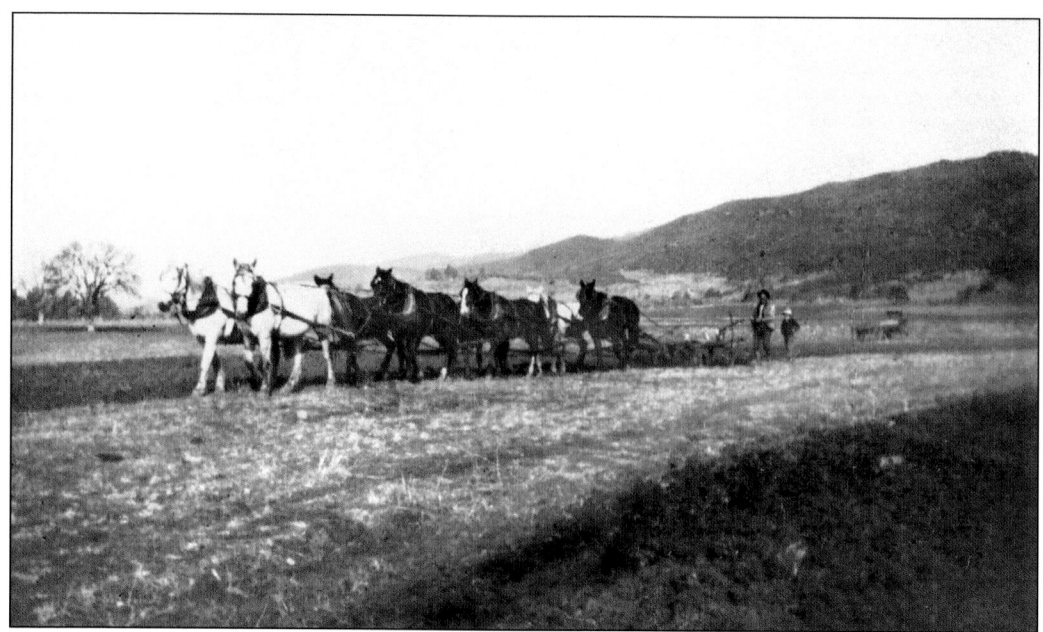

The Peach Orchard Ranch, the first in Salt Spring Valley, was established by Harris Garcelon and W. P. Allen in 1850 on the slopes of Bear Mountain. By the end of the 19th century, the ranch was owned by James and Mary Wheat and later by the Cooper family. At least 20 other farms had been settled in Salt Spring Valley by 1859, with many more to come during the copper boom. (Courtesy Calaveras County Archives.)

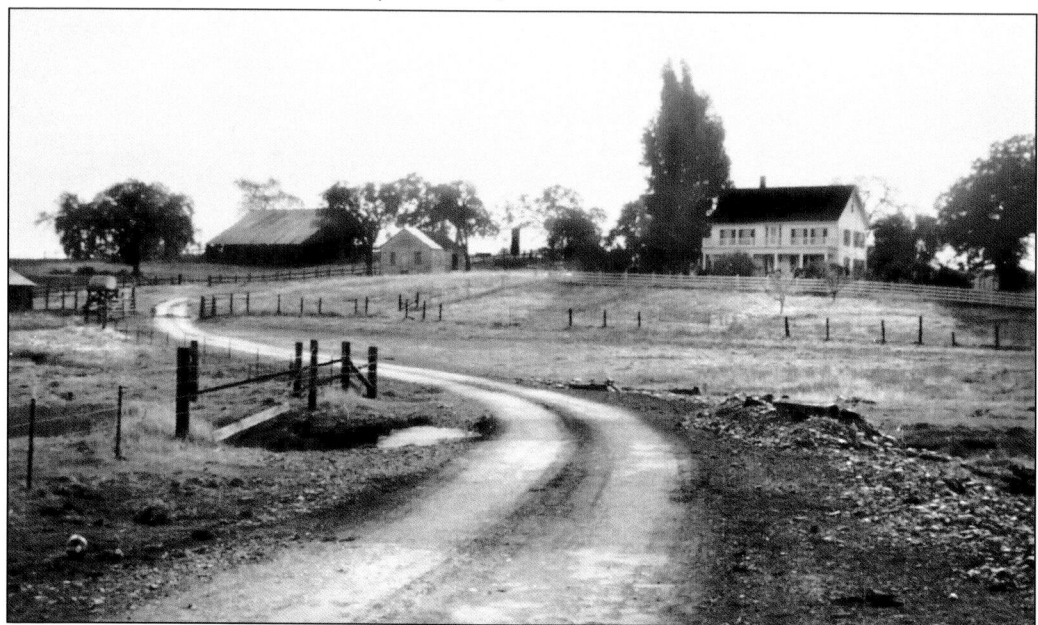

The Tower Ranch, also known as the White House Ranch, was the home of Jacob and Mary Tower and their eight children. It was also an important way station in Salt Spring Valley. Built by Jacob Tower and his partner William Bisbee, by the mid-1860s, the ranch boasted this two-story farmhouse with nine bedrooms, a schoolhouse, a bunkhouse, stage barns, a blacksmith shop, and a meat market. (Courtesy Calaveras County Historical Society.)

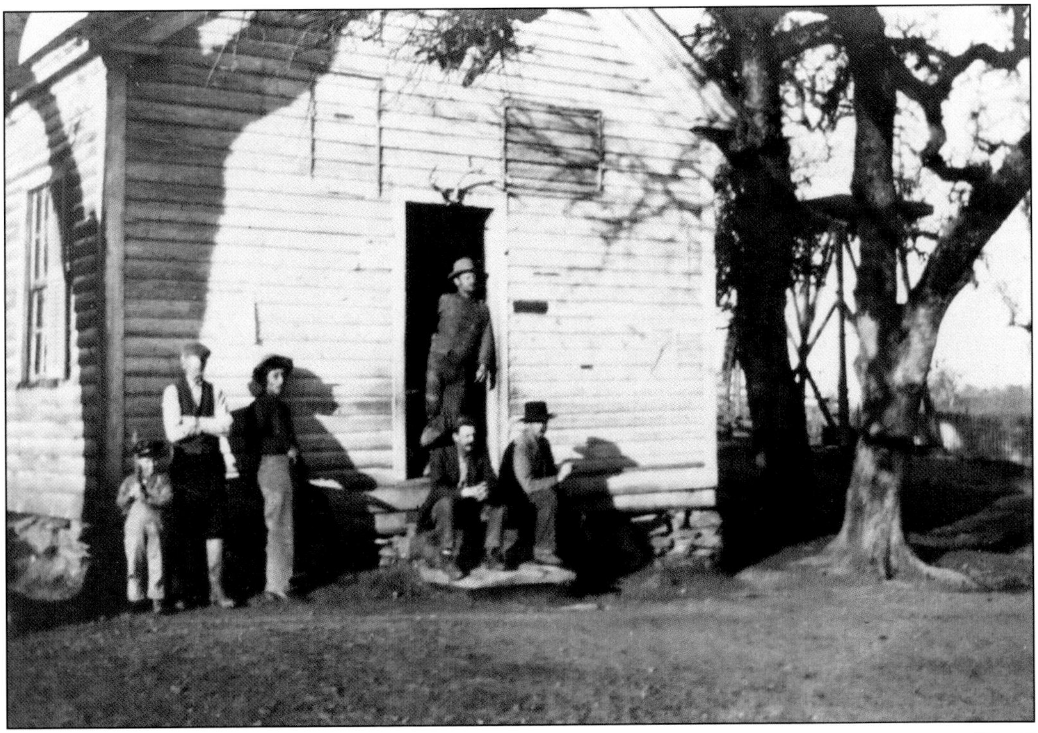

The original Salt Spring Valley School was built in the late 1860s by Tower and Bisbee near the center of the valley on the east side of Salt Spring Reservoir, centrally located for all the families of the valley. Later it was moved to the Tower Ranch at Felix, where it served as the post office for many years. Will Tower is standing in the doorway. (Courtesy Calaveras County Historical Society.)

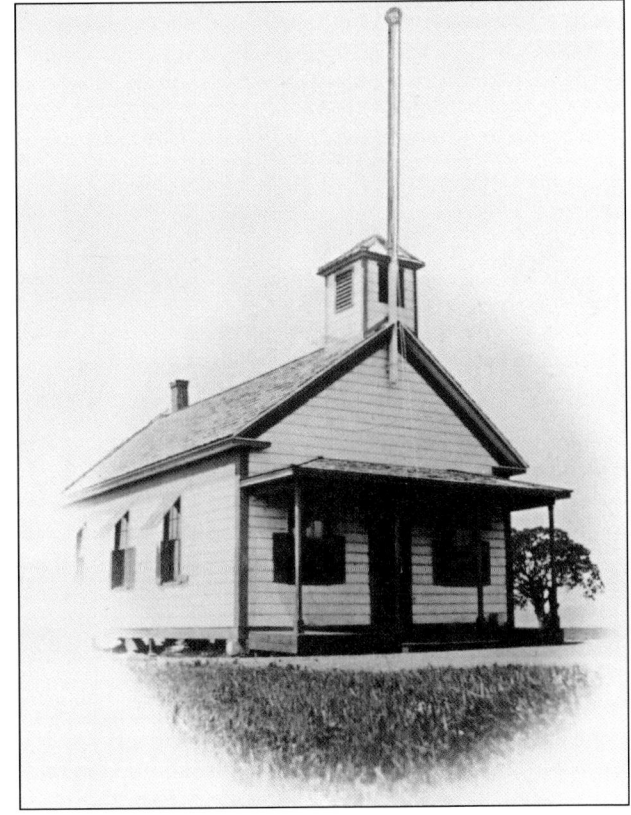

Completed in 1873, the second Salt Spring Valley School is a well-preserved example of a 19th-century Greek Revival schoolhouse. Constructed on the Tower Ranch by Jacob Tower and valley ranchers, it served the ranch families of the valley, including the Kuhns, Howards, Heizers, Boards, McCartys, Dutils, and others until it closed in 1947. *Little House on the Prairie*, other television shows, and films were made here. (Courtesy Calaveras County Archives.)

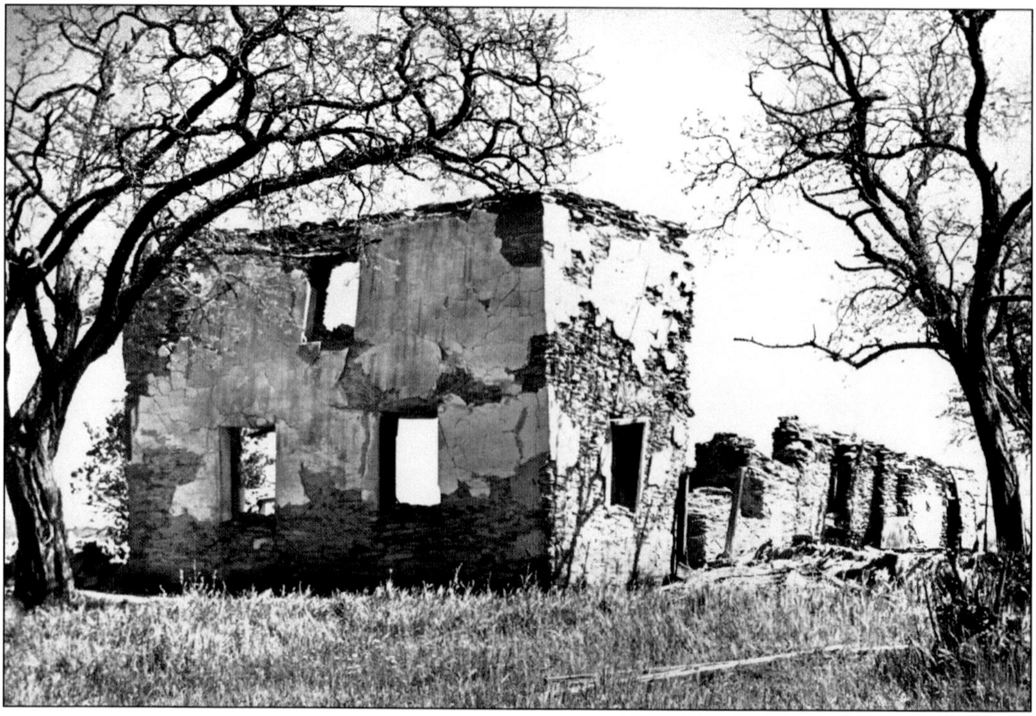

Immigrants from Switzerland, Carlo and Mary Pedroli built their stone farmhouse on a knoll beside Dry Creek in the 1860s. In ruins, it stands as a sentinel on Hogan Dam Road. The Pedrolis were just one of several families from France and Switzerland who settled in Salt Spring Valley in the early years. (Courtesy Calaveras County Historical Society.)

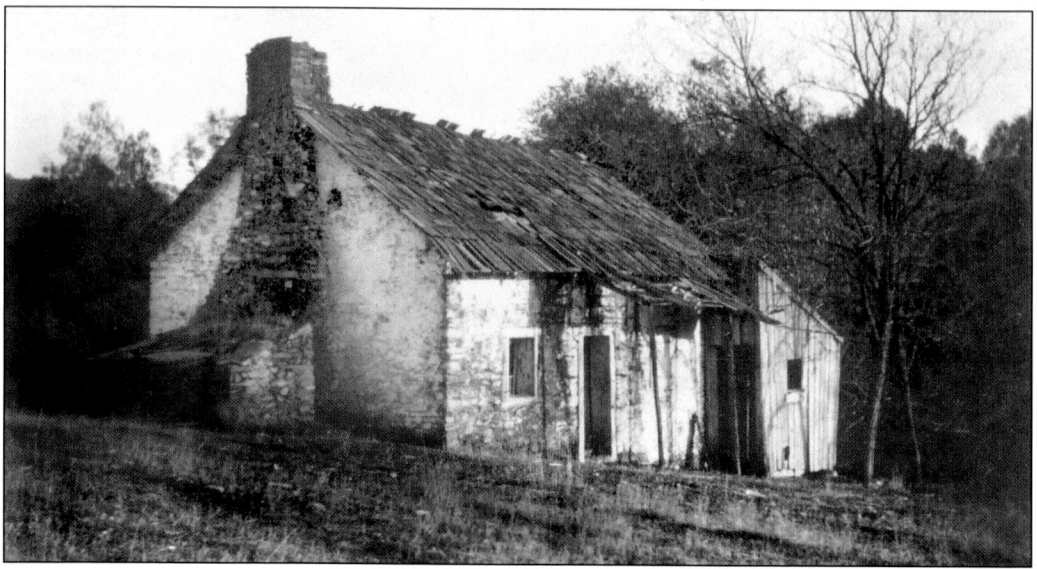

The "Lost City" was once a bustling community of Frenchmen led by Eugene Barbe, who settled on Bear Creek in the 1870s. The settlement was comprised of 10 stone buildings, an arrastra, sheds, and stone corrals. The men raised cows, horses, sheep, goats, chickens, and ducks, as well as fruit and vegetables, and mined in their shaft and along the stream drainages. Today the houses lie in ruins, beset by fire, weather, vandals, and time. (Courtesy Calaveras County Historical Society.)

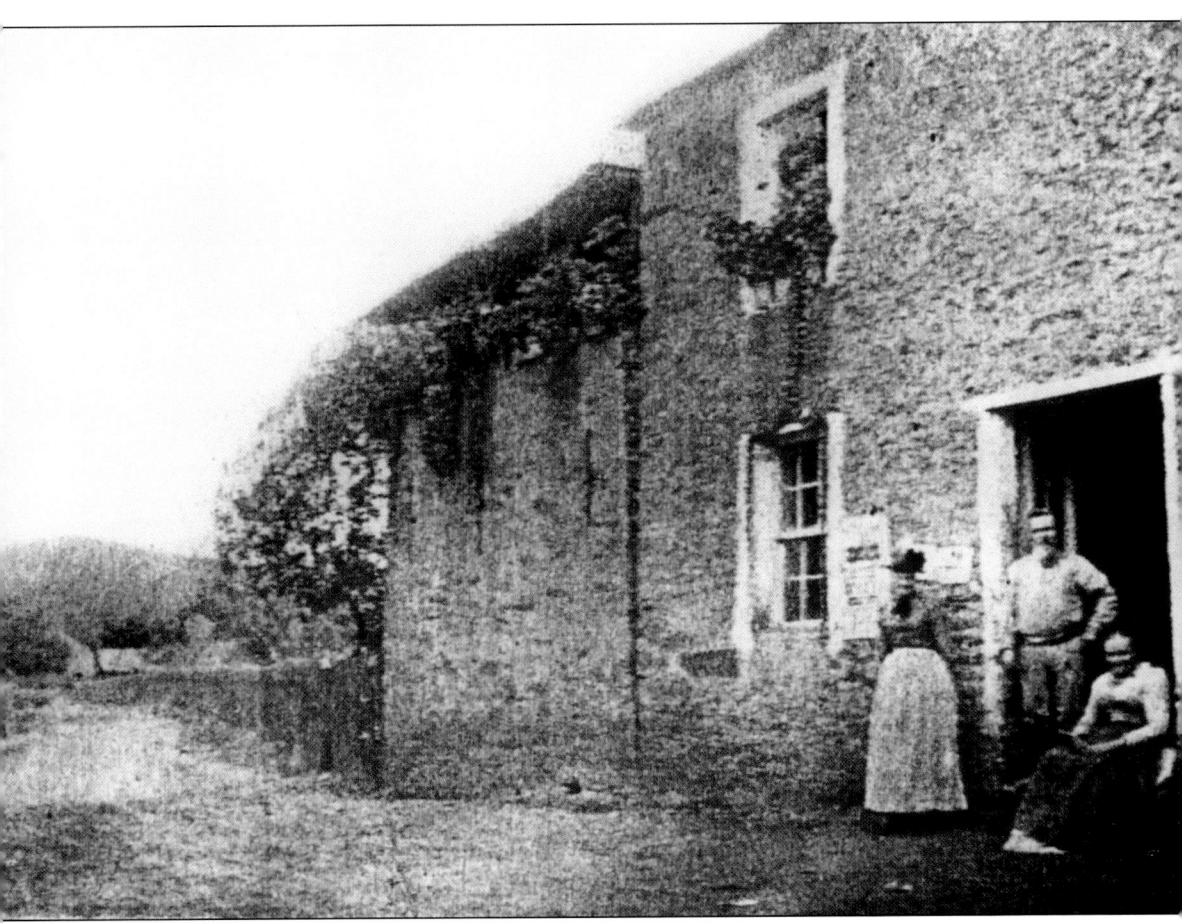

Girolomo and Louisa Romaggi and a neighbor (far left) pose in the front doorway of their stone store and residence in Albany Flat (south of Angels Camp) in the 1890s, surrounded by their ranch and vineyard. Girolomo and his partner Andrew Lee (Lertora), natives of Italy, operated the property in partnership from the 1850s; Romaggi obtained full ownership in 1878. In addition to operating a store, the Romaggi family mined for gold on their ranch, planted a large vineyard and orchard, and made wine and brandy. The family moved away in the 1920s, leaving the building to the vicissitudes of time and vandals. It now stands as a lonely reminder of the bustling days of Albany Flat, when it was a mining "hot spot," boasting hotels, saloons, and other amenities. After the placer mining played out, however, Albany Flat became home to several ranching families, including Nantz, Piper, Hanselman, Graham, Bolitho, Miller, and later immigrants from Genoa, Italy: Foppiano, Peirano, Lertora, Figaro, and others. (Courtesy Romaggi Adobe Association.)

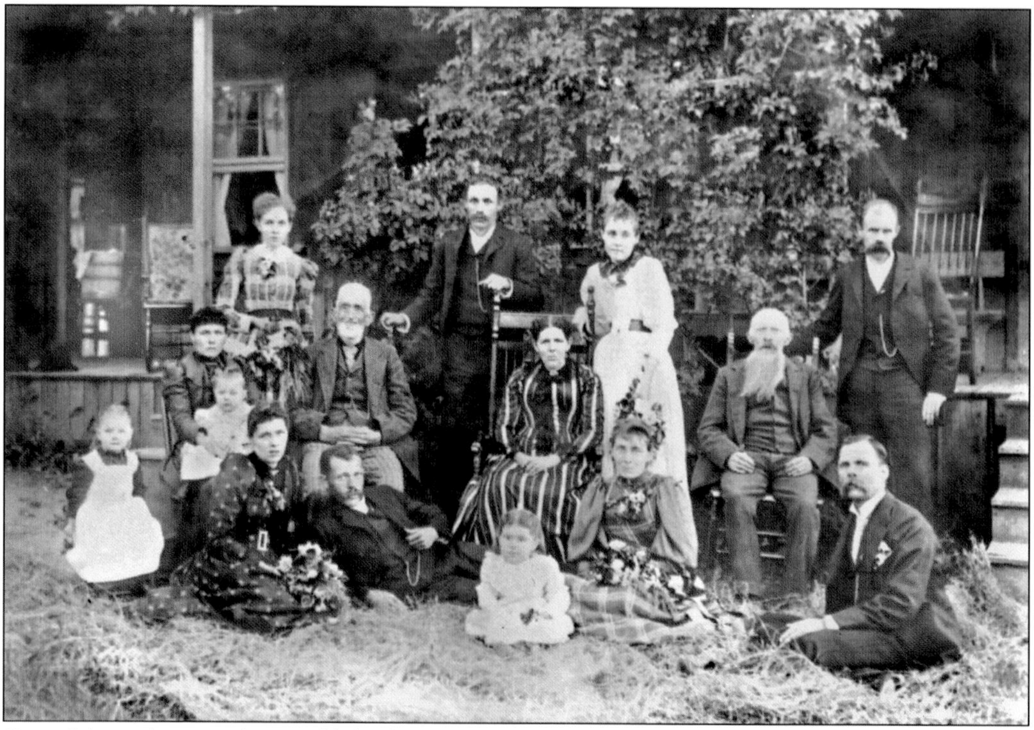

One of the earliest ranches established near Copperopolis was that of William and Lucinda Gorham, who resided on a homestead west of O'Byrnes Ferry Road in the 1860s. William's brother John and his wife, Marietta, established an adjacent ranch on Lux Creek in 1873. The Gorham ranches constituted a community sufficient unto itself, with the O'Byrnes Ferry School flourishing as long as the two families supplied the pupils. (Courtesy Calaveras County Historical Society.)

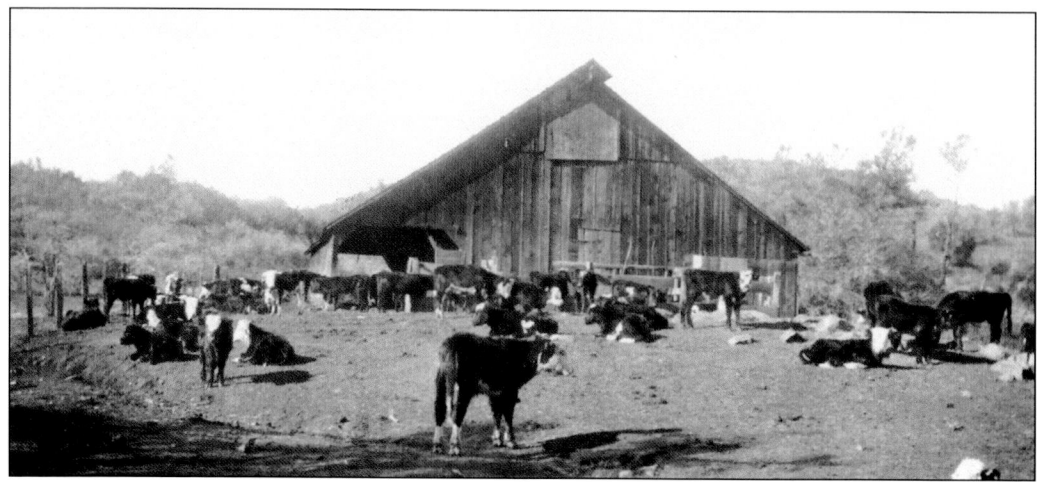

One of the largest ranches near Copperopolis was that of the Spicer family, natives of England, who settled on Littlejohns Creek in 1867. None of the five Spicer sons ever married, but daughters Mary Ann, Elizabeth, and Ellen married local ranchers. The men worked at both ranching and farming, as time and the economy demanded. Spicer Reservoir is named for their summer cattle range. (Courtesy Calaveras County Historical Society.)

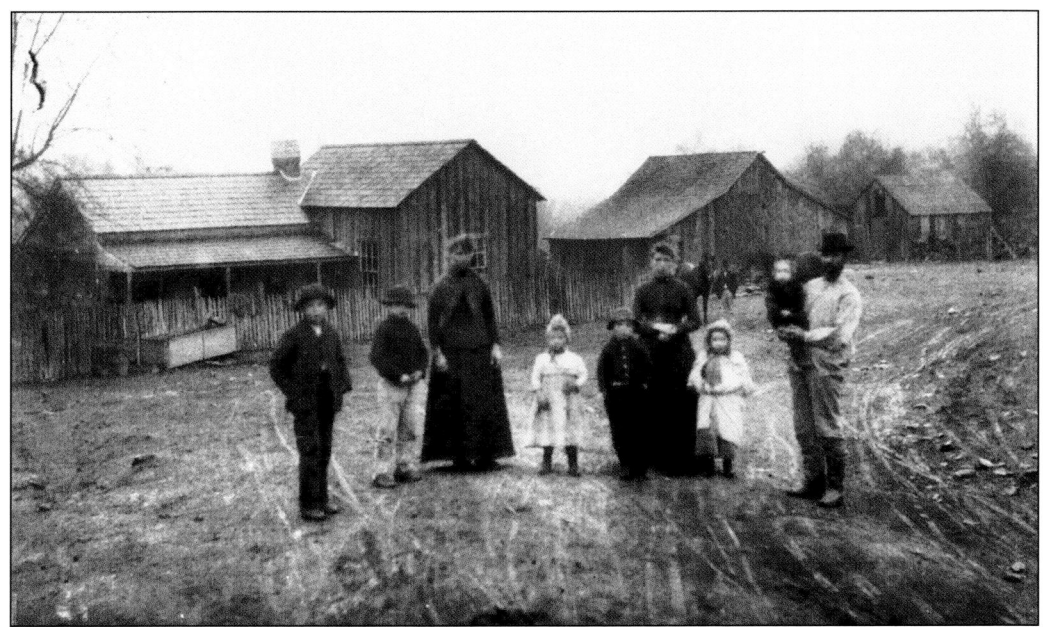

Members of the Pool family pose for the photographer in front of their way station in the 1890s. Homesteaded by Andrew and Margaret Pool in 1875 (on present-day Highway 4), the main house, where their 10 children were raised, was constructed a few years later. In addition, there were also two stage barns, two stone corrals, a pigpen, a slaughterhouse, a smokehouse, a blacksmith shop, a bunkhouse, and two other dwellings. (Courtesy Calaveras County Historical Society.)

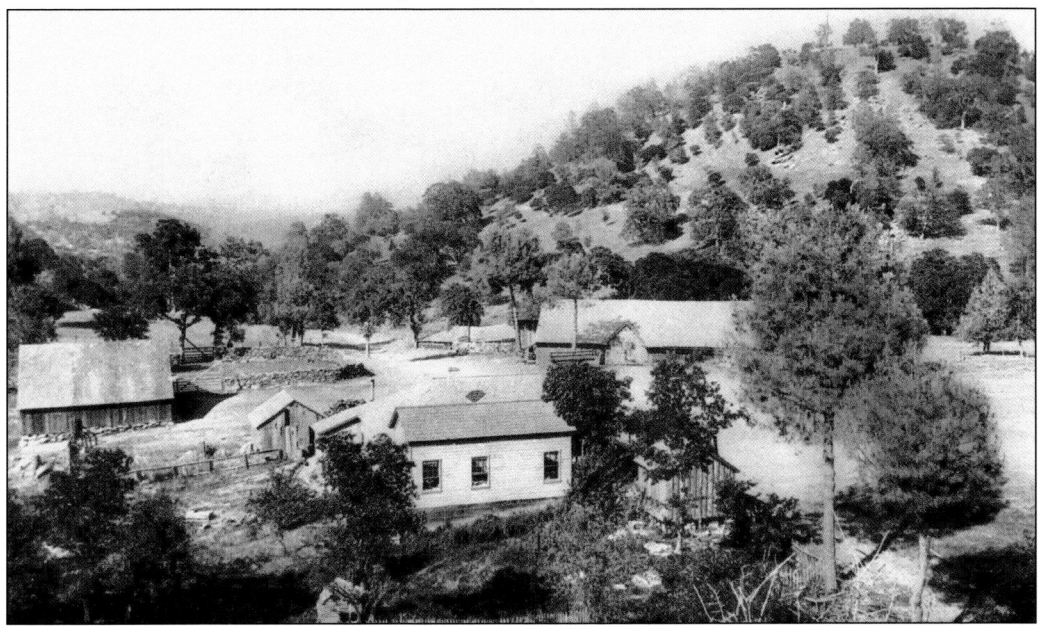

This view of the buildings, corrals, and barns at Pool Station was taken in the early 1890s. Only the stone corral remains to mark the location of this once-bustling way station on the Copperopolis and Angels Camp Road. Here travelers, as well as the horses and mules of the freight teams and passenger stages traveling from the railroad terminal at Milton to Angels Camp or farther east, stopped overnight. (Courtesy Calaveras County Historical Society.)

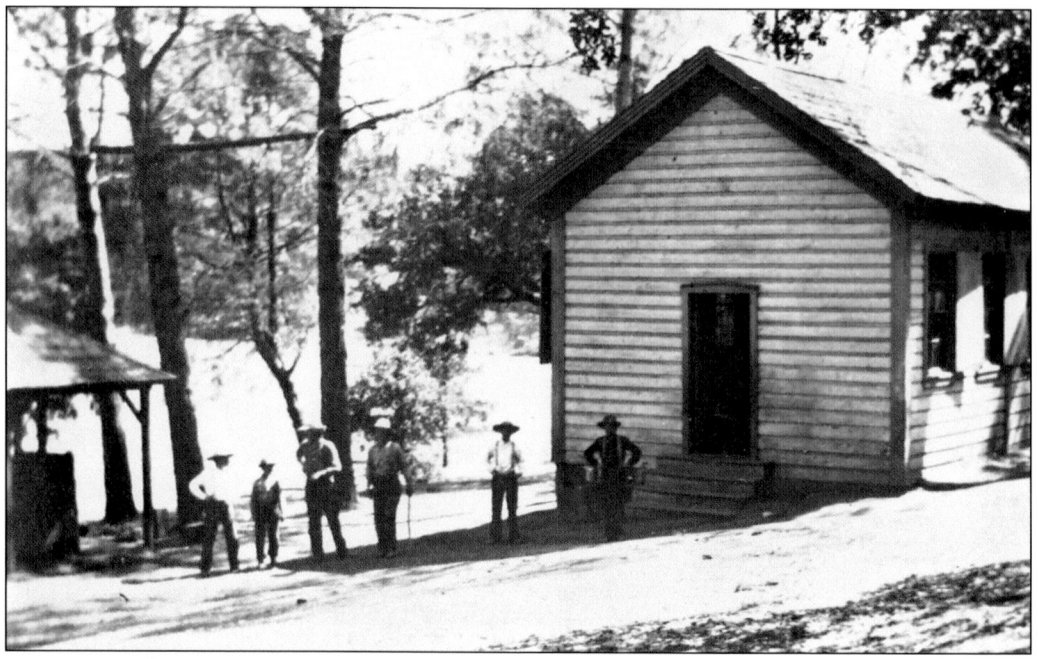

West of Angels Camp on the Copperopolis Road, the Keystone School was built in 1885 to serve the ranch families in the Nassau Valley and Pool Station areas. Located about three-quarters of a mile west of Pool Station and south of Hunt Road, the schoolhouse was active for almost 40 years. (Courtesy Calaveras County Historical Society.)

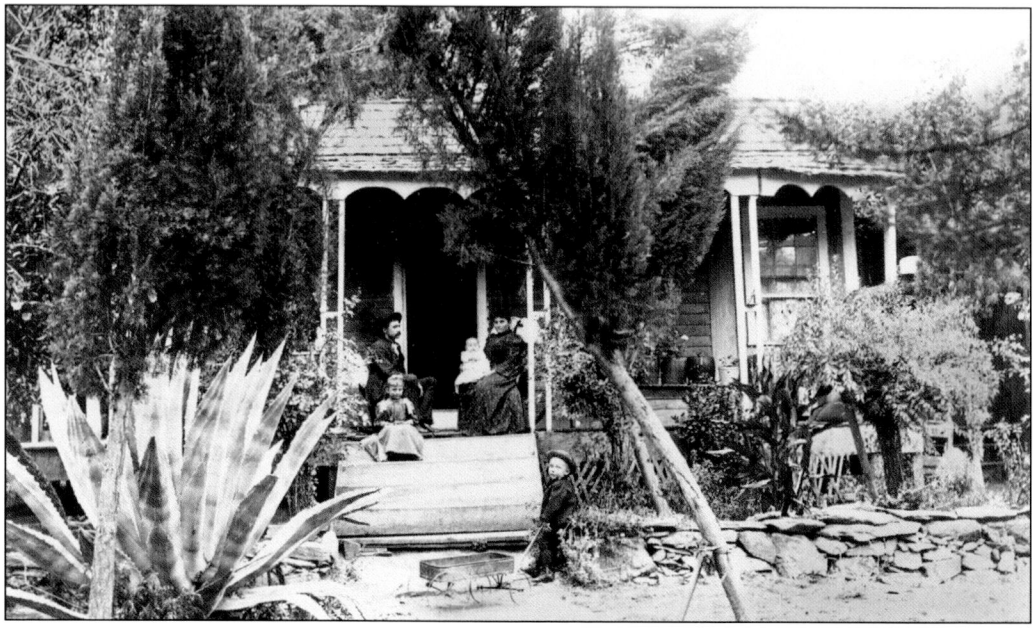

Manuel and Caroline Airola, from Genoa, Italy, are pictured at their home in Robinsons Ferry about 1870. Also shown are their children Antonia, John, and Augustine. Manuel worked as a miner, but his descendants established large cattle ranches near Carson Hill and Angels Creek and at French Camp, all near or within the Melones Reservoir. (Courtesy Calaveras County Historical Society.)

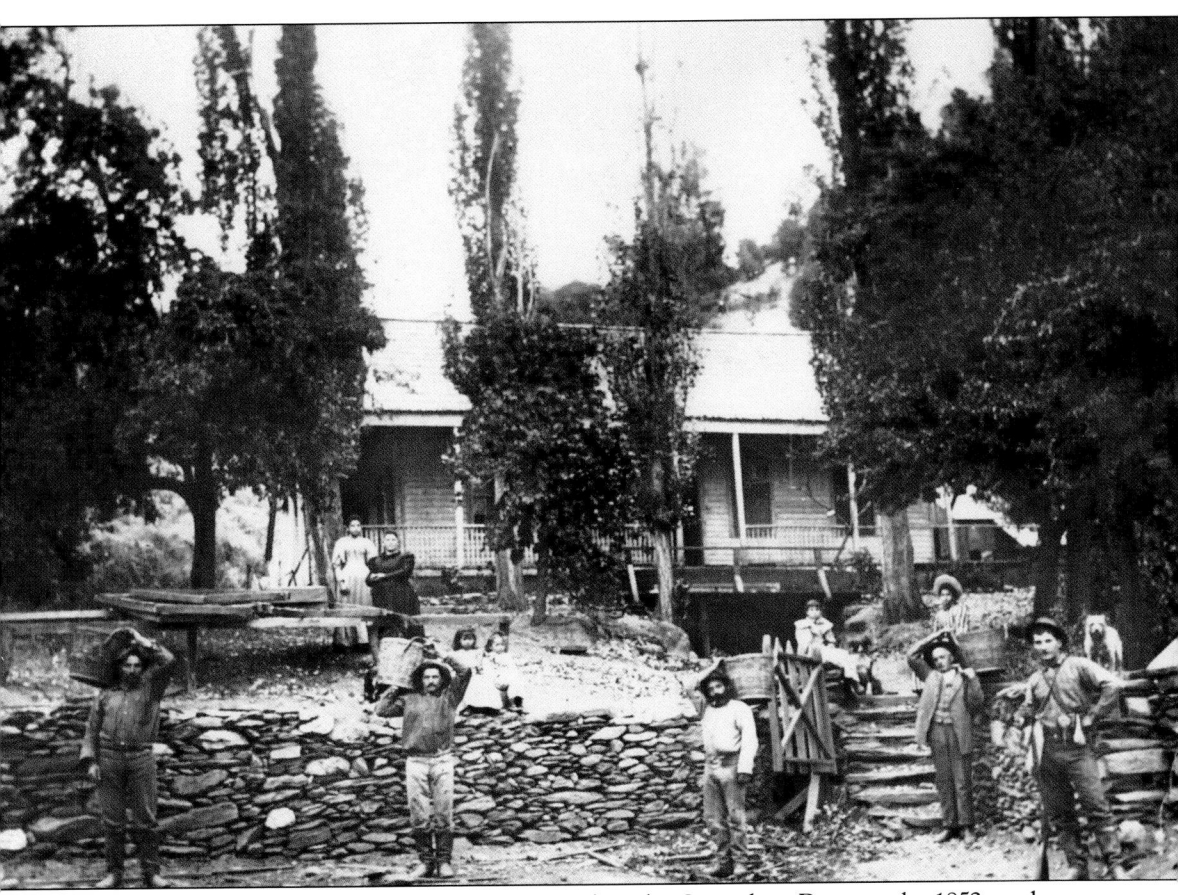

Lorenzo Pendola, a native of Genoa, emigrated to the Stanislaus Diggings by 1852, and at one time, he was the owner of Robinsons Ferry. After marrying, he and Madalina built this fine home at Robinsons Ferry in 1869, and by 1873, he owned two houses, two barns, an orchard, a vineyard, and fences, as well as an irrigation ditch. There he made wine and supplied the town and others with cabbage, beets, celery, and other row crops in winter, as well as truck garden vegetables such as peppers and tomatoes in the spring and summer. The orchard produced figs, peaches, and apples, while extra milk from his dairy cows was also sold. Lorenzo also kept up his placer mining claim at Horseshoe Bend and owned a mining and irrigation ditch from Coyote Creek. His widow, Madalina, and her five daughters—Agnes, Edith, Louisa, Angelina, and Aurelia—are pictured in the yard after Lorenzo's death in 1900, with hired hands standing below. One of the hands, John Ghiglieri, married the Pendola daughter Edith, and the couple inherited the ranch, eventually passing it on to their son Virgil. Sadly, the ranch was lost to the rising waters of the New Melones Reservoir. (Courtesy Calaveras County Historical Society.)

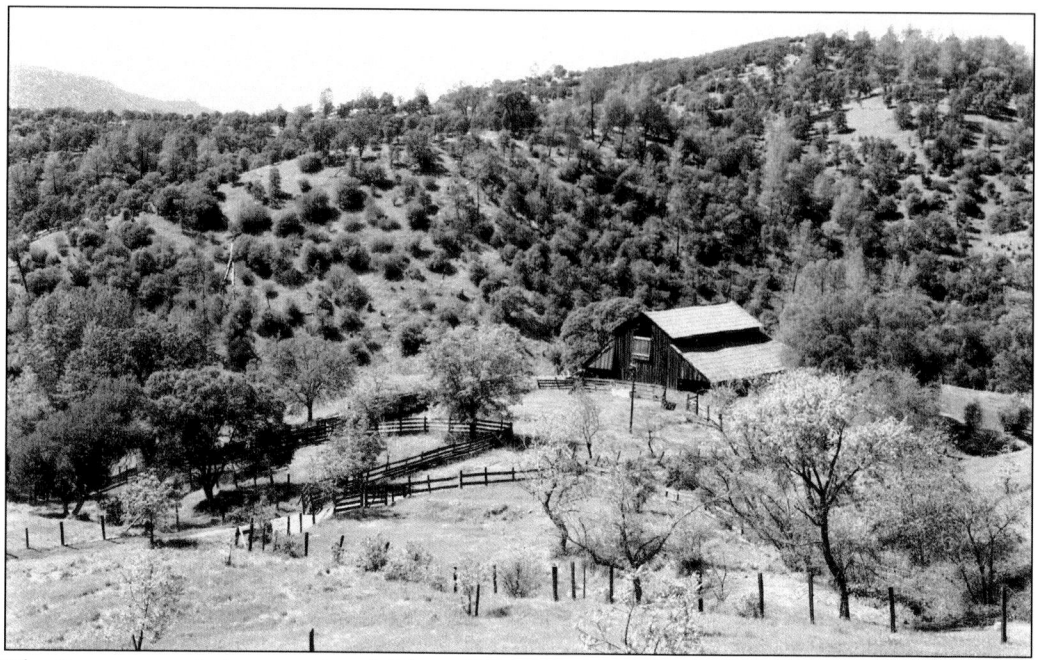

The Stevenot cattle barn on their Melones Ranch near Carson Hill is typical of such structures essential to ranchers and farmers, with its board-and-batten siding, corrugated-metal gable roof, and hay loft. Hay was stored in the center section, while the animals were fed from mangers in the shed-roofed bays on either side. (Courtesy Historic American Buildings Survey.)

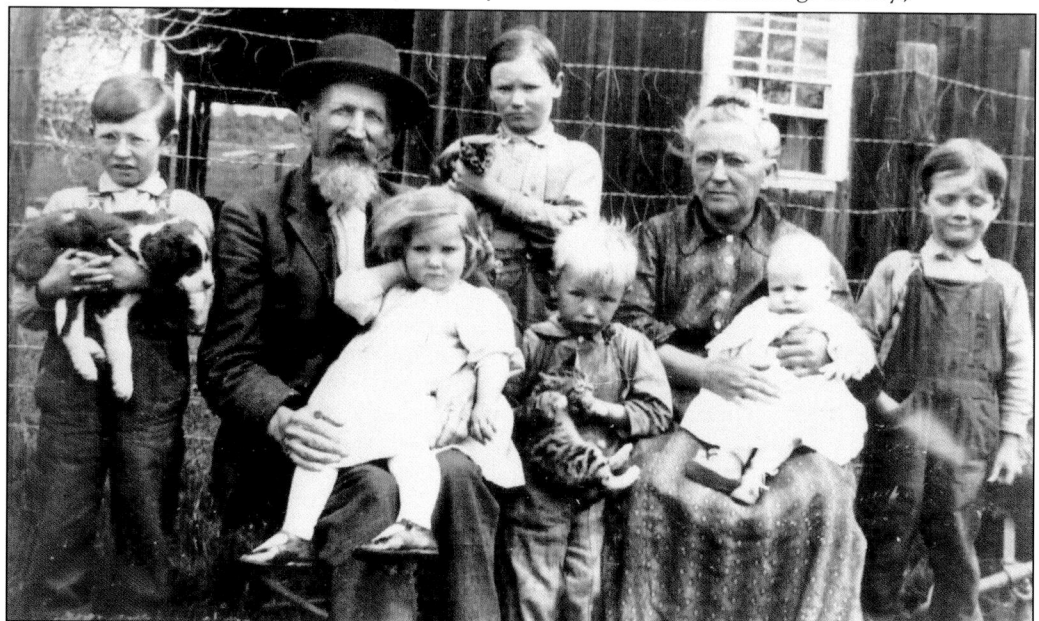

Australians Joseph and Mary Ann Whittle purchased a ranch on the old Reynolds Ferry Road in the 1860s. Their grandson Clenn recalled that the family sometimes came to town only twice a year—and then only to purchase items and foodstuffs that could not be produced at home. The Whittle grandchildren (from left to right) Harry, Ida, Don, Wint, Clenn, and Joe posed with their grandparents John and Pauline Battenfield about 1912. (Courtesy Calaveras County Archives.)

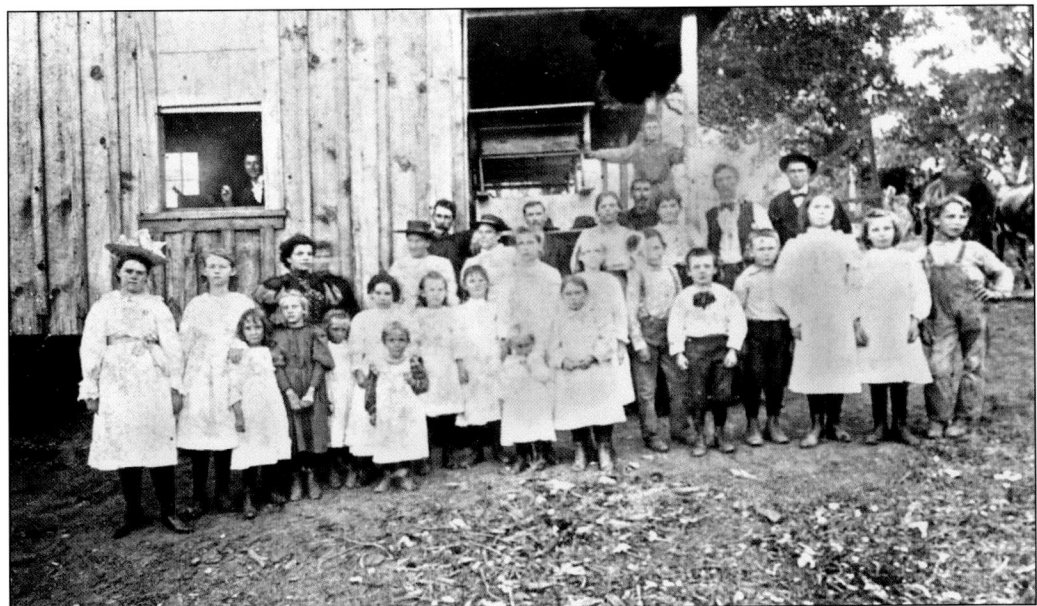

The Ramona School was organized in 1895 to provide schooling for the many ranch families in the lower Angels Creek area. The simple frame building was erected on the Reister Ranch, then moved to the Riedel Ranch near the Whittle Ranch, not far from the Airola and Battenfield ranches, as the school-age population of the children in the area waned and waxed. (Courtesy Calaveras County Archives.)

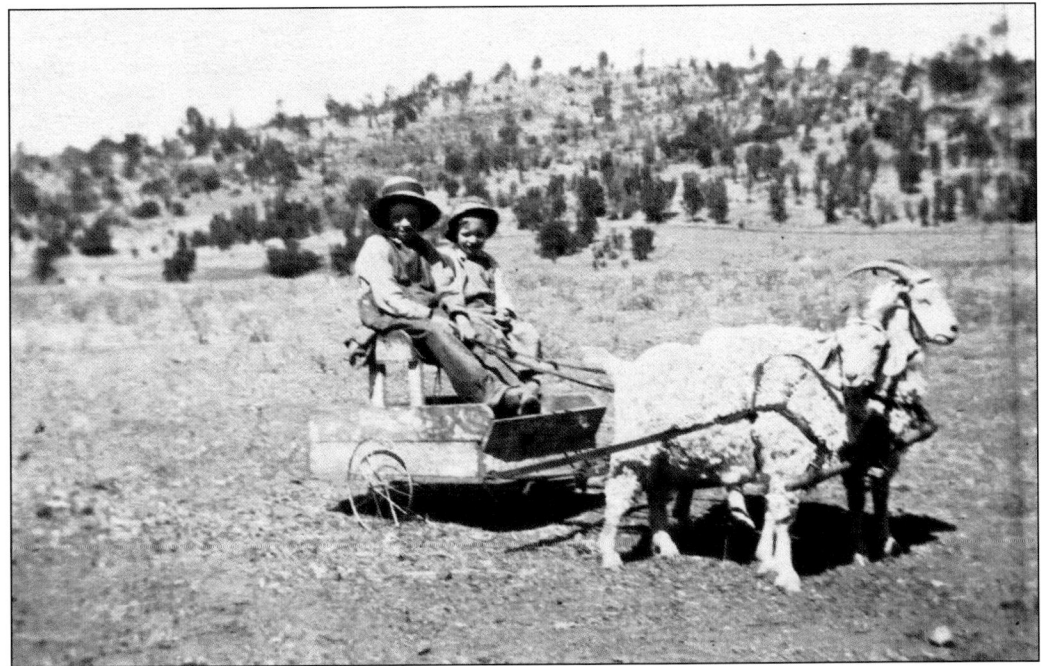

James and Martha Burnham settled in Calaveritas in the 1850s, but by the 1890s, son Fred and his wife, Nancy, had purchased a cattle ranch near Copperopolis, where they raised four sons. Sons Fred and Frank are pictured here with their goat wagon about 1910, while brothers Charles and Dahl are occupied elsewhere. (Courtesy Calaveras County Historical Society.)

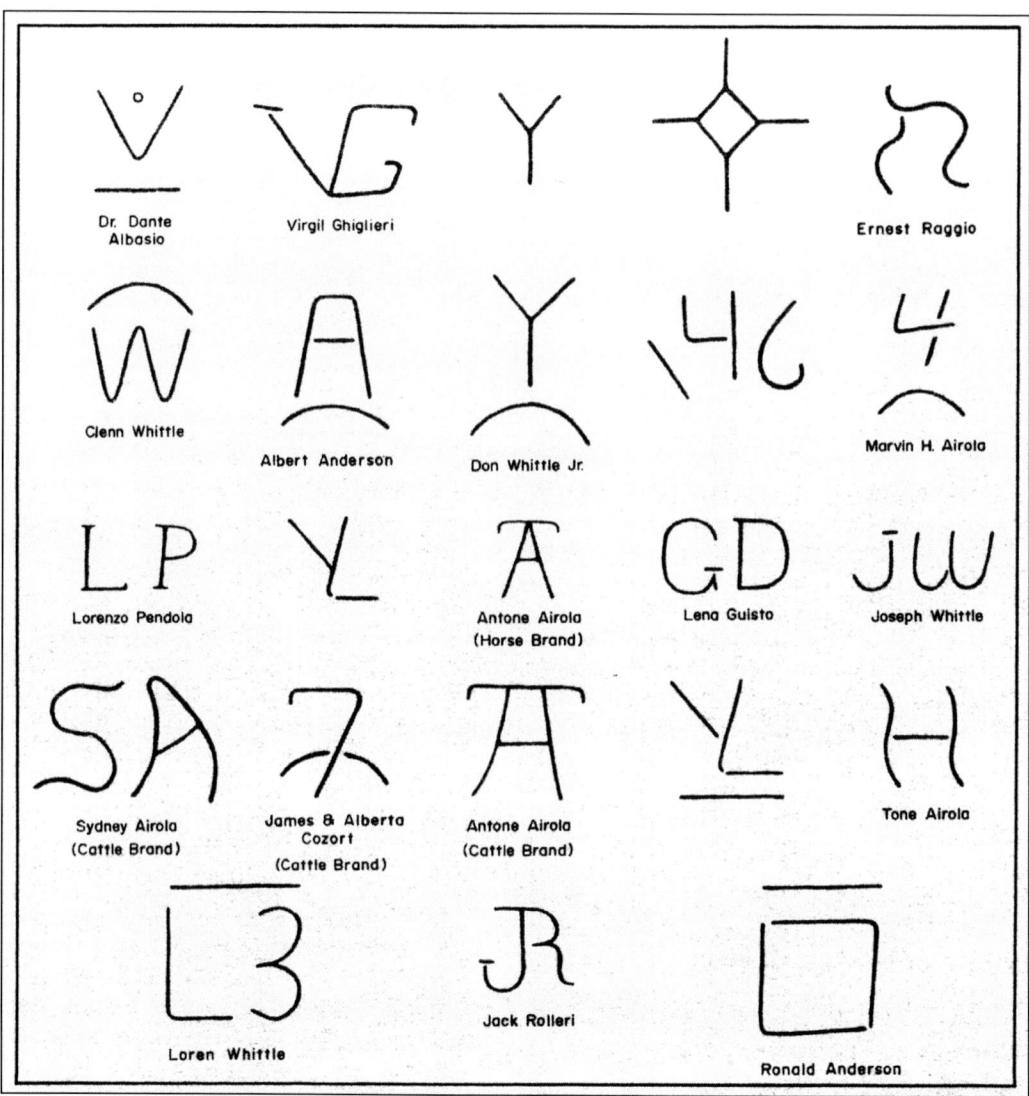

In addition to operating his ranch, Virgil Ghiglieri, a descendant of the Pendola family of Robinsons Ferry, worked as a blacksmith. Over the years, he made branding irons for his fellow ranchers, recording his work by branding his barn doors. Identified where possible, the brands are reproduced here, and the doors themselves are on display at the Calaveras County Museum, on loan from the Bureau of Reclamation. (Courtesy Julia Costello.)

Eight

Black Bart

Black Bart, perhaps the most famous stagecoach robber in American history and certainly one of the West's most fascinating outlaws, committed both his first and last holdup not only in Calaveras County, but also at the exact same spot: below Funk Hill near Copperopolis.

Wearing a flour sack with eyeholes cut in it and wielding a shotgun, Black Bart was the scourge of Wells Fargo, the express company that transported gold throughout the West. For more than eight years, from his first robbery on July 26, 1875, to his last on November 3, 1883, he was Wells Fargo's most wanted man. Yet he became a folk hero for working alone, for never firing a shot (it was said that his shotgun was never loaded), for never injuring a victim, for never robbing a traveler or a driver, for his politeness toward women, and for a few scraps of his poetry: "I've labored long for bread / For honor and for riches, / But on my corns too long you've tread / You fine haired Sons of Bitches." He signed that 1877 verse "Black Bart, the Po8" (an acronym for "poet"), and so the man known as the Gentleman Bandit began.

Who was this masked man? Wells Fargo's detectives and other dedicated lawmen did not have a clue until his final crime. Who really shot him and precipitated his capture? Some say it was a teenage stagecoach passenger; others say it was the stage driver. What happened to him after he served his time in prison? No one knows where he went or where he ended his days. Though mystery yet surrounds him, the credo he once penned in doggerel is simple enough: "Here I lay me down to sleep, / To wait the coming morrow. / Perhaps success, perhaps defeat, / And everlasting sorrow. / Let come what will I'll try it on, / My condition can't be worse; / And if there's money in that box / Tis munny in my purse."

Today his jail cell and the courtroom where he was sentenced, both at the county seat in San Andreas, continue to attract visitors. The legend of Black Bart lives on.

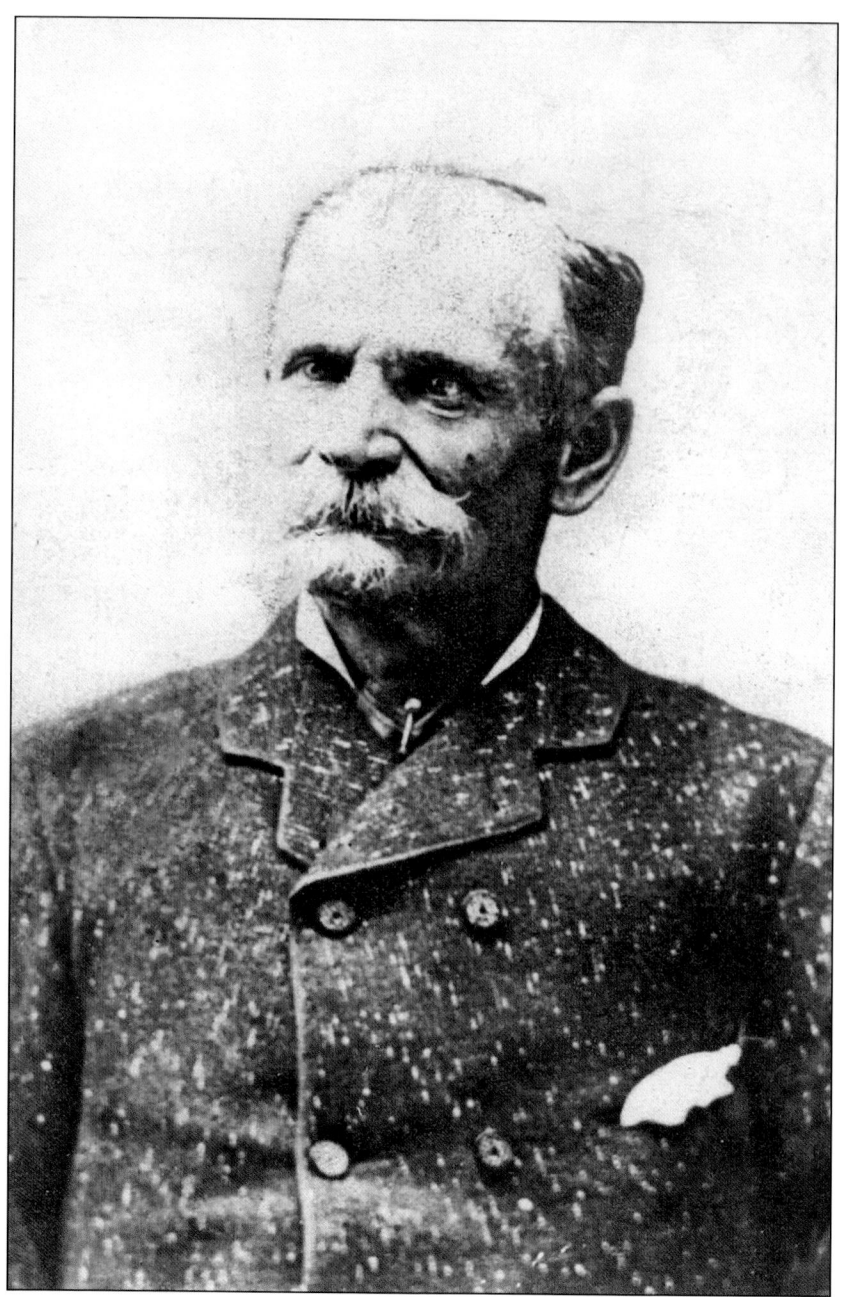

Black Bart's real name was Charles Boles. Reportedly born in either England or New York around 1829, he moved with his family to the Midwest before heading to California during the Gold Rush. But he soon returned east to Illinois, where he farmed, married, and had two daughters. He was wounded serving in the Union army in an Illinois volunteer regiment during the Civil War, and in the early 1870s, he left his family behind and again headed west, finally landing in California. In San Francisco, he was known as Charles Bolton, a dapper, soft-spoken mine owner who never drank or bragged about his success but often left town on business for periods of time. Until his capture, no one knew the 5-foot, 8-inch fellow with piercing blue eyes, who was by then in his mid-50s, was, in fact, the most wanted of men—Black Bart. (Courtesy Bill Renwick.)

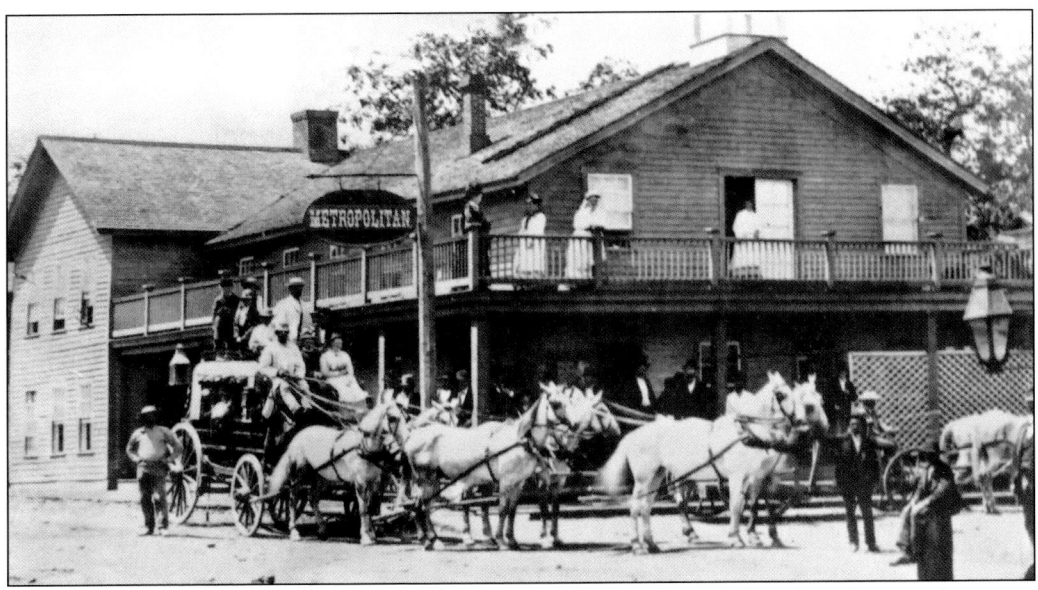

The most frequent type of stage used in the region was a "mud wagon," such as this one shown on the Roseburg-to-Redding route around the time of Black Bart's escapades. Operated by independent stage lines, they carried passengers and the U.S. mail, as well as gold bullion, coin, and notes for Wells Fargo and Company in what was called a "treasure box." (Courtesy Bill Renwick.)

REWARD!

WELLS, FARGO & CO.'S EXPRESS BOX, CON-
taining $160 in Gold Notes, was robbed this morning, by one man, on the route from Sonora to Milton, near top of the Hill, between the river and Copperopolis.

$250

And one-fourth of any money recovered, will be paid for arrest and conviction of the robber.

JOHN J. VALENTINE,

San Francisco, July 27, 1875. General Sup't.

TUOLUMNE INDEPENDENT PRINT.

The day after Black Bart's first holdup, Wells Fargo distributed this reward poster. Black Bart would be credited with committing at least 28 similar robberies from southern Oregon to California's Central Valley but largely in the Mother Lode, the heart of the great Gold Rush. The reward for his capture quickly grew to $800, a significant sum, offered jointly by Wells Fargo, the State of California, and the U.S. Post Office. (Courtesy Bill Renwick.)

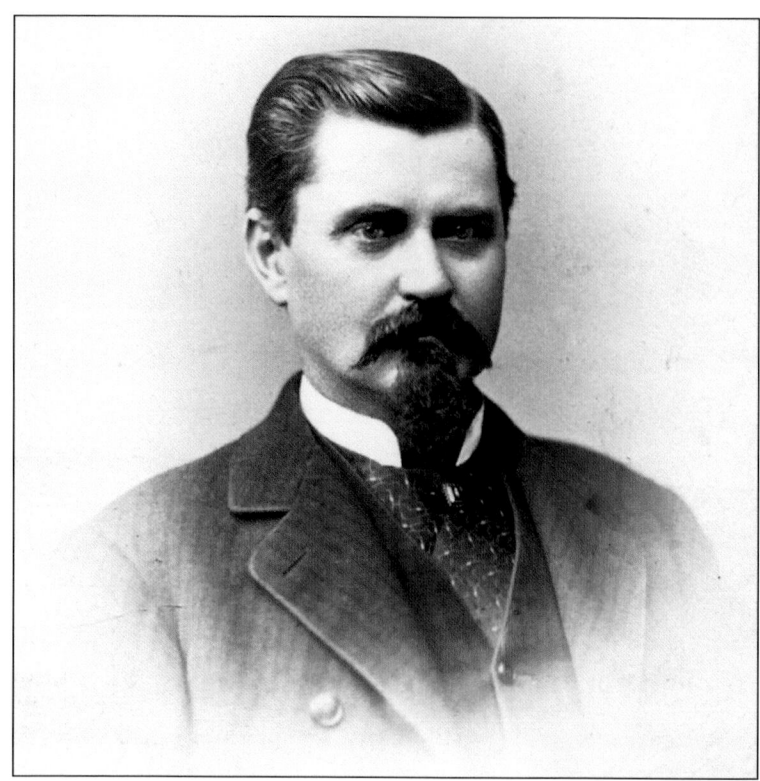

On that fateful day of November 3, 1883, honest, brave, and cool-headed Reason McConnell drove his stage from Sonora to the railhead at Milton, where connections would be made with passengers and freight, and where McConnell lived. In 1912, he authored the only eyewitness account of Black Bart's last holdup, which was finally published in 2007 by his great-grandson Bill Renwick. McConnell is about 33 in this c. 1876 photograph. (Courtesy Bill Renwick.)

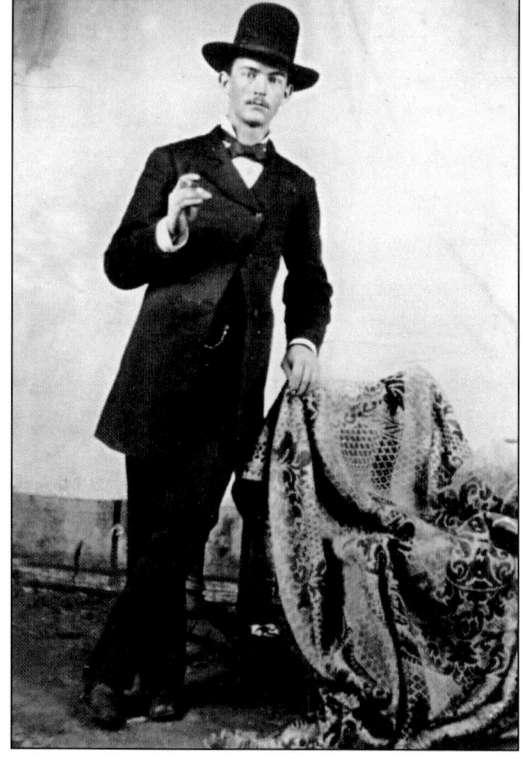

On board the stage was 228 ounces of gold amalgam worth $4,104 and gold coin valued at $553. McConnell stopped at Reynolds Ferry, and Jimmy Rolleri, the 19-year-old son of Olivia and Geralomo, who ran the hotel there, jumped on board with his .44 Henry rifle. They crossed the Stanislaus River on the ferry, and halfway up Funk Hill, Rolleri hopped off to hunt deer. (Courtesy Calaveras County Historical Society.)

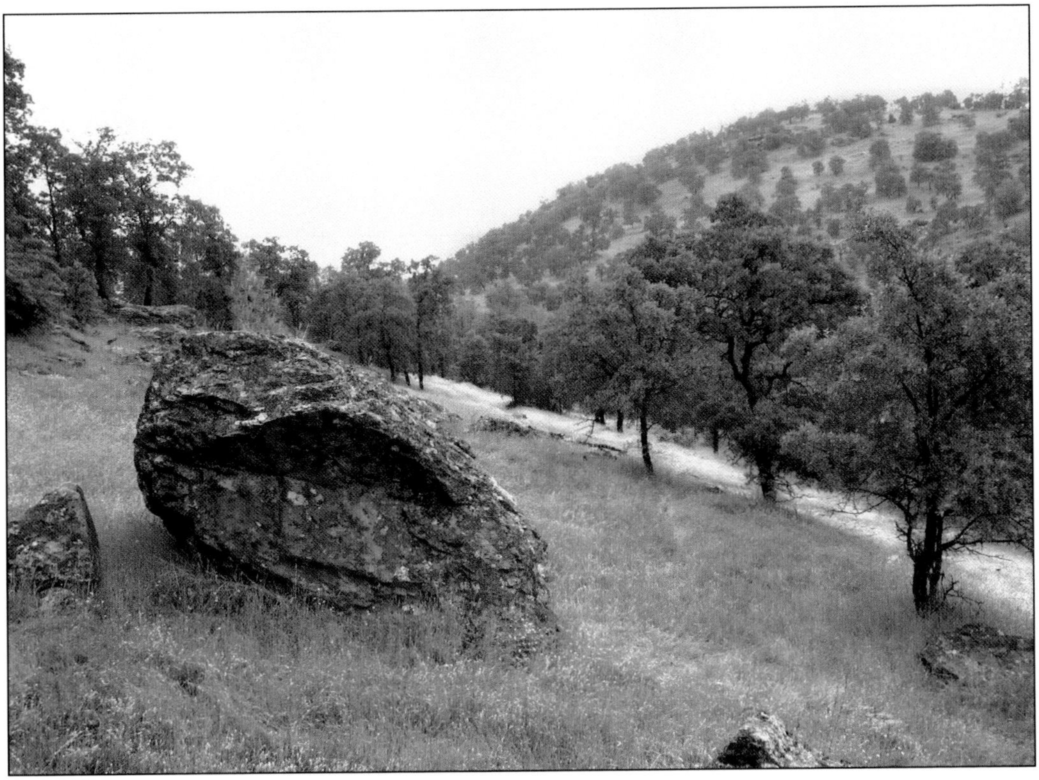

"My lead horses suddenly stopped . . . and looked towards a large rock," wrote McConnell. "As I drove up he came out with a double barrel shotgun and a white sack over his head, with two holes in it for eyes, and a slouch hat on." Black Bart waited behind the rock shown in this 2007 photograph, looking toward what was the Sonora-Milton stage road below. (Photograph by Sal Manna.)

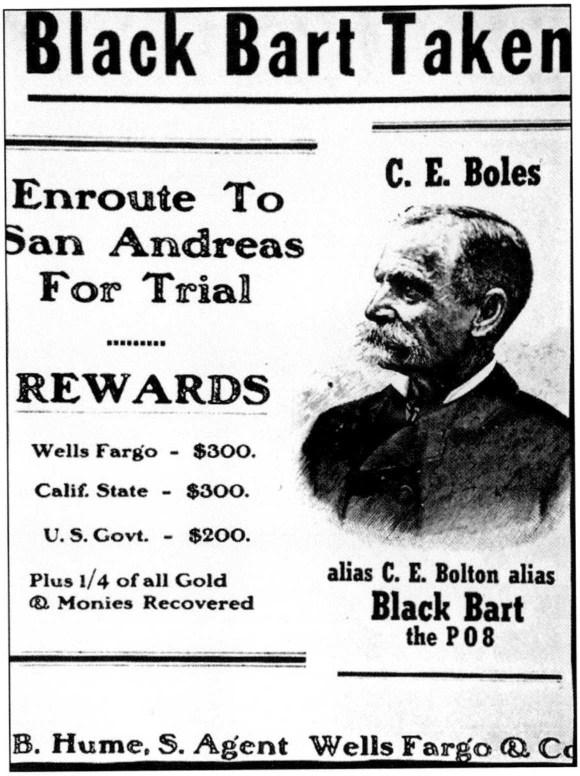

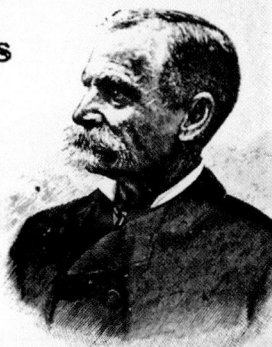

Black Bart ordered McConnell away and took a hatchet to the treasure box. But the driver found Rolleri, and they returned. "I put in four shots [with Rolleri's rifle]," wrote McConnell. Rolleri disagreed, saying McConnell shot twice but then he shot twice and winged the robber. In any case, in Black Bart's haste, he left behind a silk handkerchief with the San Francisco laundry mark F.X.O.7, which led to Charles Bolton's front door.

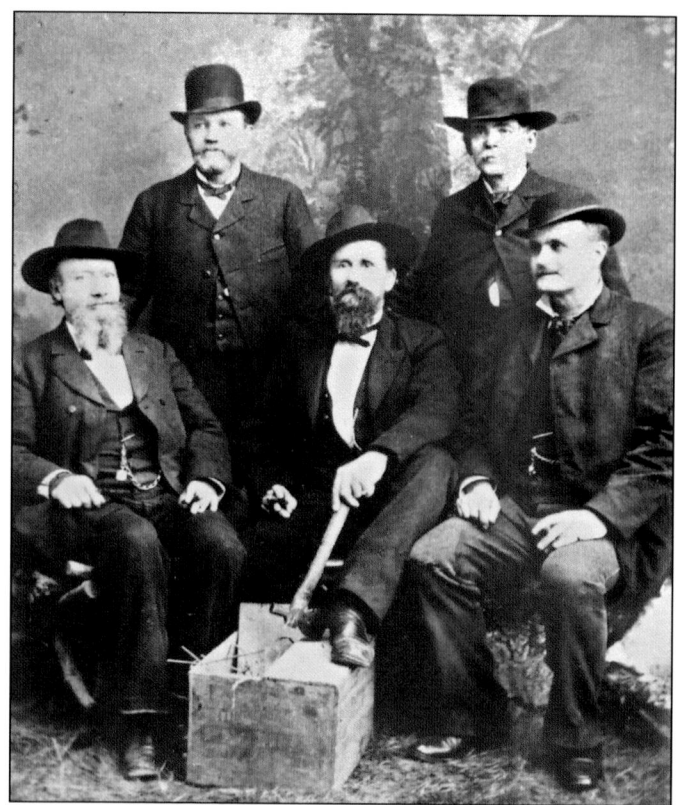

Bolton was arrested, confessed to only the last holdup, and was sentenced to six years in San Quentin. Shown here in a famous 1883 photograph titled "Cracking the Case," with the supposed treasure box, are, from left to right, San Joaquin County sheriff Tom Cunningham, San Francisco police captain A. W. Stone, Calaveras County sheriff Ben Thorn (with hatchet), private detective Harry Morse, and Wells Fargo detective J. W. Thacker. (Courtesy Calaveras County Historical Society.)

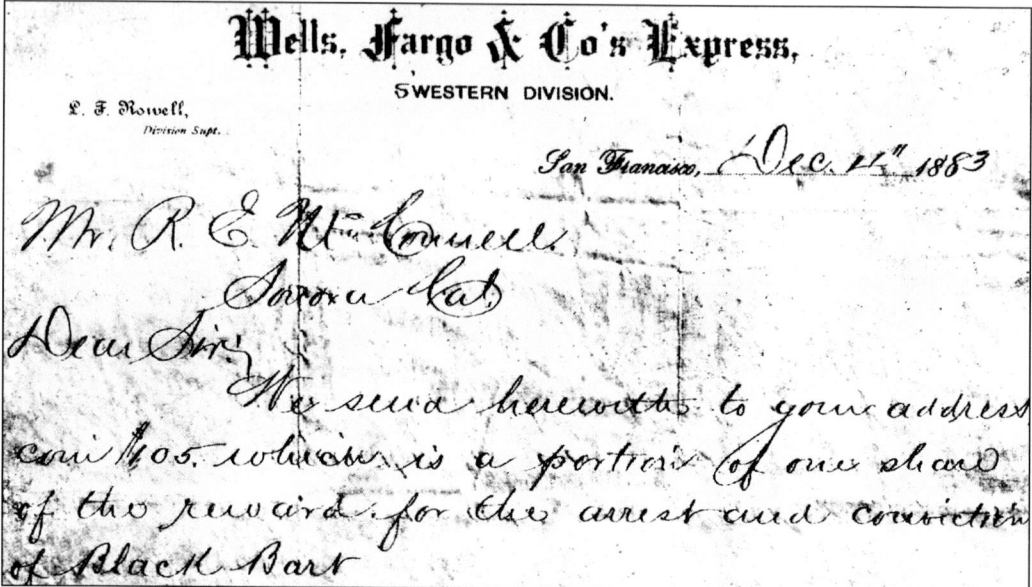

McConnell received his share of the reward and this letter of thanks, published here for the first time. Bolton served four years and two months, with time off for good behavior, and left prison on January 21, 1888. Though some claimed they saw him afterwards and that he even visited Calaveras County within weeks of his release, neither Bolton, nor Black Bart, were ever heard from again. (Courtesy Bill Renwick.)

Nine

THE IRON ROADS

Of the three railroads that breached Calaveras County, the first is one of the most obscure and never reached its intended destination, and the last is one of the most famous in the Mother Lode. The county's second railroad was the San Joaquin and Sierra Nevada, which served West Calaveras from 1882 to 1983 and is reported on in Images of America: *Northern Calaveras County*.

That first railroad came not for gold but for copper. Construction of the Stockton and Copperopolis Railroad, primarily by 500 to 600 Chinese workers, began in Stockton in San Joaquin County in November 1870. On May 1, 1871, the road was completed to Milton, and its first passenger train reached there 10 days later, the fare being 75¢ for the round-trip. But the Stockton and Copperopolis Railroad would venture no farther, never advancing to the latter locale.

A far more storied history is that of the Sierra Railway and its Angels Branch, whose construction was encouraged by mining, lumber, and even tourism interests. The road began in Oakdale in Stanislaus County and arrived in Jamestown in Tuolumne County in 1897 and then Sonora a year later.

The Angels Branch was built from Jamestown and required a trestle across the Stanislaus River and a series of switchbacks to scale the steep hillsides. The result was a 700-foot climb in elevation over 4 miles of track leading to the aptly named Gee Whiz Point and a reputation as "the steepest, crookedest, hair-raising jaunt in California." The road arrived in Angels Camp on September 10, 1902, but it too went no farther.

By the late 1930s, both railroads dwindled in importance, and by 1940, their rails were pulled up within Calaveras County. Today there is little evidence in the county of the Stockton and Copperopolis Railroad; there remains somewhat more of the Angels Branch, including the Angels Camp depot.

The Railtown 1897 State Historic Park in Jamestown, however, has kept alive the history of the Sierra Railway. Since 1982, tens of thousands of visitors have experienced a steam railroad by visiting the original roundhouse and riding one of the Sierra Railway's trains along a short section of track. Although there is not a stretch of useable track still within Calaveras County, the story of its railroads remains an important one.

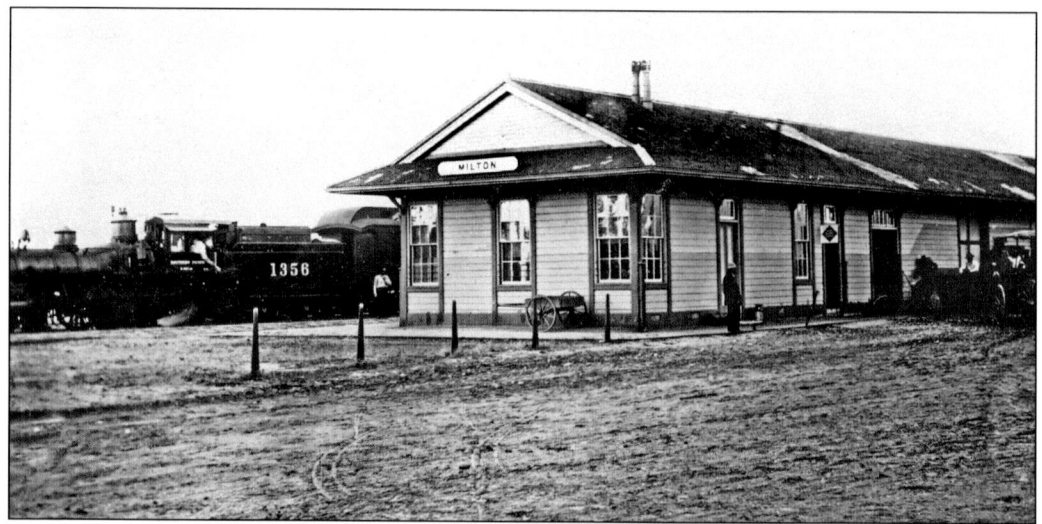

Milton, its depot shown here in the early 1900s, was named for Milton Latham, a lawyer elected to the U.S. House of Representatives from California in 1852 and the state's sixth governor in 1860. He served the shortest gubernatorial tenure—five days—when the legislature named him to a vacant U.S. Senate seat. Latham later became a railroad baron, promoting ventures including the Stockton and Copperopolis line. (Courtesy Calaveras County Historical Society.)

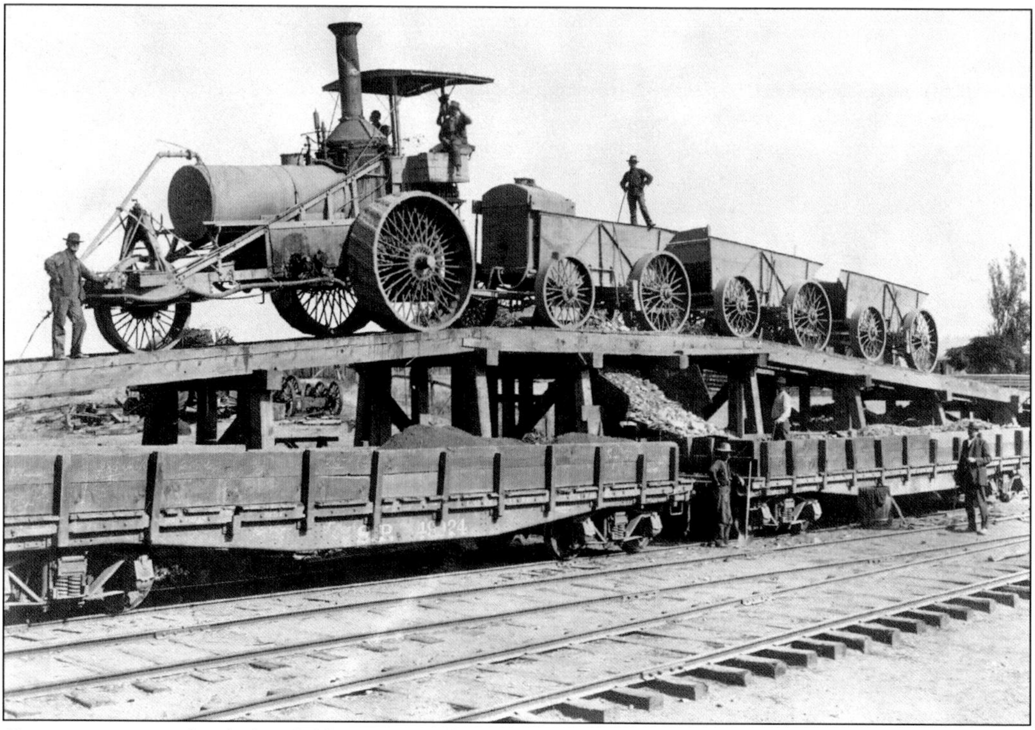

Copper ore is unloaded at Milton around 1912 from a Copperopolis mine's motorized vehicle into railcars of the Stockton and Copperopolis Railroad. The ore was then taken to Stockton, conveyed on river barges to San Francisco, and then put on steamers headed for smelters in Swansea, Wales. Before the railroad, ox teams hauled the ore to Stockton. (Courtesy Calaveras County Historical Society.)

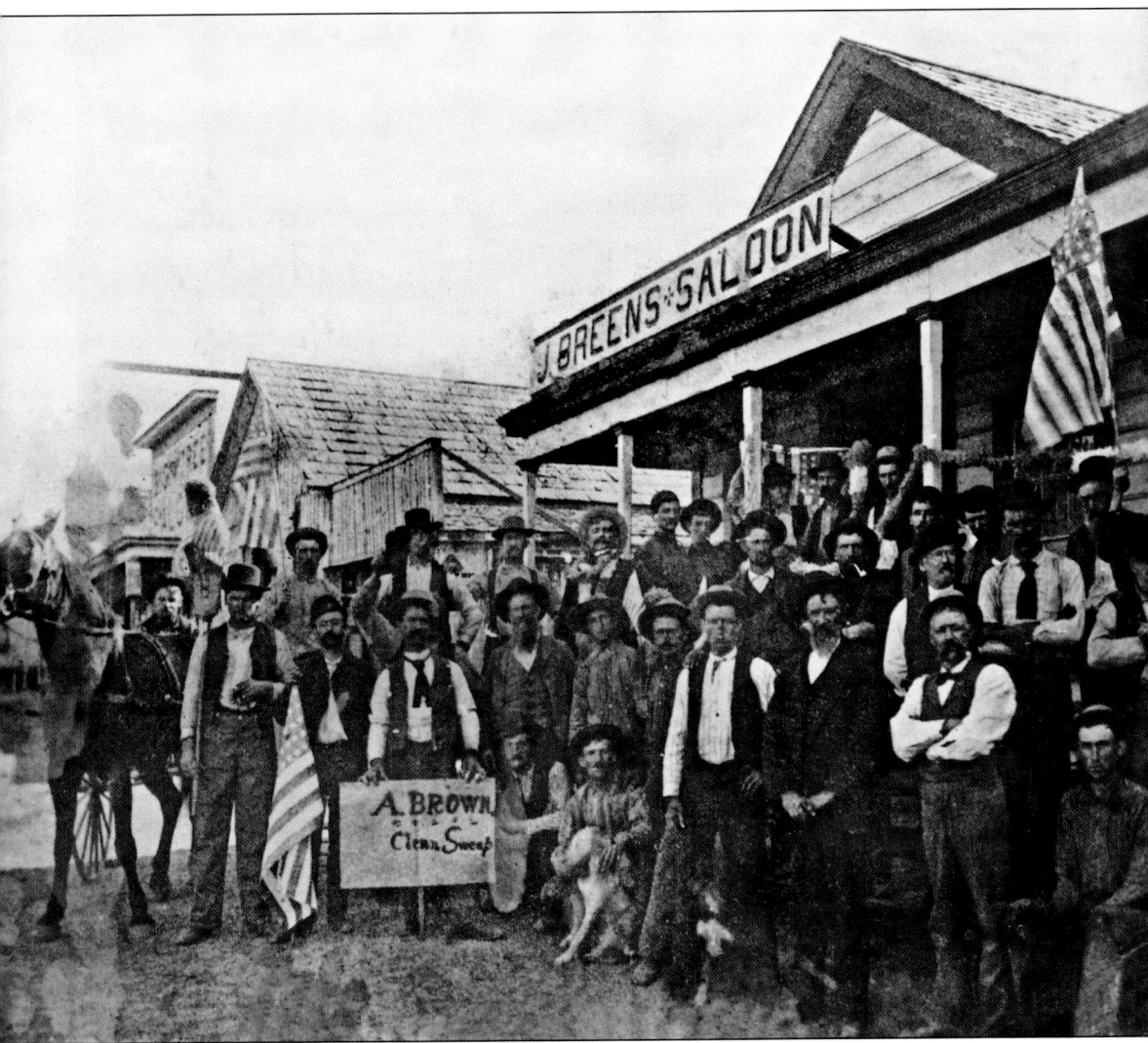

Calaveras County's first railhead, Milton was a busy place as stage lines connected the train's passengers and freight to Copperopolis, Angels Camp, San Andreas, Mokelumne Hill, and Sonora. Freight was not only gold and copper, but also cattle and sheep from the large ranches nearby. Visitors could also take popular stagecoach excursions to the Big Trees or Yosemite. In 1888, the town claimed two livery stables, two blacksmith shops, a harness shop, a Masonic hall, a schoolhouse, one church, and four saloons. The Wells Fargo agent in Milton was Alex Brown, who also ran a general merchandise store and would be elected state assemblyman in 1890. He served several terms, no doubt thanks to grassroots campaigning such as that pictured above at the saloon of Indiana Civil War veteran Joe Breen, also known as Checker Joe of Milton. (Courtesy Calaveras County Historical Society.)

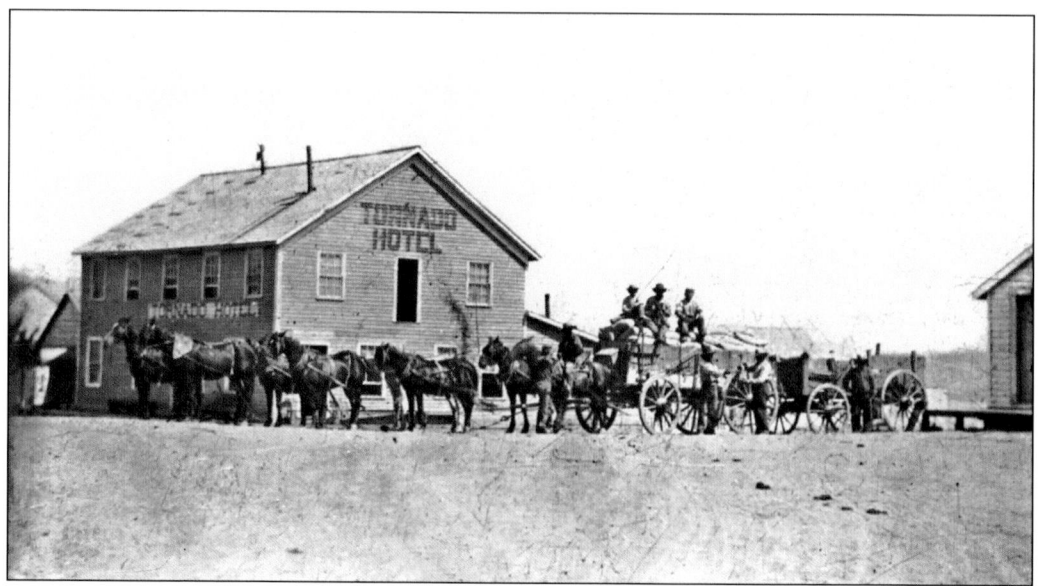

In December 1873, a quarter-mile-wide tornado touched down in Milton, blowing the new schoolhouse 8 feet off its foundation and destroying a hotel under construction. "It lasted but a few moments," wrote the *Calaveras Chronicle*, "long enough, however, to place at least half the town in ruins." When the hotel was rebuilt, seen in this photograph soon after, it boasted an appropriate name, the Tornado Hotel. (Courtesy Calaveras County Historical Society.)

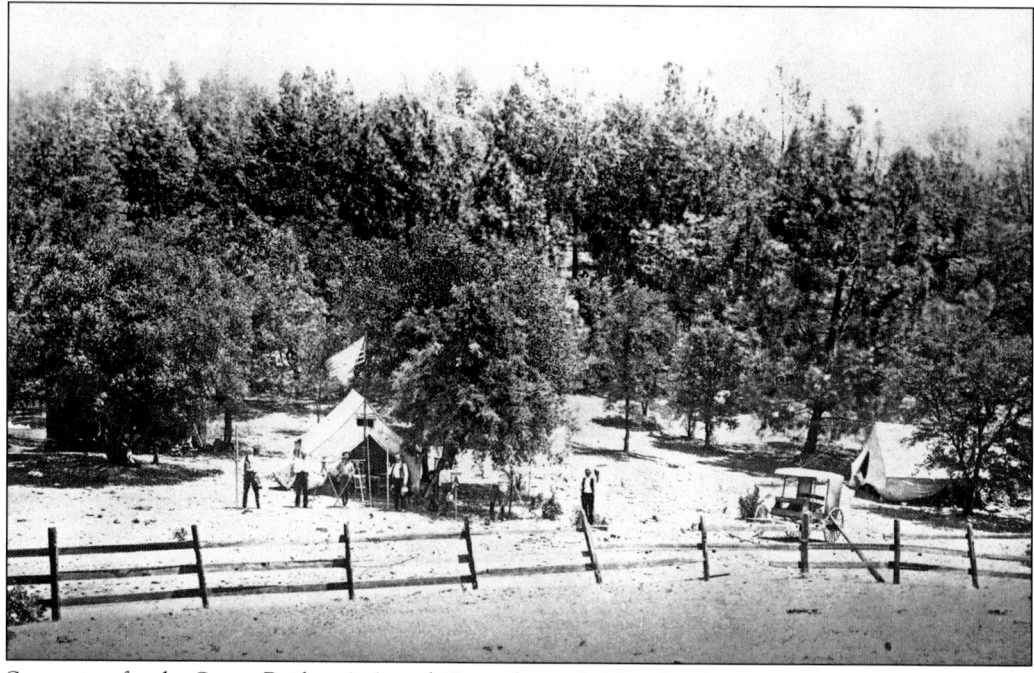

Surveying for the Sierra Railway's Angels Branch was led by chief engineer W. H. Newell, whose tent is on the left in this July 4, 1899, photograph, taken on the Stevenot Homestead. Emile K. Stevenot granted the railroad a right-of-way in return for a flag station being established there so he could hail the train to go to San Francisco. (Photograph by Emile K. Stevenot, courtesy Calaveras County Historical Society.)

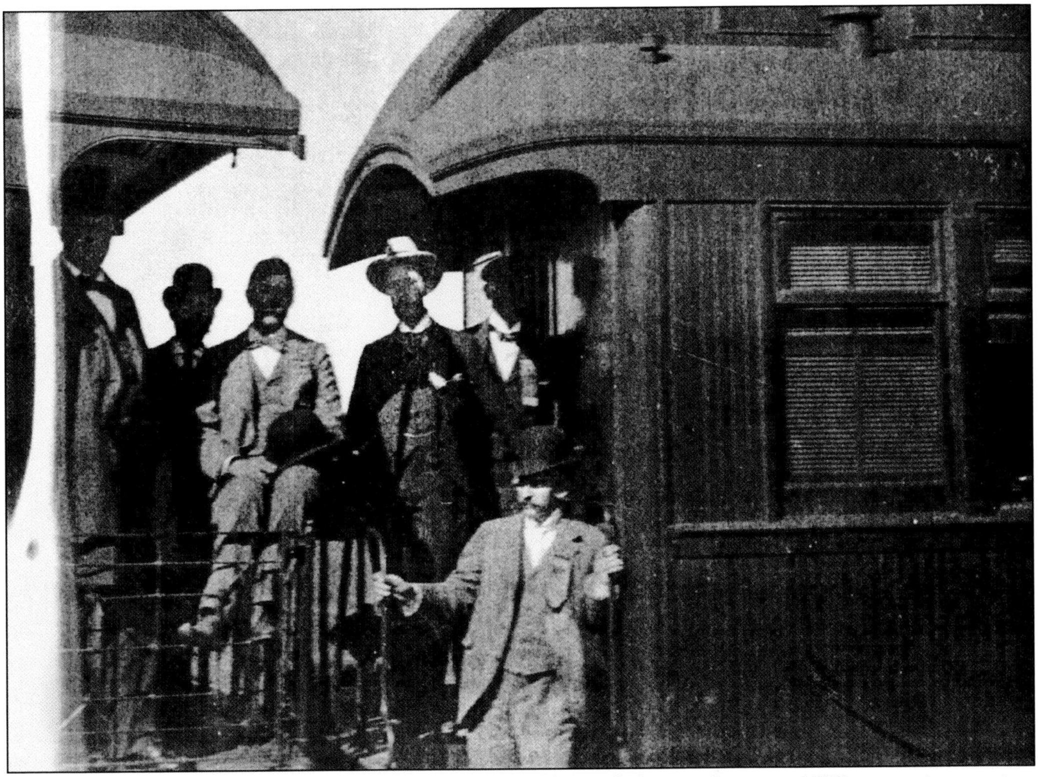

Prince Andre Poniatowski (top row, second from the right), seen here in 1897 on an inspection tour of the Sierra Railway, founded the railroad with magnate William Crocker and entrepreneur Thomas Bullock. Poniatowski, nicknamed "Prince Pint O'Whiskey," a French-born descendant of the King of Poland, subsequently built the Electra hydroelectric plant on the Mokelumne River. The plant was later incorporated into Pacific Gas and Electric. (Courtesy Wally Motloch.)

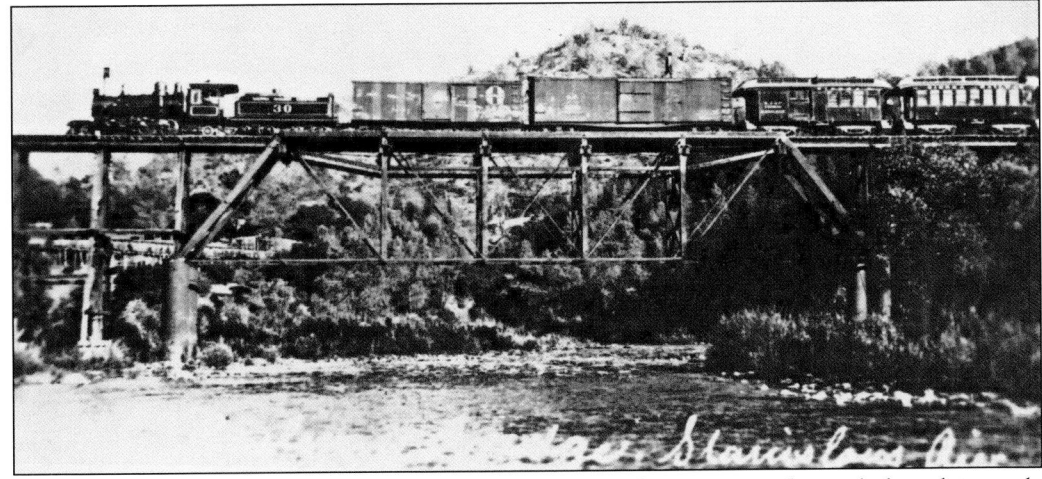

Construction of the 21-mile Angels Branch entailed an arduous 12 months, including this trestle over the Stanislaus River. The crossing of the canyon overlooking Melones was a marvelous feat of engineering. A tortuous descent, then a climb to the Calaveras rim of Stanislaus Canyon, ended at Gee Whiz Point, named for either its challenge for a train engineer or its breathtaking views. (Courtesy Calaveras County Historical Society.)

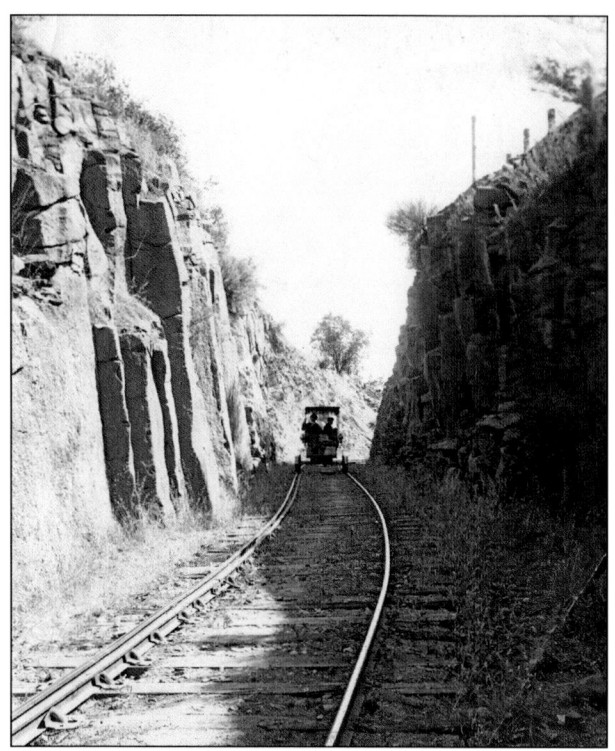

Many people, including the railway's first engineer, considered the Stanislaus Canyon impassable. His replacement, Newell, was undaunted. He conquered the canyon using switchbacks—dead ends where a locomotive could reverse direction in order to gain several vertical feet on steep grades. Other areas had to be blasted away using dynamite, such as this cut through a hill near Coyote Creek. (Courtesy Calaveras County Historical Society.)

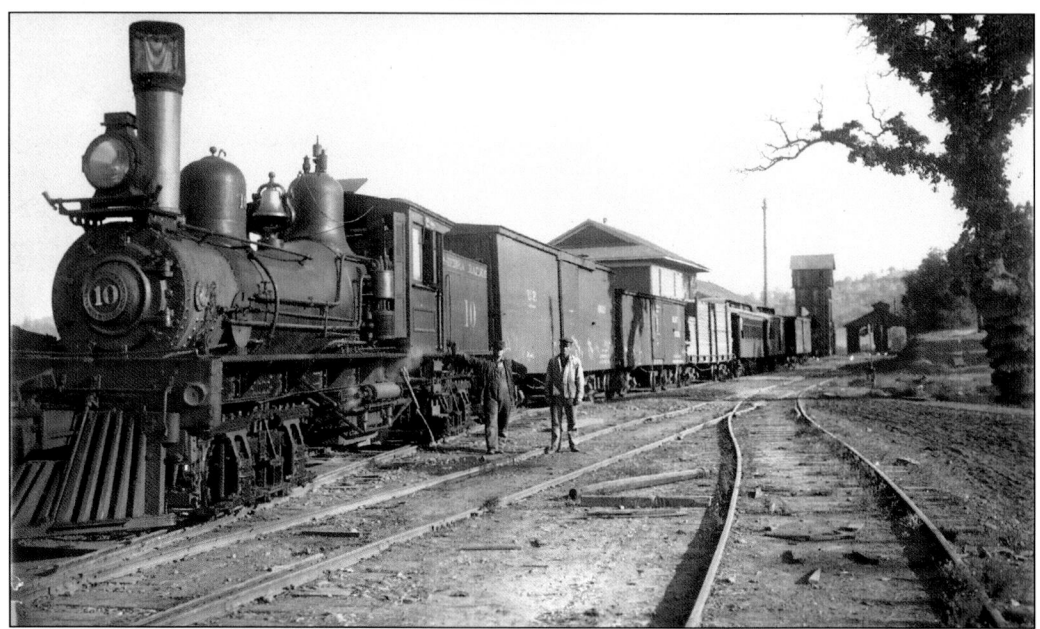

In 1902, the railway acquired this Shay locomotive, No. 10, shown at the Angels Camp depot. The Sierra's most famous locomotive, the 1891 Rogers-built No. 3 purchased in 1897, portrayed the Hooterville Cannonball in the television series *Petticoat Junction*. Sierra Railway equipment has been seen in movies, including 1923's *The Virginian*, *High Noon*, *Unforgiven*, and *Back to the Future Part III*, earning the nickname "the Movie Railroad." (Courtesy Calaveras County Historical Society.)

Ten
Frog Jump

On January 25, 1865, Samuel Clemens (aka Mark Twain), traveled from the cabin he shared with pocket miner Jim Gillis at Jackass Hill in Tuolumne County to nearby Angels Camp in Calaveras County, where everyone was rained in for nearly two weeks. To amuse themselves, the townspeople exchanged tall tales around the bar at the Angels Hotel. Twain wrote them down, including one about a frog named Dan'l Webster, who could outjump any other frog. On November 18, that tale, "Jim Smiley and His Jumping Frog," was published in the *New York Saturday Press*—and the famed literary career of Mark Twain was truly launched. In subsequent reprints, the story became known as "The Celebrated Jumping Frog of Calaveras County."

Though the first county fair was held in 1893, the first Jumping Frog Jubilee did not take place until 1928. Created by the Angels Camp Boosters to commemorate the paving of Main Street, the First Frog Jump, as it is locally known, drew more than 15,000 visitors to watch a parade celebrating the area's Gold Rush heritage and a frog jumping contest. Ten years later, the county fair and the Jumping Frog Jubilee were combined at the nearby county fairgrounds, of course called Frogtown, and have been held there in May every year since.

Twain's sense of humor and satire would no doubt appreciate a 21st-century twist. In 2003, the red-legged frog that inspired his tale, a threatened species supplanted by the Eastern bullfrog and not seen in the county since 1969, was rediscovered by the children of a cattle rancher. The descendants of Dan'l Webster had returned to the county that had made Twain renowned around the world.

Today the County Fair and Jumping Frog Jubilee remains the biggest annual event in Calaveras, and both Mark Twain and Jim Smiley's frog are colorful and celebrated symbols of the county.

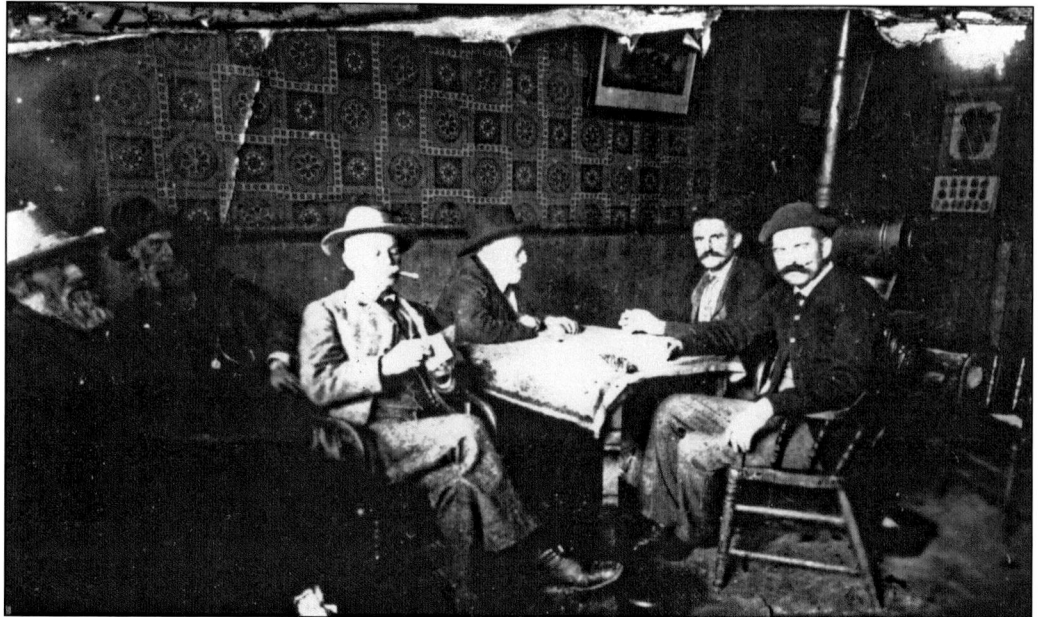

"Stranger filled C.'s frog full of shot and he couldn't jump. The stranger's frog won." Those words in Twain's notebook were written after he and Jim Gillis (third from the left, pictured in the early 1900s) heard the tale from Ben Coon. Gillis's brother Billy recalled that Twain said, "If I can write that story the way Ben Coon told it, that frog will jump around the world." (Courtesy Calaveras County Historical Society.)

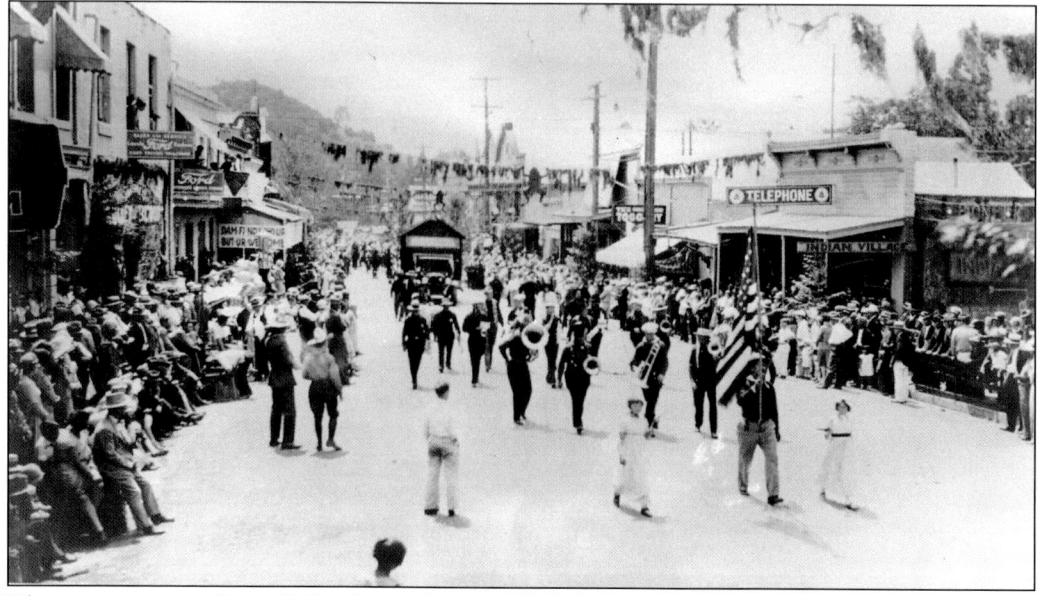

The premiere parade in 1928, shown here, included marching bands, covered wagons, oxen teams, pack trains, cowboys and cowgirls, trappers, floats, and more. Motorized equipment was not permitted. Another frequent attraction during the day was the "capture and hanging of Three-fingered Jack." Laundry of pioneer clothing was stretched on lines above the street, a tradition that continues today to announce the arrival of the county fair. (Courtesy Calaveras County Historical Society.)

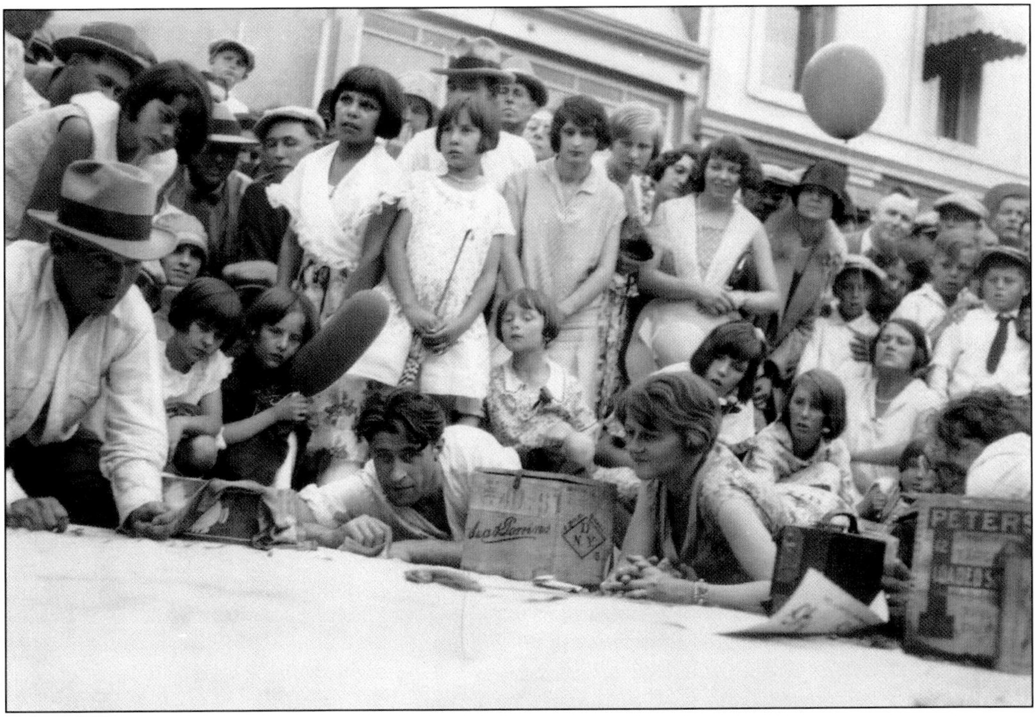

The Frog Jump became world renowned beginning with its first contest, shown here in 1928 (the young man lying on the ground is Mike Voitich and his sister Mary stands above him). They could not have imagined at the time that one day there would be a Jumping Frog Research Institute or, in 2005, a "frogumentary" titled *Jump* by fimmaker Justin Bookey. (Courtesy Calaveras County Archives.)

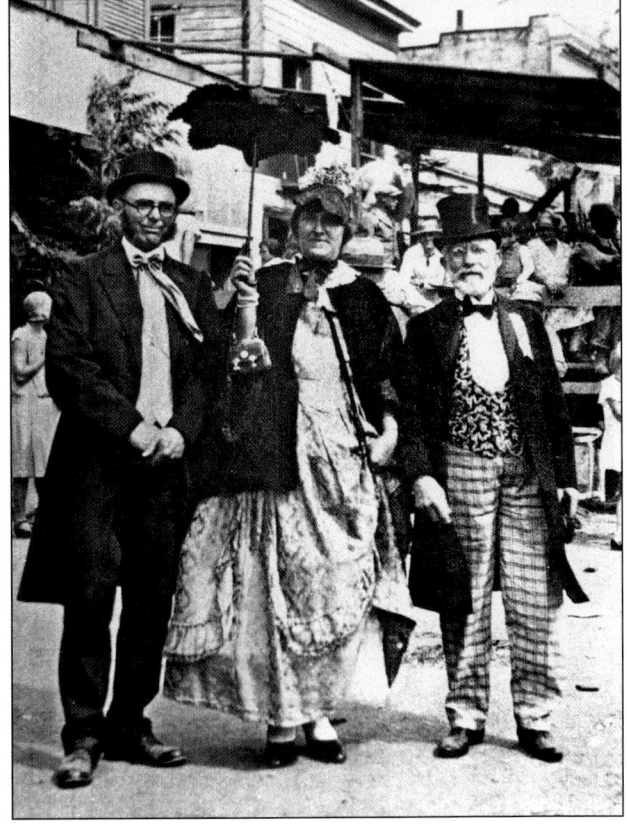

Residents and visitors would dress up as forty-niners, often portraying historic characters such as Gillis and Coon. Shown here at one of the first Frog Jumps are Harry Barden (right), Adelaide Squclatti (center), and an unidentified man. Though Barden has a trimmed beard, many men in Angels Camp would forego shaving in order to compete in the fair's Whiskerino contest for having the longest whiskers. (Courtesy Angels Camp Museum.)

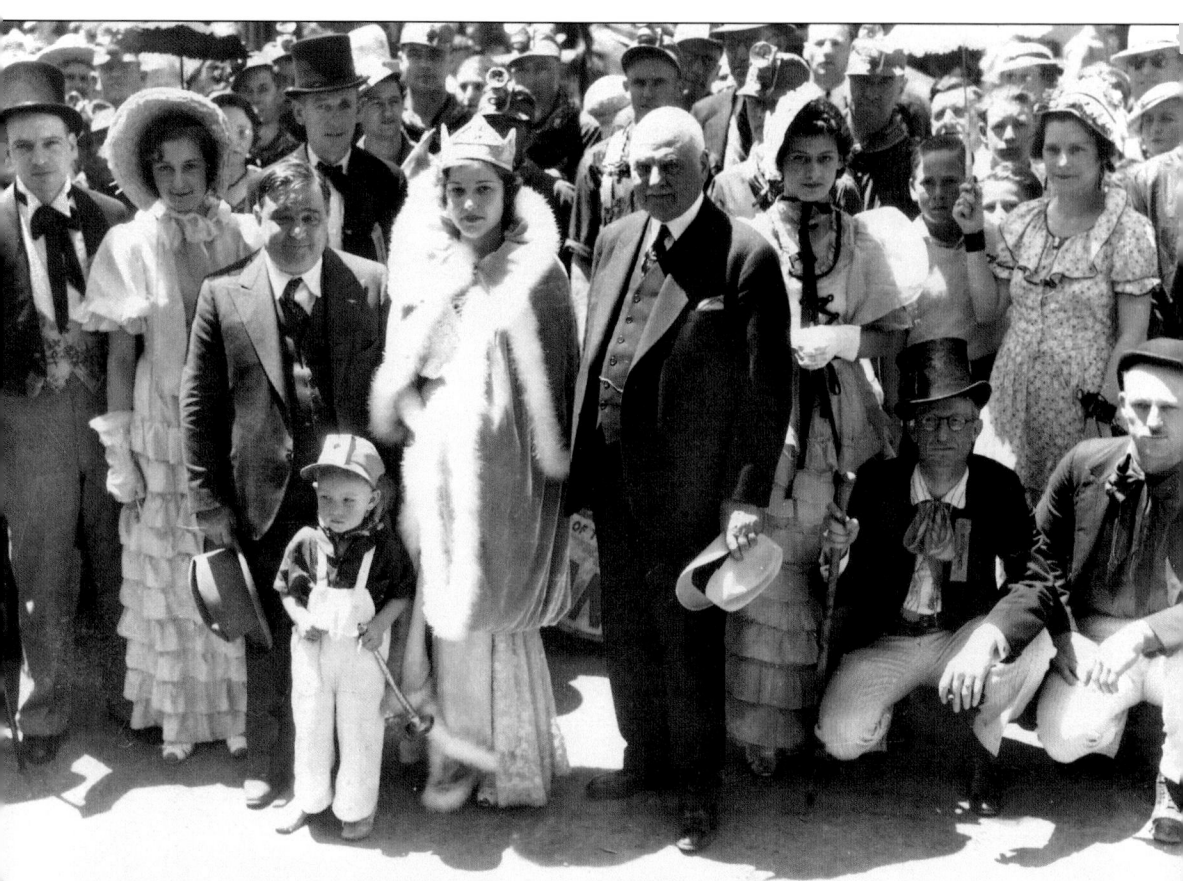

Because of its fame, the Frog Jump attracted celebrities of all sorts, from Hollywood starlets to politicians from far and wide, drawn to a publicity opportunity. In 1937, a new annual feature was the naming of the fair's Belle of the Camp. Pictured here is the inaugural honoree, Betty Cummings, an Angels Camp resident and student at Bret Harte High School, who was crowned by up-and-coming Paramount actress Marsha Hunt. To Cummings's right is Fiorello LaGuardia, mayor of New York City, and to her left, Angelo Rossi, mayor of San Francisco. Cummings wears her bejeweled crown and a gown of white satin, over which was placed a velvet robe edged in marabou feathers. Other than the difficult years of 1940–1946, the contest has been held at each county fair. Since 1956, the winner has been honored as Miss Calaveras. (Courtesy Angels Camp Museum.)

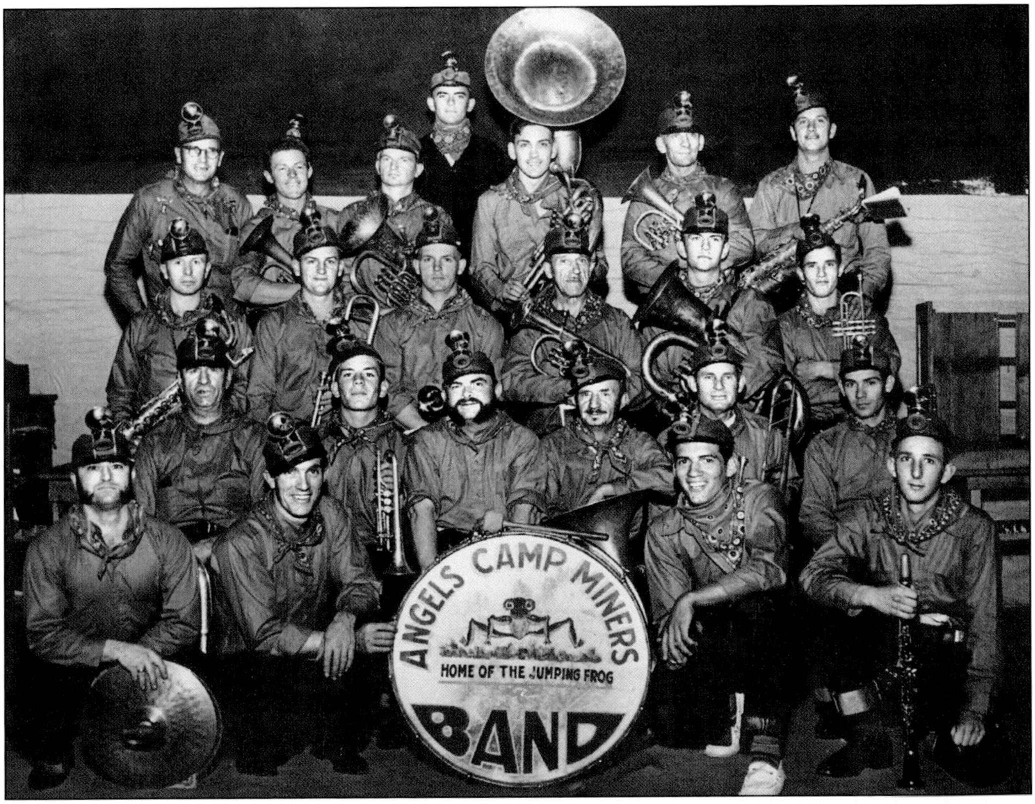

The miners' parade, which traditionally kicked off the Frog Jump, was led by the Angels Camp Miners' Band, shown here in 1937 with leader Sam Johnston. The parade was famous for taking place at night, illuminated only by the twinkling carbide lamps on the hats of the miners and large electric lights thrown onto the decorated floats. (Courtesy Calaveras County Historical Society.)

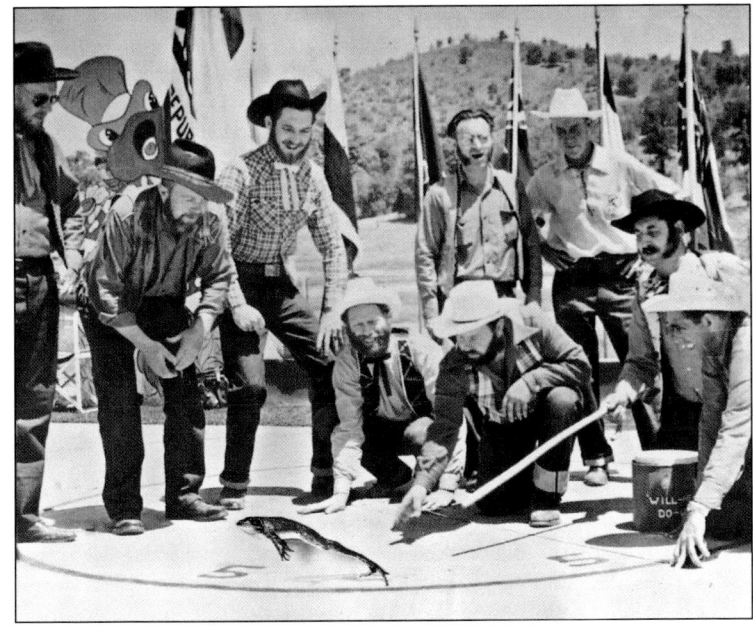

In 1938, the Frog Jump moved to Frogtown. This doctored commercial photograph was widely distributed. More recent notable events include the 1990 arrival of 13-pound Goliath frogs from Africa; three-year-old Cody Shilts, the youngest winning jockey, appearing on the *Tonight Show* in 1994; and in 2003, an unsuccessful effort by animal-rights activists to terminate the competition. (Courtesy Angels Camp Museum.)

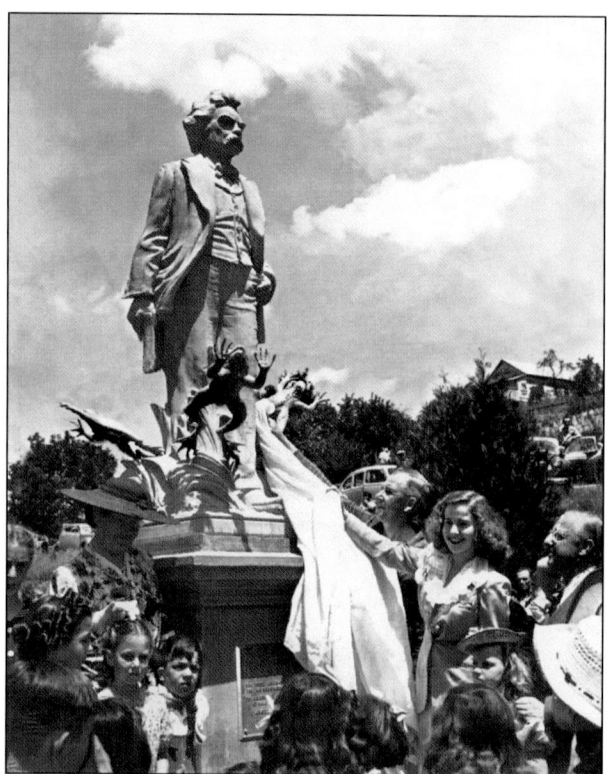

A statue of Mark Twain, with frogs at his feet, was unveiled in Angels Camp's Utica Park in 1944. To the left of the young woman stands Dr. Richard Coke Wood, a Calaveras County resident and professor at the University of the Pacific, who was a pioneering historian of the area. (Courtesy Calaveras County Historical Society.)

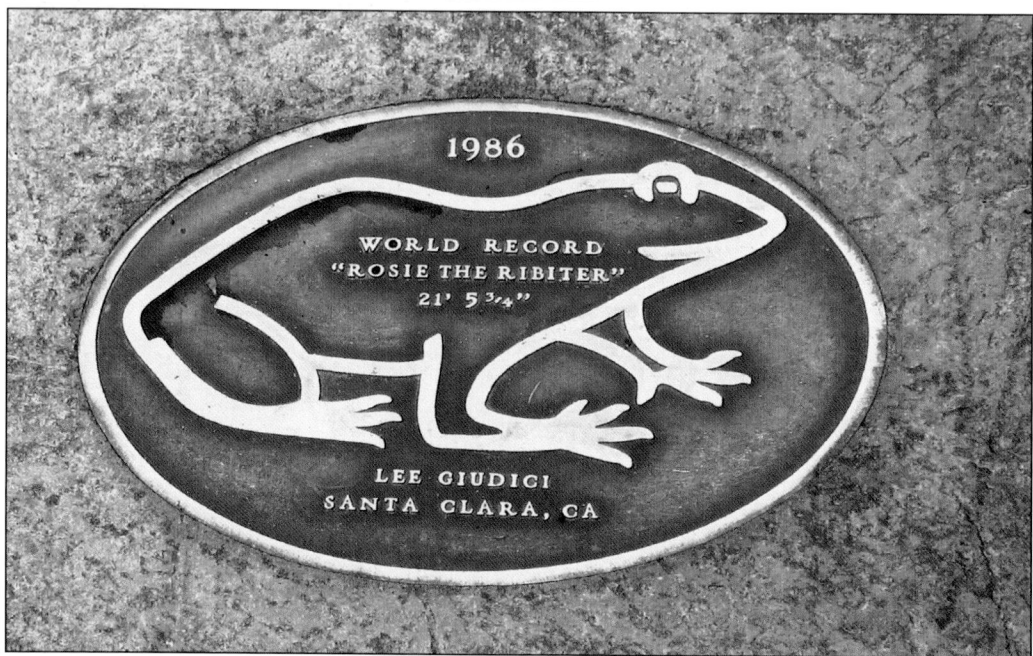

The 1928 Frog Jump was won by the Pride of San Joaquin, jockeyed (the term used for "handler") by Louis Fisher, with a leap of 3 feet, 9 inches. The current world record, 21 feet, 5.75 inches, was set in 1986 by Rosie the Ribeter, jockeyed by Lee Guidici. Each winner is commemorated on the Hop of Fame by a plaque placed in the sidewalks of Angels Camp. (Photograph by Sal Manna.)

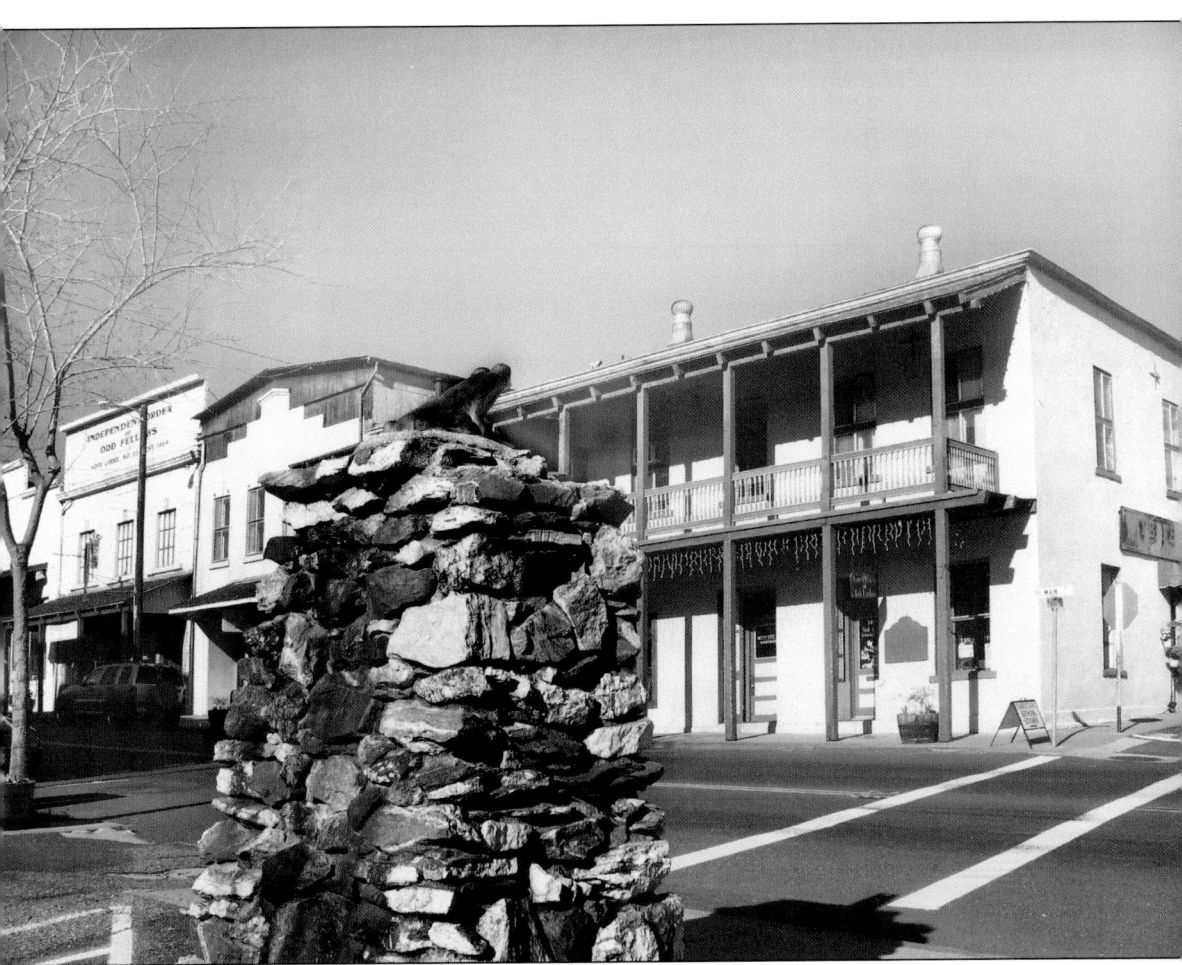

Today a statue of the frog that put Angels Camp on the map sits atop a State Historic Landmark monument and watches over the building that was the hotel where Mark Twain first heard the celebrated tale. A classic, picturesque Gold Rush town, Angels Camp has safeguarded its history for future generations through the Angels Camp Museum, the restored Altaville School, all things Frog Jump, and other visitor attractions. Though the promise of this region of Calaveras County lies beyond the frog, its past marked by gold and copper, cattle ranches, and pioneering families—and one very famous amphibian—that history has laid the foundation for an even more prosperous future. (Photograph by Sal Manna.)

Discover Thousands of Local History Books Featuring Millions of Vintage Images

Arcadia Publishing, the leading local history publisher in the United States, is committed to making history accessible and meaningful through publishing books that celebrate and preserve the heritage of America's people and places.

Find more books like this at
www.arcadiapublishing.com

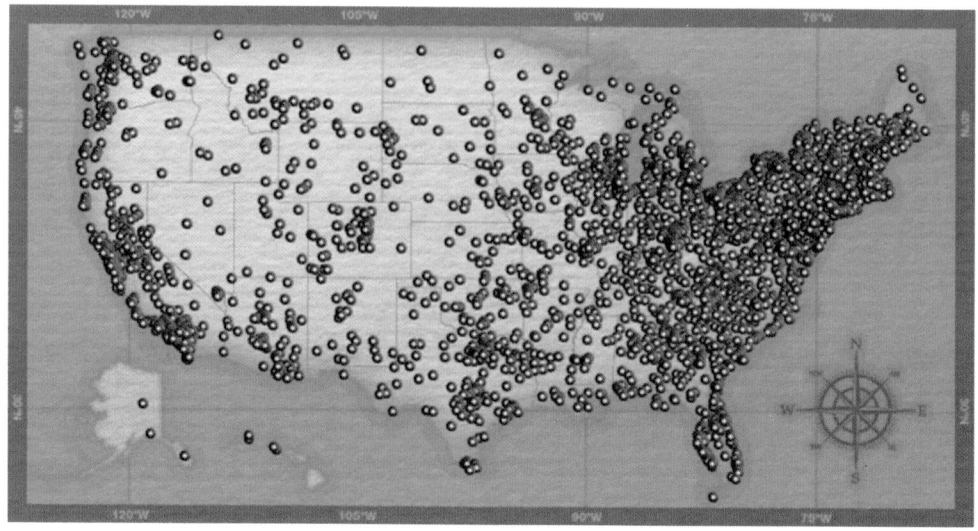

Search for your hometown history, your old stomping grounds, and even your favorite sports team.

Consistent with our mission to preserve history on a local level, this book was printed in South Carolina on American-made paper and manufactured entirely in the United States. Products carrying the accredited Forest Stewardship Council (FSC) label are printed on 100 percent FSC-certified paper.

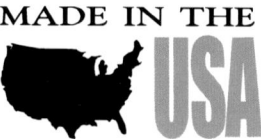